Wineries *of* Wisconsin & Minnesota

Wineries *of*
Wisconsin
& Minnesota

Patricia Monaghan

MINNESOTA HISTORICAL
SOCIETY PRESS

www.mhspress.org

The Minnesota Historical Society Press is a member of the Association of American University Presses.

Printed in Canada

10 9 8 7 6 5 4 3 2 1

∞ The paper used in this publication meets the minimum requirements of the American National Standard for Information Sciences—Permanence for Printed Library Materials, ANSI Z39.48-1984.

All maps by CartoGraphics, Inc.

Interior grape and vineyard photos courtesy of the University of Minnesota, David Hansen.

Bottle label photo, page 25, from the Minnesota Historical Society Collections/ *St. Paul Daily News*

Text design: Cathy Spengler Design, Minneapolis

Typesetting: Judy Gilats/Peregrine Graphics Services, St. Paul

International Standard Book Number
ISBN-13: 978-0-87351-617-4 (paper)
ISBN-10: 0-87351-617-6 (paper)

Library of Congress Cataloging-in-Publication Data
Monaghan, Patricia.
Wineries of Wisconsin and Minnesota / Patricia Monaghan.
    p. cm.
  Includes bibliographical references and index.
  ISBN-13: 978-0-87351-617-4 (paper : alk. paper)
  ISBN-10: 0-87351-617-6 (paper : alk. paper)
    1. Wineries—Wisconsin—Guidebooks. 2. Wineries—Minnesota—Guidebooks.
  3. Wisconsin—Guidebooks. 4. Minnesota—Guidebooks. I. Title.

TP557.M655 2008
641.2'209775—dc22

2008008754

To Michael

euoi, euoi, euoi

Contents

Acknowledgments   xi

PART 1 *Introduction: Northern Wines, Northern Vines*   3

1   Territory and *Terroir*   7

2   Juice of the Vine   13

3   Birth of an Industry   19

4   Intemperate Times   25

5   Passion and Patience   37

A Chronology of Northern Wines   48

PART 2 *Getting Started: The Winery Experience*   51

GREAT RIVER NORTH   54

Chateau St. Croix   57

Northern Vineyards   58

St. Croix Vineyards   60

Winehaven   61

GREAT RIVER SOUTH   63

Alexis Bailly Vineyard   66

Cannon River Winery   68

Falconer Vineyards   70

Garvin Heights Vineyards   72

Salem Glen Winery   73

Scenic Valley Winery   75

CENTRAL MINNESOTA 78

Carlos Creek Winery 81

Crofut Winery 82

Goose Lake Farm and Winery 84

Fieldstone Vineyards 86

Morgan Creek Vineyards 88

Olde Country Winery 90

THE DRIFTLESS AREA 93

Botham Vineyards 96

New Glarus Primrose Winery 98

Spurgeon Winery 100

Vernon Vineyards 102

Weggy Winery 104

Wollersheim Winery 106

SOUTHEASTERN WISCONSIN 109

Apple Barn Orchard and Winery 112

AeppelTreow Winery 113

Cedar Creek Winery 115

Mason Creek Winery 117

Vetro Winery 118

EAST CENTRAL WISCONSIN 121

Captain's Walk Winery 124

Kerrigan Brothers Winery 125

LedgeStone Winery 127

Parallel 44 Winery 128

Trout Springs Winery 130

von Stiehl Winery 132

DOOR COUNTY 135

Orchard Country Winery 138

Door Peninsula Winery 139

Red Oak Winery 141

Simon Creek Winery 143

Stone's Throw Winery 145

CENTRAL WISCONSIN 147

Autumn Harvest Winery 150

Burr Oak Winery 152

Lil' Ole Winemaker Shoppe 154

Munson Bridge Winery 156

Tenba Ridge Winery 157

UP NORTH 160

UP NORTH MINNESOTA 164

Minnestalgia Winery 164

Forestedge Winery 166

Two Fools Vineyard 167

UP NORTH WISCONSIN 170

Bayfield Winery 171

Brigadoon Winery 173

HookStone Winery 175

Three Lakes Winery 176

White Winter Winery 177

Woodland Trail Winery 179

Bibliography 183

Pronunciation Guide 185

Index 187

Tasting Notes 194

Acknowledgments

Traveling almost six thousand miles over the course of a year to visit the wineries described in this book was a Herculean effort made easier by the helpfulness of my partner-in-wine, Michael McDermott, who navigated the country roads of the Midwest with aplomb and was my sounding board for the historical material that emerged from libraries and archives. Thanks, Michael, for your unflagging enthusiasm for this project.

The University of Minnesota wine-breeding project scientists could not have been more helpful and cordial; thanks to Jim Luby and Peter Hemstad for elucidating grape botany. Pat Pierquet, formerly of the University of Minnesota, provided priceless insights and memories of Elmer Swenson. The archive staff at the Minnesota Historical Society was helpful and patient, as was the library staff at DePaul University, especially Pat McGrail. Research without interlibrary loan? Unthinkable!

Throughout our travels, winery owners and winemakers were helpful and friendly. They were willing to take time to answer questions, to conduct vineyard tours, and to share their expertise as well as their wine. Their enthusiasm for their craft is contagious. Similarly, the industry's two professional organizations—the Minnesota Grape Growers Association (MGGA) and the Wisconsin Winery Association—provided timely and accurate information.

A writer's friends put up with information overload at regular intervals, but my friends have proven notably patient in listening to me. They also provided hospitality and needed breaks from wine tasting. Thanks to Kerry Trask and Sherrie Richards in Manitowoc, Flo Golod and Ethna McKiernan in Minneapolis, Bonnie Wallace and Ron Hagland in Cloquet. And back on the farm, thanks to Nathaniel Moore for keeping the vines in Black Earth healthy during our absences.

Finally, thanks to Pamela McClanahan of the Minnesota Historical Society Press for her support and to the entire staff for their professionalism and expertise.

Wineries *of* Wisconsin & Minnesota

Part 1

NORTHERN WINES

NORTHERN VINES

INE. The word calls to mind vines descending red Spanish hills under a cloudless sky, white villas gleaming atop Tuscan hills, and multiethnic staffers smiling in posh California tasting rooms. "Wine" evokes French chateaux and castles on the Rhine. It bespeaks romance, culture, refinement.

Say "Minnesota," by contrast, and we imagine glacial lakes and north woods, lumberjacks and ice-fishing houses. "Wisconsin" conjures cows and red barns, cheese and beer and brats. "Wisconsin and Minnesota wine"? Surely that's the beginning of an Ole and Lena joke.

But throughout the Upper Midwest, wild vines survive harsh winters to bear fruit on long summer days. You can make wine from those grapes, as you can from any cultivated or wild fruit. Yet some people maintain that only wine made from cultivated grapes merits the name, and that only certain European varieties make good wine (what New York grower Ben Feder famously called "*vinifera* racism"). With a challenging climate that kills prestige vines, the Upper Midwestern wine industry has until recently been undetectably small. Even regional wine experts Tom Plocher and Bob Parke call the emergence of wineries here an "improbable" development.

Improbable, but occurring nonetheless, and with stunning rapidity. In the 1990s, fewer than a dozen wineries existed where almost sixty now thrive, with significant growth anticipated for at least a decade. Wineries still use apple and rhubarb, but grape-based wines increasingly predominate, made from Minnesota or New York hybrids, heritage grapes of French-American ancestry, and native American varieties.

Wineries in an emerging viticultural region will never compete with those giants of production, France and California. But local wine has aficionados among those who "think global, drink local." For such consumers, regional wines offer one clear advantage. The French have a word for it: *terroir*, the taste of the territory. To a wine drinker interested in *terroir*, a commonplace oaky Chardonnay shipped several thousand miles is less interesting than a Louise Swenson, its taste sharp and icy as a glacial stream, quaffed beside a Midwestern fire on a snowy night.

Even those uninterested in sustainable agriculture and regional identity can enjoy local wine because it offers good taste at a modest price, joined with the delights of wine tourism. Today's wine drinkers, drowning in a sea of undistinguished and indistinguishable Merlot and Chardonnay, find their palettes reinvigorated by new varietals. Sipping a nouveau-style Maréchal Foch as the aurora plays above a northern lake brings together land, season, and people in a memorable celebration. Wine tourism is a growing industry in the Upper Midwest, as more residents and visitors taste its rural essence through the region's wines.

Wine is multidimensional, encompassing geology, botany, history, and culture, and we will explore them in the following chapters. Then we visit the ten wine regions of the Upper Midwest and their scores of wineries. Whether you use this book as a guide while traveling the region's back roads or enjoy the comforts of home as an armchair traveler, make sure to taste a glass of Midwestern wine along the way.

INE LOVERS TALK about *terroir*, a French word that defies easy translation. It sounds like "territory," but that related word describes everything from a salesperson's turf to a warlord's empire. *Terroir* is more exact: it specifies the taste of a plot of land, expressed in the fruit of the vine. So important is land to winemaking that a French proverb calls grapes "tools for extracting flavor from the soil." Grapevines are among nature's most ingenious biological mechanisms for translating tiny differences in soil and weather into distinct and distinctive flavors.

Geology and climate determine *terroir*, and not just because they limit which grapes grow where. The difference between a light, fruity Beaujolais and a deep, intense Bordeaux is not merely the difference between Gamay and Cabernet Sauvignon grapes. It is the difference between rich light soils in eastern France and gravelly coastal riverbanks. These differences create the taste of the wine as much as the plant variety—perhaps more. Oenophile Ed Sbragia describes *terroir* thus: "gravelly soils produce harder wines, while bigger, softer ones come from soils richer in clay." The wealthiest winemaker cannot replace a vineyard's soil, so *terroir* is not easily altered.

All wines express *terroir*, but the French are the most energetic about promoting the concept. France restricts grape varieties by region, restrictions that derive from generations of observing which grapes grow well, which cultivation techniques succeed, and what styles of vinification enhance flavor. In newer wine regions like California and Australia, winegrowers and winemakers test varietals and try out vinification techniques, occasionally diminishing the significance of *terroir* as wines are chemically altered to create signature tastes. But to the true wine lover, *terroir* remains important as a way of describing subtle differences between wines from hallowed vineyards and from backyards as well.

The *terroirs* of the Upper Midwest have yet to be solidly defined. To understand the unique tastes coming from the region's wines, we must begin where the vines begin: with the soil.

Plain Landscapes

For the traveler seeking dramatic landforms, the Upper Midwest presents a dull first impression, nothing like the memorable landscapes of the California or New York wine regions with their picturesque hills. But those who read traces of geologic change find a fascinating narrative written on the land, and wine-lovers find distinct regions of *terroir*. Geologists use Upper Midwestern names constantly, speaking of the Algoman orogeny (named for Algoma, Wisconsin) of three billion years ago when North America's bedrock was formed from pressurized magma (molten rock), and of the Penokean orogeny (after the Penokee range in northeast Wisconsin) a few million years later, which brought that magma back to the surface. These great earth movements created our continent, which formed part of the huge land mass called Pangaea, from which the continents slowly drifted into their current locations. When North America left Pangaea, the Upper Midwest was located around today's Portugal. Not long after, an immense rift tore open between Minnesota and Wisconsin. Volcanoes erupted, evacuating so much magma that a vast valley appeared. Water pouring into this Superior syncline formed a shallow sea that lasted millions of years.

Grassy Oceans

A novice might imagine that wine grapes do not grow in the Upper Midwest because of weather; after all, chilly Minnesota will never be sunny Italy. But geology is as problematic as climate, for the region has vast areas of poor drainage with few hillsides to delight the vine. But the ancient ocean also created some good soils for the vineyardist.

Throughout the world, grapes thrive in marginal land. When planted in deep fertile loam, vines produce leaves but little fruit. So European farmers planted grapes on rocky areas near rivers, in sandy fields, on ridgetops. Because vines hate wet feet and stagnant air, grape growers learned early to plant on hillsides where rain drains quickly and fresh winds stir the leaves. Here is where Upper Midwestern grape growers face their first challenge: the region is mostly flat.

The first European visitors to the Upper Midwest were dazzled by its sweeping prairies and oak savannahs. It seemed a sea of grass. The image is geologically apt, given that ancient ocean whose tidal pools teemed with tiny shelled creatures that fell to the sea's bottom as they died. Over time, innumerable tiny skeletons, mixed with the mud of the ocean floor, formed limestone and its mineral relative, dolomite.

For grapes, limestone is a favored nutrient. But in many areas of the Midwest, that limestone was eventually covered with a blanket of silty soil, the result of ages of glaciation, putting the grape's favorite rock out of reach of its penetrating roots. Only in a few areas of the region did geological processes create favorable vineyard conditions, and these are places where vineyards cluster today.

Glaciers Change the Land

The ancient sea slowly eroded underwater mountains, creating a flat seabed, but the land we see today was finished by glacial action. No one knows why the earth's temperature suddenly dropped at the beginning of the ice ages that covered the Midwest in four great stages from two million to a mere ten thousand years ago. Instead of melting each summer, the arctic snow accumulated until the snow's weight (one hundred fifty tons per square foot) created flowing rivers of ice. At the greatest extent, a sheet of ice ten thousand feet tall covered Canada and most of the northeast and north central United States.

The ice advanced and retreated in four waves. Two million years ago the Nebraskan ice sheet covered all of Minnesota, leaving much of Wisconsin untouched but reaching as far south as Kansas City. After it retreated, tusked mammoths roamed the cold but fertile plains. Half a million years ago, the frozen mass of the Kansan ice sheet covered most of Wisconsin and Minnesota; then came an interglacial period when giant beavers and sloths lived on the plains. The Illinoian sheet (one hundred fifty thousand years ago) moved from the east to cover Illinois and eastern Wisconsin, while mastodons grazed in an untouched Minnesota. Then the Wisconsin ice sheet covered both states except for the Driftless Area. The Wisconsin buildup began a hundred thousand years ago and lasted until the geologically recent time of ten thousand years ago. Just a few thousand years before grapes were first domesticated in the ancient Mediterranean, Wisconsin was buried under ice.

Wherever the glaciers passed, they left signs of their presence. Most of the region's lakes are glacial meltwater; rolling hills were formed when retreating glaciers deposited a kind of silt called glacial drift. Ridges called moraines were created by rock deposited at a glacier's sides or end; drumlins (small rounded hills) formed when rock piled up under the moving ice. Finally, occasional huge boulders (erratics), now strewn about like a child's lost marbles, were stranded when the ice melted away.

Glaciers created the Upper Midwest we see today. They pressed the land into a swampy paste in which grapes do not thrive, although the rocky moraines provide good vineyard sites. Wine growers in the region face the challenge of finding well-drained sites with sufficient air circulation. As a result, vineyards in the Upper Midwest cluster in a few areas that provide suitable conditions for the grape: in the unglaciated Driftless Area, along the stony Escarpment, and along major rivers. For the wine tourist, this means that wineries tend to be located near other wineries, making it possible to visit several in a single day. A few wineries, however, brave the geological challenges of growing vines in less than ideal conditions and extend grape-growing beyond its typical range.

Bursting Dams, Dolomite Cliffs, and River Systems

Glacial history tells a special story in central Wisconsin. There, the Wisconsin Dells were created by the breaking of an ice dam that held back a vast glacial lake; except for the Wisconsin River bed, the Driftless Area has no glacial formations or any of the silty soil that glaciers leave behind.

Today the Wisconsin Dells have disappeared behind waterslides, but a hundred years ago the strange rock pillars and towers themselves delighted visitors. As early as the mid-nineteenth century the area attracted tourists; one promoter claimed in 1880 that the area was "one of the weirdest and strangest freaks of Nature," equivalent to the Grand Canyon. Exaggeration, yes, but the history of the Dells is both dramatic and cataclysmic.

Nearly twenty thousand years ago, the last glacier ended about four miles from the Dells. As it began to melt, an enormous lake formed, stretching to the Michigan border and ending at an ice dam located near today's town of Baraboo. Behind that dam, water built up. Recent studies show that ice dams erode from the inside until they collapse. In the Dells, the dam did not slowly melt, allowing water to drain gradually, but smashed apart from internal pressure. Water poured forth, lowering Glacial Lake Wisconsin from one hundred and fifty to fifty feet in a single day.

The force of all that water carved out strange shapes and tore an immense hole in the land below, visible now as the four-mile-wide valley of the Wisconsin River. Had people lived in the area, they could not have survived, but archaeologists believe the region was not yet inhabited. When the waters subsided, the landscape was utterly changed. Hundred-foot-tall banks now tower over river waters, and rocky hillsides worthy of vineyards abound.

The Wisconsin River valley flows through a prime wine-growing district: the Driftless Area, the Upper Midwest's only unglaciated area.

A roughly triangular area between Madison, Wisconsin, and the Mississippi River, and between La Crosse, Wisconsin, and Galena, Illinois, the Driftless Area is famously scenic. Creeks run through small valleys bounded by handsome hills. The steep hillsides, especially when formed of dolomite or limestone, create excellent wine terrain.

Wineries are also clustered along the Lake Michigan shore. Far to the east, the Niagara River rushes over a great limestone cliff. This eroded break in Earth's crust, the Niagara Escarpment, runs from there across Lake Huron, then continues down Lake Michigan to Door County. A few outliers carry vine-enhancing dolomite even farther. All along the Escarpment are fine wine areas, from Ontario to the Leelanau peninsula.

Along the Escarpment in Wisconsin the soil is thin, in some places a mere six inches deep. Although this makes for poor cornfields, such geology is ideal for grapevines, which send down rootlets into even the smallest fissures. Limestone and dolomite are the most significant rocks in some of France's most renowned wine regions, so the presence of the Escarpment bodes well for viticulture along its length.

A third, discontinuous wine district follows the region's major rivers and lakes. River systems are wine friendly, because rivers erode their banks into hills that provide drainage of water and air. But water does more; it also modulates temperature through thermal protection, so some Upper Midwestern wineries situate themselves near large glacial lakes.

The Taste of Glaciers

Winegrowers and winemakers in the Upper Midwest strive to produce wine that tastes of the region. Growers in Bordeaux have had thousands of years to determine the best grapes to grow, the best way to grow them, and the best ways to make wine from the resulting grapes; its *terroirs* are internationally known and recognized. With only a few decades behind them, Upper Midwestern winegrowers experiment and debate. Luckily, they can draw on global experience in a way that earlier winemakers could not. Local winegrowers rely on research conducted in the Baltic States and in Québec, as well as wine knowledge from California and Australia. In time, wines from the Upper Midwest will capture its *terroir:* the depth of ancient oceans, the weight of ancient glaciers, the piercing summer sun and the crisp winter winds from the north.

2

JUICE OF
THE VINE

INE" IS A PRIME WORD that descends from no other word; its nearest relative is the obviously connected word "vine." Most Indo-European words for fermented grape juice are similar, from Latin *vinum* to German *wein*. The word for wine was apparently passed along, together with vines and winemakers' secrets, through the ancient world.

No one knows where wine was first made: Some claim Russia's Georgian region, others Egypt, yet others the Middle East, perhaps Persia. But all agree that wine was not so much invented as discovered. Because grape skins carry wild yeast cells, fermentation is inevitable when grapes are left untended for a few days. Wine appeared early in human history, its discovery preceding beer as well as milk. But for the occasional glass of wine to become regularly available, the small harvest from wild grapes had to be expanded. For that, cultivation was necessary.

Taming the Vines

Left to its own devices, a grapevine grows rampant, all glossy leaves with a few clusters of sour grapes. During the Neolithic revolution, new farmers invented pruning, which encourages the vine to invest in producing fruit, as well as trellising, which offered support for heavier crops. Pruning and trellising were breakthroughs in the domestication of the wild grapevine.

Early farmers, like their descendents, also bred selectively for taste and yield. Early on, they settled on a single species that forms the basis for most wine grapes: *Vitis vinifera* (literally, "grapes for making wine"). Because grapes fertilize themselves, early developments probably came from spontaneous mutations as well as crossbreeding, wherein growers brushed pollen from one vine to another, producing seed with the strong points of both parents. Soon new grapes made their appearance: rich in taste and heavy with juice. Wine became a primary agricultural product for Greece and Rome, Egypt, and the eastern Mediterranean. Soon after, divine aspects of intoxication were recognized, with the vine becoming an important religious metaphor. The Bible is replete with references to wine, called (in the Apocryphal Ecclesiasticus 31:36) "the joy of the soul and heart" when "drunk with moderation." Proverbs (31:6) instructs us to "give strong drink to them that are sad, and wine to them that are grieved in mind." In Greece, women known as Maenads worshiped the god Dionysus (Bacchus in Rome) in secret ceremonies.

Later, wine became a symbol of transformation to Christians who drink the "blood of Christ" in the sacrament of communion. The relationship of people to the vine, established in prehistory, has never faded.

ᔛ The American Vine

When Europeans arrived in America, they found the continent overrun with grapevines. But none were *vinifera*, the classic wine grape. American vines include *riparia* (riverbank grape), *rupestris* (sand grape), *muscadina* (muscadine), *rotundifolia* (round-leaved grape), *aestivalis* (summer grape), and *labrusca* (fox grape). The last is the best known, because the compound methyl anthranilate found therein provides the familiar "grapey" flavor of Concord jelly. Europeans used to the taste of *vinifera* wines found American grapes unpalatable. As the New England writer John Lowell said in 1825, "Cider tastes good here. Wine tastes terrible."

But native grapes are vigorous and heavy-bearing, so early settlers nurtured them for juice and preserves, especially jelly. Settlers also planted *vinifera* vineyards. Although the vines seemed to adapt well at first, they mysteriously declined and died after a few years. It would be several hundred years before the source of the trouble was located.

By then, Europe's wineries were threatened by a small aphid-like ground louse, common in American soils but not in European, the very predator that had caused *vinifera* death in the New World. Europe's vines had no natural immunity to *Phylloxera vastatrix* (now named *Daktulosphaira* or *Dactylasphaera vitifoliae* but still called phylloxera by growers). When an enthusiastic winegrower imported vines from America, phylloxera hitched a ride to infect Europe's vineyards. Within a few years, ancient vineyards were dead, and Europe's wine industry was in tatters.

The geographical source of the infection, however, became the source of the cure. Growers found they could use naturally immune American roots as stock for grafting the old European varieties. The grafted vine had the hardiness of America but the distinguished taste of Europe; curiously, the "foxiness" characteristic of American grapes does not pass through the graft. From that time, *vinifera* grapes have survived only on American rootstocks.

~~ Vines in the Upper Midwest

Those nineteenth century days of anxiety and fear passed without much notice in the Upper Midwest because *vinifera* grapes, which die quickly when exposed to subzero weather, were rarely planted here. The native riverbank grape, *rupestris*, thrives throughout the region, so much so that Father Jacques Marquette commented on the "islands full of vines" that he encountered on his trip down the Wisconsin River in 1673. But *rupestris* bears small clusters of fruit that makes a harsh, sour wine. So farmers in the Midwest turned to production of country wines and ciders from fruits other than grapes, beginning an industry that survives today.

Later, growers hybridized grapes to join American vigor and French taste. Unlike grafting, where parts of a plant remain genetically distinct, hybridization mixes genetic traits of both parents. Many grape hybrids were first created during the phylloxera infestation that threatened France's wine industry. In their rush to solve the crisis, breeders relied on common *viniferas* like easy-to-grow Aramon. As a result, some French-American hybrids are rough tasting. Others, however, were bred from parents with a more sophisticated flavor profile, which came down through their descendents.

In nineteenth-century Europe, individual breeders created hybrids, with such names as Seibel, Kuhlmann, and Seyve still forming a pantheon of grapebreeders. In twentieth-century America, however, universities became the main force in hybridizing. In the east, Cornell University developed new grape varieties for the Finger Lakes and nearby areas. But western New York, while snowy, is milder than Minnesota and Wisconsin, where stretches of subzero weather can be expected at least once every winter. Thus while the southern tier of both states is marginally hardy for Cornell varieties, the challenge of growing fine wine grapes in the north remained to be solved.

Enter the University of Minnesota. In the last decade, its researchers have introduced varieties that make it possible to raise high-quality grapes in sufficient quantity to produce award-winning wines in the Upper Midwest. The first releases were from the remarkable plant breeder Elmer Swenson (see Chapter Five), the first person to breed cold-hardy grapes that were high-yielding and tasty. Others at the University of Minnesota have contributed new varieties, leading to the explosive development of the Upper Midwestern wine industry since 1990.

∿ Challenges to the Northern Grower

As a perennial woody plant, grapes are planted once, rather than annually like corn and soybeans. Thus a vineyard is a long-term investment like an orchard, with selection of site and grape varieties determining the vineyard's output for many years after planting. Grapes are planted in early spring, to permit a full summer's development before first frost. Plantings can be grafted vines, which look like sticks with a bulbous top, or rooted cuttings, which look like a few grape leaves with scanty roots. Vigorous summer growth brings vines to the top of six foot trellises their first summer.

In their second year, vines produce leaves early in the spring. Budbreak is a worrisome time for northern growers, because if frost occurs afterward, vines may die. Some varieties break bud at the first sign of warmth, which in the Upper Midwest often occurs in January. A hard freeze after a vine has sent water into its canes causes tissues to burst, with subsequent further injury from dehydration. If pruning has already taken place when freezing occurs, vines may bleed to death, unable to heal the pruning wounds.

After leaves burst forth, the vine begins to spread its canes (branches), supported by strong tendrils along the trellises' guiding wires. Grape flowers appear in clusters, each tiny green blossom developing into one grape after fertilization. By midsummer, small clusters hang from the vines. At this point, growers eliminate some clusters, so that the remaining ones will grow heavier. Canopy management—clipping of leaves that shade the clusters—also takes place.

Near the end of summer, as ripening occurs and the color of the grape changes (*veraison*), the vine slows its growth, preparing for winter. Cold-hardy varieties begin this process more quickly than do more tender grapes; some also develop a vegetable antifreeze called raffinose. Harvest can occur in early September through mid-October, depending on weather and location. Sugar content in the grapes climbs throughout ripening, while acid levels fall. When frost comes too early, the result can be an acidic, low-sugar grape, which provides a challenge to the winemaker.

After a full season of budding, bearing, and being harvested, northern grapes are ready to rest. The hardiest stay on trellises until spring, while the less hardy must be removed and buried in six- to twenty-four-inch-deep trenches. This protects them from freezing but also stresses the vines, whose trunks did not evolve for bending. Vines may also be mulched with straw or cornstalks, or protected with snow fences to capture insulating snow.

Despite the challenges of growing grapes in northern climates, more Upper Midwesterners take it up every year. In addition to the wineries open to the public, scores of small vineyards have appeared in backyards and back lots, some raising grapes for personal consumption, others for sale, yet others for an eventual new winery. It's a long way from the lands of the Bible and of the god Bacchus, but Midwestern wines are here to stay.

3

Birth of
an Industry

• • •

T HE NEW WORLD never knew wine until Europeans arrived. Although wild grapes grow rampantly, Native people did not. ferment the fruit. With the exception of Mexican pulque and Peruvian chica, fermentation was not practiced on the American continents, where sacred intoxication was based on botanicals like peyote and tobacco rather than on fermented beverages.

Nor did the earliest Europeans in the Upper Midwest ferment the juice of native grapes. In the sixteenth century, French voyageurs carried spirits with them, but there is no evidence that they made wine. When Europeans settled permanently in the region, they made fruit rather than wild-grape wine. There was, however, one exception—the man who founded the California wine industry, Agoston Haraszthy, a relentlessly energetic man who left a trail of fact and legend behind him. Was Haraszthy a Hungarian count? A swindler? A revolutionary? A greedy developer? A botanical genius?

Certainly he was an outsized character. As the great wine writer Hugh Johnson says, "No novelist could have invented Haraszthy." Haraszthy created his own legend during his lifetime, concocting "fanciful stories about himself" that could be swiftly altered whenever truth caught up with him, according to descendent and biographer Brian McGinty.

Legend holds that Haraszthy, a count and member of the royal bodyguard, fled his homeland after rashly siding with revolutionaries. He traveled through America, writing the first books published in Hungary about the New World. Arriving in Wisconsin, he built the town of Sauk City and planted a hillside of European grapes. Then, stirred by the siren call of the gold rush, he set off for California, where he created the state's wine industry, ultimately importing the Zinfandel grape from his homeland. Then he was eaten by alligators in Central America, leaving his brilliant sons to bring his vineyards into full production.

It's a great tale, and not entirely false. Although never a count, Haraszthy was a member of the minor nobility; never a member of the Royal Hungarian Guard, he did serve in the army. He had progressive tendencies but was not driven from his homeland for seditious activities. With business associates, Haraszthy did found Sauk City, named after him until the locals voted for a name they could pronounce. He did not follow the gold rush, hungry for shiny yellow metal; he always intended to develop agricultural enterprises in California. He did not personally establish the California wine industry, but he was an early winegrower. As to whether he introduced the Zinfandel grape—that issue is unlikely ever to be settled.

The claim that Haraszthy introduced Zinfandel to the New World has been a source of intense controversy. According to Agoston's son Arpad, Haraszthy brought Zinfandel from his Hungarian homeland, established it on his California estate, and spread the gospel of the grape's excellence throughout the region. But this century-old claim has recently attracted debunkers. Zinfandel appears under that name only in California, whence it migrated to Australia, Chile, and other regions. Italian winemakers claim it is their Primitivo, a claim upheld by the European Union's wine controlling board, which views the two names as synonyms. But studies in Croatia have found that a vine called Crljenak is identical to the California Zinfandel, so the vine's ancestry is disputed.

The truth does not lie directly between the pro- and anti-Haraszthy factions; there is more truth in the legend than in its debunking. While the Count may have embellished his life story, and while Haraszthy may have promoted his enterprises with an excess of enthusiasm, he was neither fraud nor swindler. Without him, the California wine industry would inevitably have begun, given that state's perfect climate for *viniferas*. But the industry would have developed differently without Haraszthy's commitment to making great wine in the New World.

Most of the Haraszthy legend centers on California, but he was also an important presence in the Midwest, to which he immigrated first. Born on August 30, 1812, in Serbia (then part of the Hungarian empire), Haraszthy came of one of Hungary's oldest families, something of which Agoston was inordinately proud. Haraszthy is believed to have studied law at the national university in Pest, which with its twin city Buda now forms Hungary's capital. Claims that he was in the Royal Bodyguard or the Diet (Parliament) seem no truer than those that he was driven out for political reasons. In 1839, Haraszthy emigrated to America, later giving many reasons for his decision to leave his native land, including the curious claim that rescuing a poet from a dungeon where he had been held for seventeen years put him in ill-favor with authorities. None of the stories can be unquestionably proved or disproved, but the likelihood is that twenty-seven-year-old Agoston simply left to find adventure and opportunity.

Agoston left his wife, Eleanora, and two children, with a third on the way, intending to be away for two years. While traveling, he kept extensive journals later published as *Travels in North America*. He wrote with special enthusiasm of his soon-to-be-home in Wisconsin, to which, he said, "Immigrants flock . . . from every corner of the earth. Every new-comer who arrived the very first year, and could afford to buy even a small parcel of land, can today boast of affluence." Of the vista that stretched before him from the hills over the Wisconsin River, he was to profess himself "firmly convinced that nowhere in the world could there have been a more enchanting place." He found it, he later said, to resemble the Danube of his homeland, although he is also said to have exclaimed, upon seeing the land, "Eureka! Italy!"

He might have been writing promotional copy for the town he was to found on the land of the Sauk (Sac) people, whose main village had stood where Haraszthy Town rose. A mere eight years had passed since a massacre ended the hopes of Native people to return to their homes and farms. With the Sauk people removed to the west, the land was open for European settlement. Haraszthy bought a section of land (640 acres) for three dollars an acre. His log cabin went up quickly, allowing the Hungarian to devote the summer to hunting.

The story grows a bit murky here, as with much Haraszthy history. Soon a second developer joined Agoston in Haraszthy Town. A new, finer home was built, and soon Agoston was engaging in new enterprises. His schemes, always ambitious and clever, were usually more than he could manage. He moved quickly, more interested in new ideas than in nailing down details.

His future was in the New World, but first he had to settle up in the Old. In a few short months, he packed up Eleanora, the three children, and his father, Károly, and disposed of their Hungarian estates. He thereafter was a fervent citizen of what he called "that magical land." After returning to Haraszthy Town, Agoston continued to expand his enterprises, which included planting a vineyard on the hills above the Wisconsin River, where today stands one of the region's most impressive wineries, Wollersheim.

Haraszthy did not, however, produce wine. Planted in 1846, the vineyard was just reaching bearing capacity when Haraszthy left for California in 1849 among the famous forty-niners moving west after the gold strikes. The vineyard was sold to a German-Swiss brick maker from Haraszthy Town named Peter Kehl. It was Kehl who erected the fine limestone home and winery visible at Wollersheim, but it appears to have been the Count himself who tunneled into the hillside to build a wine cellar, for he dug an almost identical facility at his vineyard in Sonoma years later.

Haraszthy settled in San Diego, where he planted more vineyards; wine-growing and wine-making were gaining in importance in Agoston's vision of his life in America. He was also elected to public office, first as sheriff and then as a state assembly member. Once in Sacramento, Haraszthy saw the promise of northern California and abandoned plans to return to San Diego.

Haraszthy bought land near the old Mission San Francisco, where he planted fruit. For the first time since he immigrated, his enterprise flourished. Soon he was growing table grapes, then wine grapes as well. A few years later he moved his operation to the Sonoma Valley. He became the first president of the Sonoma Horticultural Society, organized to promote wine-growing and to locate appropriate varieties for the region. By the early 1860s, his Buena Vista was one of the region's first commercially successful vineyards.

In 1861, Haraszthy went back to Europe with his son Arpad, scouting for vines and supported by the state legislature but with unclear financial backing. The pair brought back a hundred thousand vines of three hundred varieties; then the legislature refused to pay for the expedition. Haraszthy planted out the vines and ultimately recouped his investment by selling them. None of them appear to have been Zinfandel.

Nonetheless, by the 1880s, when the first California wine boom was in full swing, the story that Haraszthy had been the first to import Zinfandel into California was well established. By that time, Haraszthy had departed for Nicaragua, where he intended to build a distillery to help eliminate the family debt. But there, Agoston disappeared. His cloak was found beside a river known to be infested with alligators, giving rise to the story that he had been eaten alive. Others believe that he simply drowned trying to cross the swollen river on a felled tree.

The two most controversial claims about Haraszthy—that he founded the California wine industry and that he introduced the Zinfandel grape—can both be traced to the same source: Agoston's youngest son, Arpad. Arpad had not known his father for much of his life. Unsuited to California's rigors, Eleanora Haraszthy returned east with her children. Arpad did not meet his father again for many years, although he did accompany Agoston on his wine-gathering tour of Europe.

His inflated version of Agoston's contributions to California viticulture began in a series of articles apparently written by the bereaved Arpad. Although Arpad outstripped his father's contribution to California wine-making by creating the first commercially successful sparkling wine from the region, Arpad elaborated more and more on Agoston's reputation, although whether to enhance his own or to satisfy childish longings is unclear. It was Arpad who spread the gospel, so long unchallenged, of his father's importation of Zinfandel to California.

Agoston Haraszthy is described in every book about the California wine industry, and although he cannot be said to have had as much impact on wine-growing in the Upper Midwest, this dynamic man was the undisputed founder of the first vineyard intended for commercial use in the region. A European acquaintance of Haraszthy described him as having "a thousand ideas and the trouble with him is that he puts them all in motion." If he could see the hillside of grapes and the productive winery on the hills where he planted his first grapes, he would be proud. And then he would start dreaming of how to do more.

4

intemperate
times

HEN AGOSTON HARASZTHY headed west, the earthquake that would rock the wine world was still sixty years away.

But the ground had begun to shift under America's winemakers. By the time it brought down the nation's wine industry, the temperance movement had been active for over a century. But prohibition had not been the movement's original aim. Originally, the movement wanted to end *abuse*—not *use*—of alcohol.

Early American settlers distinguished between temperance and abstinence, the first being encouraged as a means to a better society, the second being promoted only by a few puritanical voices. Puritanical, but not necessarily Puritans, for even those somber folks were not always sober; minister Increase Mather said in 1687 that "drink is itself a creature of God, and to be received with thankfulness." Cider, wine, beer, and spirits were common and their use accepted as part of normal life in colonial America.

Throughout the eighteenth century as well, alcohol was part of public and private life throughout the country. But hard drinking by American men (accusations of intemperate drinking were almost invariably aimed at men) finally drew public recriminations. Drinking to excess, especially when it led to domestic violence and other social ills, began to be condemned by religious and civic organizations. The early temperance movement emerged, urging individuals to pray about their booze-fueled misdeeds. Usually this resulted in refraining from hard liquor or "spirits," for temperance advocates saw wine and beer as beverages of the temperate life.

Health, as well as religious belief, was invoked as a reason to avoid liquor. In 1784, Benjamin Rush of Philadelphia published his renowned *Inquiry into the Effects of Spirituous Liquors on the Human Body*, promoting the idea that overuse of alcohol could cause physical problems. Yet even Dr. Rush, who deplored alcoholic excess and curiously believed it led to gangrene, believed in temperate use of wine. "It must be a very bad heart," he wrote, "that is not rendered more cheerful and more generous by a few glasses of wine."

Inspired by ideals of physical and spiritual health, early temperance organizations focused on self-control. New recruits pledged to avoid hard liquor; some group support was available, but no attempts were made to change society. For more than thirty years, the temperance movement worked to encourage what many scholars have noted are Protestant values: hard work, repression of emotions, outward success.

From its origin through the downfall of Prohibition, temperance was predominantly a Protestant movement, bearing the values of that religious orientation into mainstream social and, later, political thought.

The Legislative Solution

In the middle of the nineteenth century, the temperance movement began to change. It had become apparent that, in a society where drinking was common, many people did not have the personal strength to remain "on the water wagon," as the early term had it, referring to wagons that brought potable water to cities. A new strategy emerged: remove the source of temptation. Instead of temperance, prohibition became the goal. If no one could purchase alcohol anywhere, even the weakest-willed backslider could live soberly.

What turned a self-improvement movement into an attempt to control the behavior of others? A strain of nativism and religious bigotry is clear, for prohibition replaced temperance as a goal just as millions of impoverished Europeans reached America's shores. Prohibition, said a California state senator, "eugenically cleanses America of a vicious element." Immigrants, especially Italians, were suspected of bearing a wine-colored taint: "When a bootlegger slips by our loosely guarded naturalization system . . . while his hands are dripping with illicit booze—and then goes from the courtroom to his still to manufacture and sell the poison that degenerates the American race—there is a clear case of fraudulent naturalization." German and Irish immigrants were similarly slandered during Prohibition debates, with the use of Communion wine in their shared religion called into question as indicating a symbolic inclination toward drunkenness.

Class also had an impact. If the middle-class Protestant American of English descent served sherry in his home, the new immigrant drank cheap spirits in a public saloon, which soon became the target of temperance organizers. Immigrants from cultures which discouraged drinking, including many Upper Midwestern Scandinavians, found themselves pitted against other immigrants; the emerging labor movement was regularly split by "dry" and "wet" factions cynically encouraged by the owning class whose own drinking was not an issue.

Gender also figured into temperance activism. If men were in the saloons, women were in the temperance halls. Some saw the ravages of excessive drinking in their homes or neighborhoods; others feared that their children would be corrupted by saloons, where gambling and prostitution often were available. By closing the saloons, such women believed, their children would pass through their tender years without falling into temptation. The temperance movement welcomed women's energies but rebuffed them as leaders. Elizabeth Cady Stanton, Susan B. Anthony, and other feminist leaders started their public careers in the temperance movement. When women found that they could not speak at temperance meetings they organized separately, as well as demanded an equal footing in mixed organizations. Some remained in temperance work, but others left it to work for women's suffrage.

Movement Toward Prohibition

National prohibition, although it lasted a mere thirteen years, was the holy grail for millions of activists for half a century. In 1908, it was calculated that the Anti-Saloon League had two hundred fifty full-time workers plus one hundred fifty support staff, located in forty-three states and territories. Added to that were tens of thousands of volunteers, including ministers and professional lecturers who conducted fifteen thousand temperance meetings annually. At the movement's height, three hundred thousand paid subscribers kept their virtuous spirits high by reading the *American Issue,* a monthly temperance newspaper.

If national prohibition was slow in coming, local victories were numerous. Wisconsin's Anti-Saloon League was launched in 1897 and, just ten years later, unseated thirty-seven legislators—more than a third of the legislature—who had voted against a temperance measure. The replacements were eager to aid the cause, and the desired bill passed easily. Within a decade of its establishment, the Wisconsin league secured passage of "dry" decisions in 800 of 1,454 communities in the state. Minnesota did even better. Its league was organized in 1898 and within a decade had virtually dried up the state: 1,200 of the 1,800 townships in Minnesota had no saloons, having been voted out by "local option."

The same was true across the land. With the turn of the millennium, almost half of the nation lived under local or state prohibition. Opposing the prohibitionists were millions of people who did not wish to change their drinking habits; most were fearfully silent in the face of the unrelenting depiction of their lives as wanton and decadent. More vocal in opposition to prohibition were the commercial interests: importers of wine, vineyard owners, bottlers, brewers, and of course tavern owners, who bore the brunt of the public protest. Early in the temperance movement, opponents of alcohol broke into saloons and destroyed them. But in 1873, the tactics turned to the more peaceful, if emotionally manipulative, technique of prayer. Business did not thrive in the face of on-site prayer services for the damned souls of drinkers, and many taverns quietly closed.

The day of success drew ever closer. For the first time since its founding, America experienced the force of single-issue politics. Using the emerging business model of departments delineated according to function and reporting to a central authority (a model derived originally from the railroads), the temperance movement changed American politics. With thousands of volunteers and a paid central staff putting out a single coordinated message, the campaign was a model of today's political campaigns and social movements. At the end, it was not merely a law that passed, but an amendment to the U.S. Constitution.

Prohibition and Intemperance

The text of the Eighteenth Amendment is brief, basically disallowing "the manufacture, sale, or transportation of intoxicating liquors within, the importation thereof into, or the exportation thereof from the United States and all territory subject to the jurisdiction thereof for beverage purposes." It also provided that both Congress and "the several States" had enforcement powers.

Ratification was rushed through state legislatures, the temperance supporters showing their political muscle in state after state. Just a year after passage, thirty-six states had ratified the amendment, all the rest except Rhode Island ratifying later. On January 16, 1919, Prohibition became the law of the land. One year to the day later, enforcement began.

Or did it? Legislating social change is far easier than policing it. From the start, Americans who were determined to drink found ways to do so. Although the popular image of reckless drinking in speakeasies and moonshiners outrunning federal agents on narrow country roads was the case only in the later period of Prohibition, enforcement was problematic from the start. Shared authority between state and federal government, as well as lack of a national enforcement department, meant a grid of overlapping jurisdictions and possibly contradictory regulations. Within a few years, the limitations of national Prohibition would be revealed.

Many in America never signed on to the Prohibition agenda. As the New York wit Charles Hanson Towne put it, it was "the last thing in the world the American people expect to have come upon them. . . . It was like predicting a world war—which eventually came about; it was like dreaming of the inconvenience of a personal income tax—which also came about." Surprised to find that they lived in a land where their private lives were controlled by law, Americans revealed their pragmatic streak. Those who wished to drink, had access, and could afford it, drank; those who did not wish to, lacked money, or could not find a provider, did not. The law controlled behavior less than did funds, access, and personal belief.

Enter Andy Volstead

Someone had to craft federal legislation to define how the new amendment was to be enforced, and that someone was Andrew Volstead of Minnesota, who wrote the law that became known by his name. He was shortly thereafter recalled by his constituents and lived the rest of his life in self-imposed obscurity. Perhaps because of the ultimate failure of Prohibition, no book-length biography of Volstead has ever been written and only a few articles published since his death on January 20, 1947. Facts about his life are scattered in files in Washington, D.C., and in his home state. The man so vilified for Prohibition remains a historical cipher.

The child of immigrant Norwegian farmers from near Oslo whose name in the home country was Wraalstad or Vraalstad, Andrew John Volstead was born October 31, 1880, in southeast Minnesota. Although his parents hoped he would enter the ministry, Volstead went into law after graduating from St. Olaf College and the Decorah Institute in Iowa. He also became involved in Republican politics, especially after opening his law office in Granite Falls, where he served as both city and county attorney, as mayor, and as president of the board of education.

Thin and quiet, hardworking, not given to self-promotion, Volstead had a reputation as a kindly man. During his early Granite Falls days, Volstead married Nellie Gilruth, through whom he became active in the Congregational Church. It is unclear what influence Nellie had on his drinking habits, but shortly after moving to Granite Falls Volstead became a teetotaler who made regular contributions to the Anti-Saloon League. He was not, however, particularly vocal about his support; he never gave a pro-Prohibition speech, either before or after writing the Volstead Act.

First elected to Congress in 1902, Volstead was an unobtrusive presence, working for his home district on issues like opposing reciprocity for Canadian wheat and crafting legislation that favored agricultural cooperatives. Over time, through seniority, he attained an important position: chairman of the House Judiciary Committee. It was in this role that Volstead was to make his mark.

Accounts vary about how much of the Volstead Act was actually written by Volstead. Some historians claim that the act was not written by Volstead himself but by the lawyer for the Anti-Saloon League, Wayne B. Wheeler of Ohio. Others say that the hardworking legislator, presented with an unpopular assignment for his committee, sat down and wrote the text himself. Volstead never commented about the source of the bill's wording, except to take responsibility for its problems.

Volstead, the very face of Prohibition to its opponents, in retrospect is an unlikely champion. According to the Congressional Record (July 8, 1919), he "never made a prohibition speech" before the Eighteenth Amendment passed. He had been opposed in his own district by the Anti-Saloon League because he was viewed as insufficiently "dry." He retained his seat but did not forget the slight. In 1920, after Prohibition had been enacted, the Anti-Saloon party wrote asking for an endorsement. He responded with a tart refusal.

The Act That Bears His Name

From obscurity, Volstead was catapulted into notoriety. The Volstead Act specified that no one could "manufacture, sell, barter, transport, import, export, deliver, furnish, or possess any intoxicating liquor . . . to the end that the use of intoxicating liquor as a beverage may be prevented," with the definition of "intoxicating" set at .5 percent alcohol. The law did not forbid consumption of alcoholic beverages. Nor did it forbid the possession of previously acquired liquor, which meant that the wealthy put aside substantial wine cellars in advance of enforcement and continued to enjoy a lavish lifestyle during it. Sacramental wines could still be manufactured and sold, as could liquor prescribed by a physician (a loophole that resulted in a huge increase in scripts for spirits).

Also allowed was the home manufacture of wines, which resulted in the Mondavi family leaving Minnesota to become a force in California wine-making. Cesare Mondavi, a native of Italy who saw the energetic manufacture of home wines during Prohibition by other immigrants on the Iron Range, left Virginia, Minnesota, for Lodi, California, late in Prohibition with the intention of providing grapes for the home wine-making industry—which grew by 400 percent during Prohibition years. He founded C. Mondavi and Sons, a fruit-packing business that shipped grapes back east. His son Robert, born in Virginia, later became one of the premiere winemakers of the nation. Home wine-making, which became common during Prohibition, was the starting point for many commercial wineries in the Upper Midwest.

Volstead's act had harsh penalties, with fines of up to a thousand dollars at a time when the average annual wage was approximately fifteen hundred. To provide for enforcement, more than a thousand federal agents were trained as part of the Prohibition Bureau of the U.S. Treasury. Thus began the short strange period of the Great Experiment—an experiment that was shortly to fail in a grand and historic way. On October 28, 1918, the bill was passed into law—over the veto of president Woodrow Wilson.

The Experiment in Action

Volstead's papers are preserved in seven boxes at the Minnesota Historical Society library. The first boxes reveal him to be an articulate and meticulous, if sometimes argumentative, proponent of laws that would support his own constituents, especially farmers like his parents. Carefully typed four- and five-page responses to constituents who demanded an explanation for his votes are frequent in his early years in Congress. But although the files grow thicker after the Volstead Act was passed, responses from Volstead himself almost disappear.

It is impossible to exaggerate the vitriol of the letters addressed to Volstead by those who identified him with Prohibition. "Andy Gump," as his opponents dubbed him, carefully preserved evidence of the public's hatred of him. A few penciled postcards praised Volstead as a divine agent, like the one from an unnamed "100% American" who wrote that "God is back of prohibiting any and all evil. Everything to gain and nothing worth losing to lose." But more often, the cards read like this: "Why don't the fanatical Prohibitionists buy the saloons with their millions and run them as they see fit instead of legislating them out of business." Or this: "You will go to hell soon, you damned loafer. . . . You are bribed by the Coca Cola Slop Makers." Or this, to "Czar Volstead, White House, Washington D.C.": "Why the H . . . don't you have statue of liberty removed form [sic] N.Y. Harbor. . . . Give it to Ireland as a present."

Threats against Volstead's life were common. "Now your dirty work is finished," one unsigned card read, "I am not a saloon man, but I like my beer and wine, I never was drunk in my life. I have a family but you have made a Bolshevik out of me. We will clean the country of ALL TRAITORS. . . . You say the War is not OVER? Well, in War Time, TRAITORS ARE SHOT." Or another: "Dear Sir: I am sending this letter to you and others that if you Don't Repeal your Prohibition Law you made in thirty days you are a *Dead* one you are going to be Blowed to Pieces they are there watching you for a chance. *One of the Gang.*" Or this, addressed to Volstead, prohibition lunatic, Washington D.C.: "Andy Volstead—you old Sonofabitch—you have run the limit. We propose to *get you.* This is *no* threat, but a timely warning."

No replies are preserved to these threats. Occasionally, the old articulate and self-assured Volstead could be heard responding to a supporter, as when in 1921 he wrote a constituent, "Permit me to thank you very much for your kind letter of the 13th instant, together with copies of your poem entitled 'Prohibition Does Prohibit.' There is every reason to believe that public sentiment is steadily growing in favor of the law and that with the growth of such sentiment will come more effective and successful administration of its provisions."

He could not have been more wrong.

Failure of the Great Experiment

Volstead was not the only one to presume, on the basis of a few quiet years after Prohibition was passed, that a new day was dawning. Morris Sheppard, a "dry" senator from Texas, famously gloated, "There is as much chance of repealing the Eighteenth Amendment as there is for a humming-bird to fly to the planet Mars with the Washington Monument tied to its tail." But soon Prohibition was so clearly a failure that the Great Experiment ended with the only complete repeal of a constitutional amendment in the nation's history.

At the end of Prohibition, drinking was almost as common as before. Before the wartime restrictions were imposed, Americans annually consumed 1.69 gallons of beer, wine, and spirits; under restrictions

(1918–19) that dropped to .97 gallons. Consumption reached its low point of .73 gallons in Prohibition's early years (1921–22), less than half the prewar level, but by 1930 consumption had almost recovered, with 1.14 gallons drunk per year per American.

From the start of Prohibition, illegal distilleries and transportation of alcohol were common, and vast profits soon brought in criminal elements. Al Capone's Chicago gang, which ran booze throughout the Midwest, was one of many criminal enterprises that profited from Prohibition. Because drinking itself was not illegal, speakeasies flourished, leading a generation of young Americans to enjoy a scofflaw existence.

Where did the booze come from, and how was it transported? In addition to the illegal manufacture of spirits—illegal stills blew up as regularly as meth labs do today, and with similarly tragic consequences— there was a huge traffic in contraband spirits coming in from abroad, estimated at more than a million gallons smuggled in each year late in Prohibition. Minnesota, with its border with Canada, was a source of considerable illegal importation; residents of the International Falls area saw rum-running across Lake of the Woods and saloon boats moored just over the international boundary. In Detroit, the liquor trade was so blatant that a "Prohibition navy" was formed by energetic foes of Demon Rum. Watery battles between the two sides grew so extreme that Chicago social activist Jane Addams remarked dryly that "What the prohibition situation needs first of all is disarmament."

Lawbreaking became common, and an enforcement industry thrived. Over a half-million arrests were logged by federal agents by 1929. Amendments to the Volstead Act raised penalties to five years in jail and ten thousand dollars, but the traffic continued unabated. States and municipalities began to withdraw active support for enforcement, and crime syndicates made fortunes in smuggling and distribution. Finally, anti-Prohibition sentiment began to swell throughout the country, until in 1932 the Democratic Party endorsed repeal, which led to a landslide for the party in that year's elections. As soon as the new Congress had been seated, the Twenty-first Amendment rushed through, with "drys" specifying that state legislatures be specifically avoided in the ratification process, out of dread that the "wet" contingent would hold up approval. Instead, for the only time in the nation's history, state conventions were authorized, with representatives directly elected to vote on the issue. Throughout the land, "wet" delegates were sent forth, and little more than eleven months after its introduction, the Twenty-first Amendment repealing Prohibition was passed.

Volstead's Fate

Prohibition ruined Volstead's political career. He was reelected upon the heels of the successful passage of the Eighteenth Amendment, but in the next election faced a tough reelection battle that he narrowly won. He returned to Washington to craft his single most important piece of legislation, the Capper-Volstead Cooperative Marketing Act of 1922, called "the Magna Carta of the American cooperative movement." But he could not live down his connection with the act that bore his name.

Although he never changed his support for Prohibition as a means of effecting positive social change, Volstead found that little he did erased the negative connections with his name in the minds of voters. In 1922, the Rev. O. J. Kvale ran against Volstead in his home district on the curious claim that, according to the *New York Times*, he was "dryer than Volstead." Kvale had previously run against Volstead as a Republican, but in the following election he ran as an independent and thrust Volstead out of the seat he had held for twenty years.

Volstead descended into obscurity. He declined invitations, some highly paid, to be a public speaker in support of Prohibition. Returning to Granite Falls to practice law, he quietly removed the skulls, bottles, and other litter daily placed on his home's fence. He removed himself so thoroughly from the public debate over alcohol that when, not long before his death, he was asked to help keep a liquor store out of Granite Falls, he declined to participate. Invalided in his final years, he died in 1947 and is buried in Granite Falls.

The Lasting Impact

The National Prohibition Act was repealed, but its impact on vintners and grape growers has never ceased. With the end of Prohibition, Wisconsin winemaker Glenn Spurgeon says, the nation developed fifty new forms of Prohibition. Each state has different, often contradictory, regulations about the manufacture and distribution of wine, beer, and spirits. Perhaps most importantly, the heritage of Prohibition has influenced the American perception of alcohol as something racy and immoral. Unlike Europeans, who believe no good meal should be served without an appropriate wine, Americans are not as a group used to drinking wine with meals. Drinking is connected to what is now called "partying," or drinking to excess. Winemakers in the Upper Midwest and throughout America still battle ghostly images of speakeasies and wild flapper behavior, remnants of a brief failed experiment in social control. Wine, once viewed as the beverage of moderation, became associated with lawless behavior—an association that lovers of wine still struggle to erase.

T THE TURN OF THE CENTURY, forty years after Agoston Haraszthy had abandoned the Upper Midwest for California and four years after Andrew Volstead was elected to his first term in Congress, the University of Minnesota launched a grape-breeding program.

No one was thinking about wine. It seemed unlikely that fine wine could be effectively grown in California, much less the Upper Midwest. Many parts of Minnesota were "dry" by local option, so the future market for any wine, local or imported, was unclear. But there was always a demand for table grapes for eating or juicing or jelly-making. As a land-grant college, the University of Minnesota was mandated to help develop agriculture in the state. So, in 1908, the U's M. J. Dorsey got to work on grapes.

Grape breeding requires immense care and patience. Grape flowers are self-fertile, which means breeders must tweeze off the stamen (male organ), a process called emasculation, then brush fertilizing pollen from another plant on the pistils (female organs). The flowers are tiny, so this process requires patience and persistence. The newly fertilized flowers must be labeled with the parents' names and protected from random pollen with an envelope or other barrier. By summer's end, each grape produces several seeds, which may vary greatly, some useless but others with the potential to improve the line.

Grapes are slow to mature. Once seed from a promising cross is obtained, it must be planted and nurtured for at least three years before its fruit can be evaluated. If further crossbreeding is necessary, add another three to five years to develop the next generation. Some hybrids are the result of as many as six or seven generations of crossbreeding, as much as fifty years of methodical work.

When the University began its program in 1908, its aim was to produce grapes hardy enough to withstand the Upper Midwest's continental climate, especially its intensely cold winters. A vine that gives up the ghost at twenty below zero is not hardy enough. But the grape must also ripen early, because winter can arrive in a rush in the region. Disease-resistance is also desirable. And, of course, the grape has to taste good.

Dorsey and later A. N. Wilcox based their breeding on *Vitis labrusca*, the grape that gave rise to the popular Concord, the gold standard for jellies. It took almost forty years, but in 1944 the University released Bluebell. A thick-skinned small blue grape, Bluebell's pink juice makes a pretty jelly. Bluebell is still grown in Upper Midwestern farms and gardens.

Having bred one table grape for Minnesota, however, the University ceased its breeding program, although Wilcox maintained the breeding stock. Efficient rail transportation meant that more produce was imported from other regions, especially California. Attention turned to other fruits, especially apples like the Haralson and Prairie Spy, with which California could never compete.

A Grape Breeder Is Born

Five years after the University began breeding Bluebell, a farm couple in Osceola, Wisconsin, welcomed a son. They were neither wealthy nor educated, but they encouraged their child's curiosity. A natural scientist, Elmer Swenson would eventually ignite the imaginations of a new generation of grape growers and winemakers. He never left the farm to study botany; he spent his life as a Wisconsin dairy farmer. But his passion was clear. Peter Hemstad, now a grape breeder at the University, remembers Elmer saying, "I guess cows are okay. But I prefer grapes."

Swenson's interest began in childhood. His grandfather Larson had a small vineyard where young Elmer helped pick grapes for juice and jelly. While in grammar school, Elmer discovered that Grandma Larson had a copy of *The Foundations of American Grape Culture* by T. V. Munson, a classic text. Elmer read avidly about how vines could be crossbred and propagated. The serendipitous appearance of a classic book by a Texas plant breeder on a small farm in rural Wisconsin allowed for the germination of Swenson's later career.

As a young man, Swenson dabbled in grape breeding. He had a farm to run, the 120-acre Larson place that he inherited from his maternal grandparents. He had a young wife, Louise, whose name would later be given to one of Swenson's grapes. Yet he found time for the patient work of crossbreeding his grandfather's grapes with some wild grapes (*Vitis riparia* or riverbank grape) that were used locally for wine. The results of his first attempts at breeding were surprisingly good: "grapes hardier than Janesville" (a jelly grape named for a Wisconsin town) "and quality comparable to Beta" (a cross of Concord and *riparia*), according to wine historian David MacGregor.

When World War II came, Elmer's brothers went into the service while he stayed on the farm. Then another serendipitous event occurred: the University of Minnesota announced an open house for farmers. Swenson saw the U's experimental vineyard, now over forty years old, with its many unnamed varieties set out in neat rows. For a young man whose passion for grapes had been viewed back home as a curious hobby, the sight must have been stirring. Swenson took home five cultivars, including the unnamed Minnesota 78 that formed the genetic basis for his later releases.

Cuttings in hand, Swenson went back to Osceola. Twenty-five years passed. Peter Hemstad picks up the story: "In 1969, Elmer came back with a basket of grapes, the best of what he'd bred. Now, people come by all the time, some guy with a grape that 'grandfather brought over from the Rhine Valley,' that turns out to be a Beta. It was different with Elmer. His were unusually good grapes. Instead of the couple of minutes of cursory chitchat, the faculty talked for an hour, then offered him a job."

With no academic credentials, it was impossible to appoint Swenson to the faculty, but he was willing to join the staff as a gardener. With that title but working as a member of the research faculty, Swenson worked on apples, the most important crop at the time, as well as grapes. "There was no separate job for grape research at the time," Hemstad explains. "It was a low priority." The grapes that Swenson brought over from Osceola were planted in the experimental vineyards, where they underwent testing and further breeding. The University did not authorize the work and had no budget for it but did not discourage it either. Swenson forged ahead, hand-fertilizing grapes and patiently waiting to see the results.

The results made agricultural history. Swenson and the University jointly released two grapes: Swenson Red (1977), a cross between Minnesota 78 and the French-American hybrid Seibel 11803, makes a hearty rustic wine; Edelweiss (1980), bred from the original Minnesota 78 crossed with an Ontario grape, makes a fruity Riesling-like white wine. Of the latter, breeder Pat Pierquet says that Edelweiss "will one day be recognized as Elmer's most lasting contribution to the Midwestern wine industry. Edelweiss has been widely planted throughout the Midwest and New England and is used to make a very tasty white wine. A Nebraska winery won Best of Show with their semisweet Edelweiss at an international wine competition—quite an accomplishment for a grape variety bred and developed by a Wisconsin dairy farmer!"

Because Swenson was primarily interested in breeding table grapes, he used *Vitis labrusca* in his breeding, the grapes with the "grape jelly" taste that some wine fanciers deplore. Swenson "wasn't really a wine person. He never made wine, and very rarely drank any wine," Peter

Hemstad says. "I would encourage him, 'C'mon Elmer, have a taste,' and he'd do just that, have just a taste."

The joint Swenson-University release benefited both. The University's prestige made people take notice, where the release of a grape by a Wisconsin dairy farmer might have made little impact; the University got a plant breeding genius for the price of a gardener. For nine years, until 1978, Swenson worked at the University's Horticultural Research Station in Excelsior, going home to Osceola for weekends. "He said they were the happiest years of his life," Hemstad says. After retiring from the University, Swenson released more hybrids: table grapes Trollhaugen, Petite Jewel, Summersweet, and Lorelei; and wine grapes Swenson White, Prairie Star, St. Croix, St. Pepin, La Crosse, Alpenglow, Shannon, Brianna, Esprit, Sabrevois, Kay Gray, and Louise Swenson. Swenson himself never named varieties, which went by labels like ES 31-2t; the names were bestowed by other growers with Swenson's approval.

Swenson remains a beloved figure to winegrowers in the Upper Midwest, many of whom cherish memories of him. He was generous with other grape lovers, readily giving grafts to anyone who showed enthusiasm. David Macgregor describes the aging Elmer as working "down four acres of tightly spaced vines, knowing the number, parentage, and history of every one without reference to records, though bemoaning his failing memory." He was a kindly man, "the kind who mowed the grass in the church cemetery, every week, without expecting thanks," Hemstad remembers.

When Elmer Swenson died in 2004, his funeral brought together scientists, winemakers, farmers, and neighbors at the little rural church in Wisconsin where he had worshiped all his life, all mourning the loss of a Midwestern original, a man who through passion and patience had changed the face of the northern wine world.

Grapes on the Riverbanks

University research did not stop after Swenson returned to Osceola. A graduate student in horticulture, Pat Pierquet, was getting ready to do his master's thesis. Having assisted Elmer in the vineyards since 1975, Pierquet had come to recognize the limits of available breeding stocks. Unlike Swenson, Pierquet was a winemaker interested in breeding high-quality wine grapes. Like many in the industry today, Pierquet started as a hobby winemaker when he was a forestry student at the University of Wisconsin in Madison. He bought his supplies from Bob Wollersheim and bought acreage for a vineyard with Dave Mitchell, Wollersheim's business partner—acreage that is now planted partly in grapes that Pierquet bred.

Most previous breeding, both in Minnesota and earlier in France, had been done with *Vitis labrusca*, the fox grape. But *labrusca* offers several difficulties for northern winegrowers. Firstly, it is not necessarily cold-hardy, although it grows in such areas as Ontario. More important in terms of wine, the grapes have a specific taste that is considered unpleasant by many wine drinkers, the so-called foxy flavor. Pierquet, as a winemaker, knew that to breed grapes that winemakers found exciting and wine drinkers appreciated, he would have to look beyond *labrusca*.

Among other native American grapes, one held promise. *Vitis riparia*, the riverbank grape, is extremely cold-hardy, growing all the way up to Québec. The species has many varieties, including disease-resistant ones that could form breeding stock. But *riparia* also presents challenges. The fruit is small and not especially juicy. The stems are long, and the fruit is sparse on them. The leaves are heavy and often hide the fruit.

Oh, yes, another thing: *riparia* tastes awful. It's strong and sour. "I remember first tasting one when I was a kid," Peter Hemstad says, "and saying 'eeww, where are the raspberries?'" High in acid and low in sugar, the grapes are difficult to make into good wine.

But they live through cold, and they bear fruit despite the rigors of northern winters. So Pat Pierquet, with the approval of faculty mentor Cecil Stushnoff, set out to gather as many clones of *riparia* as he could. He didn't need to harvest whole plants; grapes grow easily from cuttings. In a canoe, he paddled around the rivers of Minnesota, collecting and carefully cataloguing hundreds of *riparia* vines. "I like the stories about me finding vines in the Boundary Waters, but they're not true," Pierquet laughs. "Actually most of the collecting was done on the rather mundane Minnesota River, not far from the Minneapolis suburbs. I did take a trip to Manitoba though, and got some wild vines from the research station there."

In the fall of 1975 and 1976, when the riverbank grapes were full of fruit, Pierquet collected fruit from grapes that seemed clearly disease resistant and carefully noted their location. A dozen or so individual vines seemed promising enough to travel back to the lab with him, where they were tested for sugar and acid levels. The grapes that seemed most suitable were brought into the University vineyards and propagated, then examined further. The hundred or so clones of *riparia* that Pierquet selected now form the backbone of the University's breeding collection.

One of those vines stands out in Pierquet's memory. "It had the highest sugar content of any wild grape we'd found," he recalls. "And it had huge clusters. We labeled it Riparia 89. It was from the Minnesota River near Carver, between Minneapolis and Mankato." He crossed that grape with a French hybrid called Landot 4511 (or Landot Noir), a complex, deeply tinted red grape. The seedlings looked promising, so he set them out in the experimental vineyard to mature.

Then Pierquet left the University and wine-breeding behind. After spending several decades in industrial research, he returned to the wine world in 2007, first in Illinois, now in Ohio. In the interim, one of the seeds that he bred decades earlier has become the single most-planted northern grape. Here is how Pierquet describes the next stage in the development of Frontenac: "There were twenty-seven seedlings. In wine breeding, you think you're lucky if you get one good vine out of five thousand attempts. But we got an exceptional vine out of twenty-seven seeds." Because of the extreme variation among seeds from fruit crops like grapes and apples, they are propagated through cuttings rather than by seed. Yet that same variability makes a huge pool of useful varieties available as well.

Breeders select constantly. They examine hundreds, even thousands, of immature vines for the traits they are hoping to encourage. Vines that seem slow to grow, or with poor quality fruit, are pulled out to make room for new prospects. Because of the long time lag between making the initial selection and public introduction of fruit, grape breeding is a true team effort. As Pierquet moved away from breeding, others continued to develop cold-hardy grapes for the northern winemaker. But Pierquet's part was vital, for from his original collection of *riparia* clones, all new releases from the University of Minnesota have grown.

The Tipping Point

With the development of cold-hardy wine grapes, the tipping point for Upper Midwestern vineyards had been reached. Several pioneer grape growers began planting the new varieties as well as French-American hybrids in both Minnesota and Wisconsin. Winemakers began to experiment with the new breeds and to share the information, especially important because most wine-making techniques were designed to use with *vinifera* grapes while the new hybrids were heavily *riparia*. In 1976, the Minnesota Grape Growers Association (MGGA) was formed, providing a network for those involved in growing and making regional wines.

It was MGGA that, in 1984, convinced the Minnesota state legislature to appropriate $125,000 annually for a grape-breeding program at the University of Minnesota. The growers pointed out that, in addition to the value of the crop, grapes bring income to rural areas through agritourism. Urban people might not drive far to see a soybean field, but a winery—now that's a tourist magnet. Somewhat bemusedly, the legislators approved the appropriation.

The University already had a plant breeder, Jim Luby, who had earned his undergraduate and graduate degrees at the University's St. Paul campus. Like most breeders, Luby was able to apply his expertise to many plants, all of which reproduce in a roughly similar way, but his energies were spread thin between teaching, advising graduate students, and working with several different plant breeding programs that included apples, blueberries, and strawberries as well as grapes. Despite his demanding schedule, Luby had been involved with the breeding and release of the University's first post-Swenson effort: Frontenac. A hardy vine that grows readily in the north, the red-wine grape was enthusiastically adopted by northern growers after its release in 1996 and is now widely grown in the United States and Canada.

With the new appropriation, the University was able to hire another breeder, one with special expertise in grape breeding. Peter Hemstad, a Twin Cities native, had always been fascinated by grapes and had elected to do his graduate work on the species at the prestigious Cornell University, which had introduced many wine grapes used in the Finger Lakes region. At the time, he had no idea that grape breeding was likely, or indeed possible, in Minnesota. But when the University of Minnesota offered him the job in 1985, he leaped at the opportunity.

Not long after he arrived, lightning struck. It was harvest time, and the graduate student and part-time workers were hard at work in the vineyard. The protocol was to toss on the ground any grapes that looked wrong: discolored, strangely formed, or half-unripe. The harvest crew was shorthanded, so Hemstad grabbed a clipper and got to work himself. One of the rows he harvested was the single row of Frontenac.

Hemstad was picking along the row when he suddenly saw something strange. "There was one cane on a single vine of Frontenac," he remembers. "The grapes were a different color, a soft amber. I picked one and squeezed it into my hand. The juice was clear. It was a Gris."

Frontenac is a red grape called a *teinteur*, a "tinter," because unlike most red grapes that release pale juice, its juice is red. The clear juice of the single cane meant that the vine had mutated. Mutations happen all the time in the grape world, most of them useless or even damaging. A leaf form may alter slightly, or a slightly different hue might be detectable in the skin of one branch over another. In most cases, the mutation is too slight to be noticed. Had someone other than Hemstad been picking from that vine that day, the odd-colored fruit might have been discarded and, in pruning, that single cane would have been cut off. Frontenac Gris, officially released in 2003 and now planted throughout the Upper Midwest and Canada, has not appeared spontaneously on any of the other hundreds of thousands of Frontenac vines now being grown. Every vine of Frontenac Gris has been propagated from that single mutant cane.

"Northern Pinot"

Lightning has not struck twice in the University vineyard, but the methodical work of grape breeding has yielded several other important new varieties that are being grown in vineyards throughout the region. The first, released in 2002, was La Crescent, a sweet white grape that was another team effort. Peter Hemstad had the idea of the cross, but Elmer Swenson had the right vines. So Swenson did the actual breeding; Hemstad evaluated the seedlings and selected out the one that became La Crescent. Because Swenson had bred a sweet white named La Crosse, for the Wisconsin river city beneath the Mississippi bluffs, the University named its new grape for the sister-city in Minnesota. La Crescent has been made into a highly regarded dessert wine.

Even more exciting to growers was the release, in 2007, of the heralded Marquette. In its heritage is a *riparia* collected by Pat Pierquet, bred to Pinot Noir. The vine has been planted extensively in the region since its release, and wines made from it should be available within five years. Pinot Noir is a highly regarded *vinifera* that is marginally hardy in the north; some growers have helped it survive Upper Midwestern winters by burying it. A premium red wine, Pinot Noir brings its distinguished heritage to the Minnesota collection, making Marquette the first truly high-bred hybrid.

Although the grape is new to the public, it has been extensively tested over more than a decade in the most rigorous fashion: it has been made into wine. The addition of an oenologist, Anna Catherine Mansfield, to the University staff has enhanced the work of developing northern wines even further. Trained in the chemistry of wine-making, Mansfield takes the new grapes that show promise in the field and tests them to see how good they will be for wine-making. Those who have tasted wine made from Marquette sing its praises as breaking new ground for northern growers.

A Bright Future

The wine-grape experimental vineyard is based at the Minnesota Horticultural Research Station in Excelsior, just west of Minneapolis, the same place where Elmer Swenson did his groundbreaking work. Tens of thousands of vines clamber up their trellises, each carefully catalogued as to its genetic heritage. Several rows of *vinifera*—Cabernet Sauvignon, Chardonnay, and the like—stand before the station's main building. "We use those for pollen," Hemstad says, a bit dismissively. "We bury them every year. Some are more than thirty years old. We have shown that, with enough work, you can grow *vinifera* vines here."

But Hemstad and the other researchers are not interested in high-maintenance grapes. They do not coddle their thousands of experimental vines with special irrigation systems, extensive spraying, special pruning techniques, or winter burial. "We are looking for hardy, disease-resistant plants," says Hemstad as he walks through the vineyard on a sunny late summer day. "That one—look at the amount of foliar phylloxera, compared to the one next to it." The diseased vine will be torn out and destroyed, to leave room for other, hardier vines.

"Look at that one," he says, pointing to a vine voluptuously hung with huge clusters of pale green fruit. "Look at how open the plant is. How easy to pick it would be. That one has promise." The process of plant breeding is ruthless, for among the tens of thousands of plants the vineyard will produce, only one will meet the standards for release to the public.

Cold-hardy, disease-resistant—and good for wine-making. Some nice-looking hardy vines are simply terrible tasting. "I remember the one that tasted like a tomato," Jim Luby winces. The variety of possible grape tastes is broad enough that the Minnesota researchers will be at work for many decades to come. "I'd like to see a Muscat-like wine," Hemstad says. "And of course something like a big Cab. And a spicy wine like a Gewürztraminer. And . . ."

And the rows of possibilities stretch out before him, each of them a possible ancestor of another new grape that will create great northern wine.

A Chronology of Northern Wines

1846	Agoston Haraszthy arrives in Wisconsin.
1848	Agoston Haraszthy leaves Wisconsin.
1908	University of Minnesota grape-breeding program begins.
1913	Elmer Swenson born.
1944	Bluebell table grape released by University of Minnesota.
1967	von Stiehl Winery opens; first winery in Wisconsin.
1972	Bob Wollersheim buys Haraszthy vineyard.
	Three Lakes winery established.
Early 1970s	Jim Pape opens Stone Mill Winery (now Cedar Creek).
1974	Door Peninsula Winery established.
1977	First Minnesota farm winery license issued.
1978	First Alexis Bailly wines released.
	Swenson Red released by University of Minnesota.
1980	Swenson retires from University of Minnesota.
1982	First Spurgeon vintage released; Scenic Valley Winery established.
1983	Northern Vineyards established.
1985	Orchard Country Winery established.
1989	Woodland Trails Winery established.
1990	Cedar Creek Winery established.
1991	Botham Winery established.
1992	St. Croix Vineyards established.
1993	Morgan Creek established.
1995	Bayfield Winery, Winehaven, Trout Springs Winery established.
1996	White Winter Winery established.
	Frontenac released by University of Minnesota.
	Wisconsin State Fair Wine Garden opens.
1998	Forestedge Winery established.

2000   Kerrigan Brothers Winery established.

2001   Lil' Ole Winemaker, Aeppeltreow Winery established.

2002   Chateau St. Croix, Red Oak Winery established.

        La Crescent released by University of Minnesota.

2003   Fieldstone Winery, Simon Creek Winery established.

        Frontenac Gris released by University of Minnesota.

2004   Falconer, Cannon River, Vetro Winery, Weggy Winery, Autumn Harvest Winery, Apple Barn Winery, Tenba Ridge established.

2005   Vernon County Vineyards, Burr Oak Winery, Two Fools Vineyard established.

2006   Olde Country, Brigadoon, HookStone established.

2007   Garvin Heights, Salem Glen, Crofut Family Winery, Goose Lake, Captain's Walk, LedgeStone, Parallel 44, Munson Creek established.

        Wine Country Exhibit opens at Minnesota State Fair.

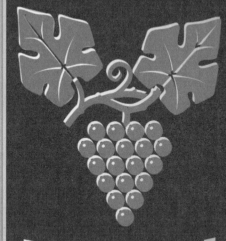

Part 2

RINKING TEACHES MUCH ABOUT WINE. You learn to distinguish dry from sweet, soft from hard, higher or lower alcohol, or varietal tastes—but not the relationship of vine to soil, and of winemaker to both. For that, you must see vineyards. You must visit wineries.

This book's aim is not to hold up a single ideal but to celebrate the variety of options in the region. Wineries that make fruit wines appear alongside those making grape wines; wineries that import juice or grapes appear with wineries that use locally grown fruit. Some wineries handcraft their wines in small batches; some use commercial-sized fermentation vats for large-scale production; a few contract out winemaking and focus on sales and promotion. Some are gift stores with a tasting counter; others are sleek facilities offering wine only. Some are converted barns; others are town storefronts. Some feel like Tuscan villas; others like cabins in the north woods. These wineries are, literally, incomparable.

Wineries that have no tasting rooms do not appear here; look for their wines at restaurants and wine shops. Vineyards alone were also excluded, although some are open for public events. Finally, new regional wineries will continue to open; the industry's unprecedented growth shows no signs of slowing. To find new wineries, check in with the Minnesota Grape Growers Association (www.mngrapes.org) and the Wisconsin Winery Association (www.wiswine.com).

When you visit these wineries, expect to learn; wineries are the wine industry's educational arm. If you are a newcomer to wine touring, do not be concerned if you see others swirling and sniffing, swishing and spitting. Ask what they're doing, imitate them, or ignore them. If you have questions, ask the server. In small wineries, that might be the winemaker or grape grower, eager to share hard-won knowledge.

Visitors are typically offered a "flight" or sequence of wines, usually from white to red and from dry to sweet. These standard procedures help ensure that one wine is not overpowered by an earlier one. The "pour" size is standard in each winery: a mouthful, never a full glass. Wineries usually limit the wines to be sampled, a decision that has to do with availability. Finally, both custom and, in some cases, law demand that only pourers serve the wine. Never help yourself.

As for spitting: most people don't. Serious wine tasters who want to keep their senses sharp spit out wine after tasting. For the majority of people, swallowing is the common practice.

There is no one right way to enjoy a winery visit, but there are things to avoid. Never enter a vineyard without permission. Many wineries provide picnic tables and patios, but some are not legally permitted to allow off-site food, and of course drinking wine from another winery is poor manners indeed. Remember that tasting rooms are not designed for partying but for sipping. Do not hog the bar if others await their turn and, if you plan to visit more than one winery in a day, designate a driver for safety. Loudly comparing a winery to the fancier place you visited in Napa Valley is boorish. So is complaining about the size of the pour. And remember that wineries are not charity operations; when you find something you enjoy, bring a bottle home.

Great River North

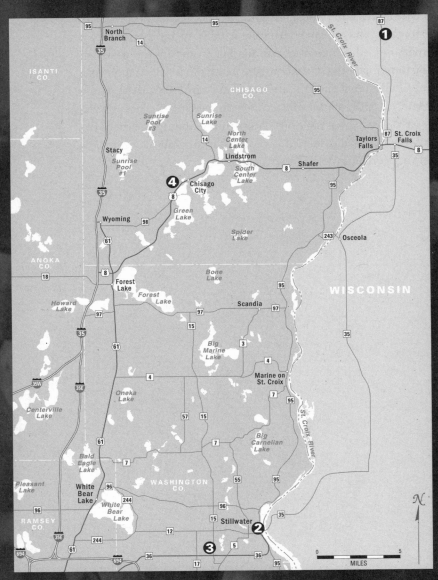

1. Chateau St. Croix 2. Northern Vineyards
3. St. Croix Vineyards 4. Winehaven

IN EAST CENTRAL MINNESOTA, a river cuts gorges and bluffs into glacial flatlands. There, a cluster of wineries takes advantage of natural vine-pleasing soils and slopes. These wineries are close to Minneapolis and St. Paul, in a region filled with history, culture, and recreational opportunities.

During the St. Croix phase of the last ice age, around twenty thousand years ago, ice sheets reached the edge of this region, from which the St. Croix River carried the water of the huge glacial lakes Grantsburg and Duluth. Its waters slowly fell as the glaciers melted, leaving stepped gorges that show the sequence of old riverbeds. The river rises near Gordon, Wisconsin, passes through a wide glacier-formed valley to the dam at St. Croix Falls, then enters the gorge of the Dalles. Farther downstream, the river widens at the Minnesota riverfront town of Stillwater to form Lake St. Croix.

Stillwater is a charming river town steeped in history. Originally inhabited by Ojibwe and Dakota peoples, Stillwater saw its first European settlement in 1939, when a mud-plastered cabin was erected by Joseph Renshaw Brown, known as Joe the Juggler for his fiscal finagling. Brown was soldier, fur trader, trading post proprietor, and finally lumberman. Minnesota was then part of Wisconsin Territory, and Brown served as representative to its legislature. Agitating for a distinctive Minnesota identity, he organized the Stillwater Convention of 1848, which sent Brown's good friend Henry Sibley to Washington to plead for establishment of a Minnesota Territory. Sibley was later elected first governor of the state.

In Stillwater's early years, the river was filled with logs for the town's lumber mills. Legend has it that river rafting began there after an accidental release of hundreds of logs. Men discovered that they could control the logs by riding on top, directing the flow with poles as they raced along with the river current. Always dangerous, river rafting was also financially rewarding. Stillwater boomed with the trade of well-paid raft pilots.

After logging declined, Stillwater faced the same fate as other Upper Midwestern towns; even the invention of the toaster by a Stillwater mechanic did not slow the steady economic slide. Then Stillwater reinvented itself as a destination for tourists from the Twin Cities, and now a score of antique shops and bookstores share the downtown with upscale restaurants.

Stillwater has a special place in Upper Midwestern wine history because of the Last Man's Club, formed by thirty-four Civil War veterans. Their regiment had suffered greatly during the war, with many soldiers killed at their first battle at Bull Run. In 1885, survivors vowed to dine together every year on the battle's anniversary, July 21. Thirty-four chairs were set, to be draped with black after a person died. Before the ritual toast Mrs. Samuel Bloomer, widow of the company's color sergeant, ceremoniously displayed a rosewood box containing a bottle of Burgundy, vintage unrecorded, which had been set aside for the last living member of the regiment.

For the next forty-two years the group met annually, until only three Last Men remained: Peter Hall, 89; Charles Lockwood, 86; and John Goff, 85. They held their final meeting in 1927, three aged men surrounded by thirty-one black-draped chairs, and Hall made their formal toast: "Men love their country now, but our dead comrades loved it most." Reports from the time say that the bottle was opened then and shared among the survivors.

But *Time* magazine in 1930 reported that the last Last Man, Charles Lockwood, opened the wine that year. "He filled his glass," the magazine reported, "held it aloft and recited as the Club had specified long ago: "The camp fire smolders—ashes fall; The clouds are black athwart the sky; No tap of drums, no bugle call; My comrades, all, Goodbye!" Then he took a drink, tears running down his cheeks. But the wine had turned so sour he could only take a sip. Lockwood, who died five years later, commented thus on the experience, "We should have saved ourselves a bottle of old Irish whiskey instead." The emptied bottle now belongs to the Washington County Historical Society.

CHATEAU ST. CROIX

Imagine a castle in one of Europe's great wine regions, rising like a great stony mass above a river's banks. Visitors sip a glass of wine on a terrace above the formal gardens, perhaps watching a game of polo on the spreading lawns. Young entrepreneurs Laura and Troy Chamberlin visited castles like that and a dreamed of bringing home that regal lifestyle. Wine was part of that dream, so they began looking for a location for a winery. When they found it, Chateau St. Croix was born.

Built on the design of a winery in Burgundy, Chateau St. Croix opened in 2003. Its small vineyard, planted in Elmer Swenson grapes, is dedicated to production of ice wines. Developed in Germany in 1794, ice wine requires that growers leave grapes on the vines until they freeze, naturally concentrating the sugars. The process requires perfect weather, to say nothing of protection from birds and other predators.

Most of the wine at Chateau St. Croix is made from grapes imported from California and vinified to suit a variety of tastes: an unoaked Chardonnay, a Sonoma Cabernet Sauvignon, and an American Muscat dessert wine. Chateau St. Croix has also found a niche as a location for wedding and business events.

Wine stands at the center of Chateau St. Croix, but Laura and Troy see it as only part of the lifestyle that charmed and inspired them. Art and sport are important as well. A spacious, light-filled gallery shows off the work of area artists. Beyond the winery, a polo ground stretches out and ponies practice. If that does not bring forth visions of European elegance, it's hard to say what would.

Chateau St. Croix

1998A State Road 87 • St. Croix Falls, WI 54024 • 715-483-2556 • www.chateaustcroix.com

Location: Directly north of the town of St. Croix Falls on State Road 87.

The Tippling Point

A 2005 study by Scarborough Research Group found that one-third of wine drinkers boast a household income in excess of $75,000, while almost half have some college education—both figures considerably higher than the American average of $42,228 and 24 percent, respectively. Wine consumers also tend to be better-traveled than average Americans.

Although the average wine drinker remains older than the average beer drinker, a 2005 Gallup poll discovered that, for the first time, wine has overtaken beer as America's most popular alcoholic drink. Younger and less wealthy Americans have turned to wine for several reasons. Health and dietary information presents wine as an appealing alternative to supposedly high-calorie beer. Innovative marketing and blending techniques also appeal to younger consumers.

Then there is the so-called Starbucks effect, wherein younger consumers are undeterred by complex wine selection decisions. Finally, the cultural influence of such media events as the popular movie *Sideways* have helped younger consumers identify not only with wine drinking, but also with wine tourism. So the person standing next to you at a wine-tasting may as easily be a tattooed and pierced twenty-something as a tweedy old fellow with pretentious pronunciations.

Hours:

June 1–October 15:

Monday, Wednesday, Thursday, noon–5:00 pm

Friday and Saturday, 11:00 am–7:00 pm

Sunday, noon–4:00 pm

October 16–May 31:

Monday, Wednesday, Thursday, noon–5:00 pm

Friday, noon–5:00 pm

Saturday, noon–6:00 pm

Sunday, noon–4:00 pm

Closed Tuesdays, major holidays, and the first three weeks of January

Tasting: Complimentary

Tours: Every half-hour, on the half-hour, $5

Signature wines:

Cheesehead White: full-bodied "wine for the rest of us"

Merlot: award-winning California red

Jaune d'Or Port: tawny port aged in French oak

Events: Occasional; see website.

NORTHERN VINEYARDS

The sleek tasting room of Northern Vineyards occupies a small section of the building on Stillwater's main street. The rest is the domain of winemaker Robin Partch. Wine is in his blood: his grandfather and father were German winemakers in Missouri, until Prohibition destroyed a flourishing industry. A former science teacher, Partch was once a hobby winemaker with a small patch of vines. That was then: now Partch dedicates himself fulltime to fermenting and bottling the output of cooperating vineyards in Minnesota and Wisconsin. Surrounded by tanks and accompanied by his Siberian husky Spot, who greedily laps up spilled wine, Partch creates individual varietals and blends.

Partch helped organize Northern Vineyards with Dennis Martin, cooperative president and holder of the oldest farm winery license in Minnesota. Like many in the cooperative, Martin wanted to grow grapes but was uninterested in making wine. Then in 1983, Martin and other growers found themselves unable to sell their grapes for the price they had anticipated. Making wine from those grapes was a logical next step, but finances and lack of wine-making experience limited individual growers. Together, they were able to gather both funds and expertise to launch what is now one of Minnesota's biggest producers of local wine.

At first Partch ran the wine-making operation part-time, but the enterprise soon became too much for a weekend winemaker with a vineyard 140 miles away. In 1998, Partch went full-time to vinify Minnesota-grown grapes. The biggest challenge is that cool climate grapes tend toward the acidic. Long autumns permit grape sugars to increase while acids diminish. But who can predict an Upper Midwestern season? Sometimes harvest waits for the perfect balance, but sometimes early cold forces the picking of still-acidic grapes. Partch uses several techniques, including use of acid-lowering yeasts, to bring the wine into balance. Production of sparkling wine, often a recourse in similar regions of high acidity, is an option Partch is disinclined to pursue. "Often sparkling wine is bad still wine. I'd rather just make good wine."

Demand for Northern Vineyards' wine exceeds the supply of local wine grapes, so Partch buys selected grapes from California and New York growers. He is unusual among Midwestern vintners in using the Italian Barbera grape, which he selected because "it tastes like it could have been grown here." Northern Vineyards sells most of the winery's output to local and regional buyers. At the long oak bar, visitors can sample from the variety of offerings or purchase wine to take upstairs in good weather. There on the expansive deck, picnickers watch the lift-bridge open for passing boats. And if anyone spills any wine, Spot is right there to lap it up.

Northern Vineyards Winery

223 N. Main Street • Stillwater, MN 55082 •
651-430-1032 • www.northernvineyards.com

Location: North end of Main Street in Stillwater.

Hours:

March–October:
Sunday, noon–9:00 pm
Monday–Thursday, 10:00 am–8:00 pm
Friday and Saturday, 10:00 am–9:00 pm
November–February:
Sunday, noon–7:00 pm
Monday–Thursday, 10:00 am–7:00 pm
Friday and Saturday, 10:00 am–8:00 pm
Closed Thanksgiving, Christmas, and New Year's Day

Tasting: Complimentary

Tours: By arrangement

Signature wines:

Old Vines Maréchal Foch: rich, fruity, intense, and dry
St. Croix Reserve: dry and elegant
Prairie Smoke: dry, oaky Minnesota La Crosse

Events: Sunday concerts on the deck in good weather; December cheese and chocolate festival.

The Cooperative Movement

Many French wines come from cooperatives that combine grapes from many small vineyards, but Northern Vineyards is at present the only wine cooperative in the Upper Midwest, a region that, with its Scandinavian heritage, has historically been friendly to cooperatives. On the Iron Range, a cooperative park still functions, created in response to anti-Finnish prejudice. Early-twentieth-century newspapers derided Finnish immigrants as "jack pine savages" whose socialist tendencies made them inassimilable. Saloons on the Mesabi Range bragged that "no Indians or Finns" were admitted. Finns responded by building a series of cooperative enterprises that outsold competitors. In this spirit, in 1929 the Finns decided to organize a cooperative park as a place to hold the ethnic summer solstice celebration. Within a year, they found land near Hibbing where they constructed buildings and pavilions. Mesaba Park still exists and, although member-owned, welcomes the public.

Not far away, Cloquet occupies an important position in American cooperative history, because its cooperative society provided consumer goods including food, furniture, coal, and gas. Until the middle of the twentieth century, nearly half of Cloquet's residents were co-op members, the highest percentage of any town in the nation.

Producers' cooperatives, as distinct from consumers' cooperatives, are common in agriculture. Dairy cooperatives such as Land O'Lakes help maintain quality and high prices for farmers. Beet farmers, alfalfa producers, even biodiesel farmers have joined together for mutual assistance. Will the Upper Midwest become like the Côtes du Rhône, where the small vineyardist joins with others to create and market regional wines? Don't be surprised to see more cooperatives springing up in the region in coming years.

ST. CROIX VINEYARDS

What three things make a successful Midwestern winery? Location, location, location, right? Not really. You need land, yes. Then vines, and the knowledge of how to make them grow. Finally, organizational and business sense. And the three don't necessarily come in a single package.

Location helps, especially if that location is smack in the middle of one of Minnesota's most popular tourist destinations. Chris Aamodt had land in that ideal location: Aamodt's Apple Farm, a picturesque well-tended twenty-seven-variety orchard with a century-old barn just west of Stillwater. But he was not especially interested in wine.

Lawyer Paul Quast knew wine, and he was an organizer, in charge of the wine division of the Minnesota State Fair. He also knew Aamodt's because he had worked there as a teenager, picking apples and directing traffic during festivals. But he did not know how to grow vines.

For vineyard knowledge, who better than University of Minnesota wine breeder Peter Hemstad? Hemstad yearned to get into the winery business and had taken to driving around the metropolitan outskirts looking for a likely vineyard site. When Quast and Hemstad met through the State Fair, the three vital ingredients were brought together.

St. Croix Vineyards was born in 1992—relatively early for Upper Midwestern wineries. At the time, the new cold-hardy grapes had not been released, so the vineyard was planted in the French-American hybrid Maréchal Foch. Many of the original eight hundred vines survive, although managed differently now. "Every fall we pruned after harvest—imagine, we'd be exhausted, but out there cutting them down. Then we pinned them down and covered them with straw. In spring, we'd take out the straw and find the mice. The straw kept them warm, and we had helpfully brought the canes down for them to dine on."

That was then. Everyone said you had to bury the vines, so they did. But after a few years Hemstad tried leaving a few vines standing. "They had no mouse damage, so after awhile we came to the conclusion that it was more effective not to pin them." The method is now accepted procedure.

There were other experiments too, like the Chardonnay period. "We had to bury them every winter. It was a labor of love," Hemstad laughs. The wine won awards, but after ten years, it was time to move on. "We had proven that, with enough effort, you can grow *vinifera* in Minnesota." But the new Minnesota varieties were available. "We thought the world would be more excited about a really new wine than about having one more Chardonnay on the shelf." Out came the Chardonnay, and in went Frontenac Gris, La Crescent, and Marquette.

St. Croix Vineyards' white wines include Seyval and Vignoles, both French hybrids; reds include Frontenac rosé, as well as a Maréchal Foch aged in American oak. An apple wine tips the hat to the orchard beside the vineyard. The orchard heritage is also evident in the tasting room, which adjoins the apple barn. At St. Croix Vineyards, past and present flow together seamlessly, and the promise of the future is almost tangible.

St. Croix Vineyards

6428 Manning Avenue • Stillwater, MN 55082 • 651-430-3310 • www.scvwines.com

Location: Directly west of downtown Stillwater; a half mile north of State Highway 36 on Manning Avenue.

Hours:

Mid-April–July:
Friday and Saturday, 10:00 am–6:00 pm
Sunday, noon–6:00 pm

August–October:
Monday–Saturday, 10:00 am–6:00 pm
Sunday, noon–6:00 pm
November–December:
Monday–Saturday, 10:00 am–5:00 pm
Sunday, noon–5:00 pm
Closed January–mid-April

Tasting: Complimentary

Tours: Free 45-minute public tours, 1:00 pm, first Saturday of each month from May to December

Signature wines:
Seyval: fruity, light French variety
Maréchal Foch Reserve: dry, medium-bodied, aged in oak
Raspberry Infusion: red dessert wine, sweet but balanced

Events: Early September grape stomp.

WINEHAVEN

A half century ago, Kevin Peterson was looking for a part-time job. He found it when a farmer hired him to tend beehives. Peterson discovered he had a knack for it and eventually built up a multistate business as part of the Sioux Bee honey cooperative.

Like many in agriculture, Peterson started looking for a product to enhance profits. He found it in the ancient beverage called mead: wine made from fermented honey. In 1995, Peterson and his wife, Cheri, founded Winehaven. Today their sons have joined them. Kyle, who studied at Cornell University, joined his dad on the wine-making team, while Troy serves as tasting room manager, creating an ambiance that led to Winehaven's five-time status as Minnesota's friendliest winery.

Located just off the main road into Chisago City, Winehaven's oldest vineyards are planted on sandy loam soil with varieties developed by Elmer Swenson of nearby Osceola. Peterson and Swenson were friends, brought together by a shared Scandinavian heritage and a passion for grapes. Other Winehaven varieties include the French-American Maréchal Foch, as well as Minnesota-bred Frontenac and Marquette. The popular *vinifera* variety Riesling occupies some vineyard space, but Peterson acknowledges that it's risky in Minnesota and requires more care than the other plantings.

Three Rivers Wine Trail

Many wine regions have "trails" to show tourists the way from one winery to the next—an idea based on the fact that people enjoy seeing more than one winery in a day or weekend. By working together, six wineries on the Three Rivers Wine Trail hope to help tourists find their way.

Unlike a packaged tour, a wine trail is self-guided. Map in hand, Minnesota wine tourists can now wend their way from Winehaven to Northern Vineyards to St. Croix Vineyards, all in an afternoon. The southern part of the wine trail includes Alexis Bailly, Falconer, and Cannon River Winery (see Great River South)—again, easily accomplished in a day. Both sections of the trail are within an hour's drive of the Twin Cities.

Following a wine trail helps the traveler understand the area's wines more fully; otherwise, why not just go to a bar? As the landscape unfolds between destinations, the wine tourist begins to see distinctions of terrain and to imagine its influence on *terroir*. With its dramatic river scenery and friendly wineries in historic towns, Three Rivers Wine Trail is the first of what is likely to be a series of such trails in the Upper Midwest.

In addition to that vineyard, new plantings take advantage of a milder lakeside microclimate. This section, with rich soil and natural protection from potentially damaging winds, was dubbed the Deer Garden by Swedish settlers in the late nineteenth century; Winehaven's signature blends are named for this area of the farm.

"We like to say we have happy grapes," Kevin Peterson smiles broadly as he talks of the vineyard expansion. "I've seen up to three weeks' difference because of the lake effect," including both bud-break and harvest. He is optimistic about the future for the Midwestern wine industry and for Winehaven in particular. Their wines continue to include mead made with native basswood honey, a specialty product given the short blooming period of the trees. The mead, offered in both medium and semisweet styles, keeps alive the experience of a young Kevin Peterson in his first job in Chisago City half a century ago.

Winehaven

9757 292nd Street • Chisago City, MN 55013 • 651-257-1017 • www.winehaven.com

Location: 35 miles north of the Twin Cities, on the outskirts of Chisago City, north of Green Lake.

Hours:
April–December:
Sunday–Tuesday, noon–5:00 pm
Wednesday–Saturday, 10:00 am–5:00 pm
January–March:
Saturdays only, 10:00 am–4:00 pm

Tasting: Complimentary

Tours: By arrangement

Signature wines:
Deer Garden White: medium-dry easy drinking blend
Maréchal Foch: Minnesota grapes make a light, medium-dry wine good with food
Honeywine: semisweet variety presented to Swedish royalty in 1996

Events: Early December, holiday festival; March, Cabin Fever Day; April, New Vintage Days; July, Raspberries and Wine Festival; August, Rhubarb Frenzy; early September, Fall Fever Day and Harvest Tour; October, Dessert Wine Experience.

Bees and Wine

Winehaven's labels feature a small stylized bee, a nod to the family's honey business. In Scandinavia, where grapes are not native, honey formed the base for wine. In the hive, honey is too sterile for fermentation to occur—any stray yeasts die a speedy death—but harvested honey attracts moisture from the air. In such diluted honey, wild yeasts find a rich source of nutrients. There was probably no inventor of mead, but rather a discoverer who dared drink the fermented stuff.

Mead has fallen out of favor today, in comparison with the fruits of the vine. But honey wine casts its sweet alcoholic cloak over newlyweds taking their "honeymoon." Although the etymology is disputed (some sources claim the term refers to the speedy waxing and waning of love's pleasures), most say that ancient brides and grooms were provided enough mead to keep them drunk for a month. In such traditions, the honeymoon was over when the wine was gone and stark sober reality had to be faced.

1. Alexis Bailly Vineyard 2. Cannon River Winery 3. Falconer Vineyards
4. Garvin Heights Vineyards 5. Salem Glen Winery 6. Scenic Valley Winery

BENEATH DARK BROODING BLUFFS above the Mississippi, Minnesota finds its most picturesque wine country. Geologically distinct from the rest of the state, the river bluff country shows none of the telltale signs of glaciation: it was never ironed flat under the weight of ice, there are no lakes filled with glacial melt or big granite boulders strewn about, the soil is not rich glacial till but lean and rocky. Streams and rivers have eroded the land into hills and valleys, creating panoramic vistas unlike anywhere else in Minnesota.

The predominant features of the landscape were formed, in geological terms, only recently. Five hundred million years ago, the area lay under a shallow sea whose sandstone bed forms the region's lowest rock layers. Above the sandstone rests a cap of dolomite formed from the skeletons of sea creatures whose bodies sank into the muddy bottom and decayed. After the sea retreated, the dolomite formed the land's floor for eons, until the glacial era ended. Ten thousand years ago, when the Mississippi drained the melting glaciers, enormous water pressure undercut the hard dolomite, which broke off in vertical fractures, forming sheer faces visible on hillsides and bluffs today.

In this region, the Mississippi joins with smaller rivers like the St. Croix and the Chippewa. Lake Pepin—not a lake but a natural widening of the river—is a playground for boaters; waterskiing was invented there in 1922, by a local daredevil who strapped lumber to his feet and grasped a clothesline tied behind a speedboat. Other sports are also popular, especially fly-fishing. With 680 miles of designated trout streams, the area is among the nation's top locations for brown and rainbow trout.

Migrating water birds fish these waters too. The Upper Mississippi River National Wildlife Refuge, a 261-mile-long stretch of marshes and sandbars, sees millions of birds pass through in spring and fall: white pelicans, great egrets, sandhill cranes, night herons and other exotic breeds. Year-round residents—eagles, ruffed grouse, and wild turkeys—are also visible in the mixed oak-hickory and maple-basswood forests.

Bicyclers and hikers enjoy a well-established trail system that ranges from gentle to steep terrain. Those interested in botanizing find a wealth of possibilities, including the unusual "goat prairies," so named because they grow on slopes so steep it seems only goats could graze there. Wine tourism, although in its infancy, joins antiquing, gallery hopping, and theatergoing as regional attractions.

Located near the Twin Cities, southeastern Minnesota has been a haven for harried urbanites for more than a century, but its longer economic history includes fur trading, pottery, and farming. As early as 7000 BCE, Paleoindians settled there; later Mississippian peoples (500–1650 CE) created rock art and mound complexes that suggest an affluent, ritually sophisticated culture. During early historic times, the region was occupied by the Sioux, who traded with the French fur-seeker Pierre Esprit Radisson.

Although voyageurs ranged through the Upper Midwest, the Mississippi was central to French-American culture, with several permanent settlements, including one founded on Prairie Island near Red Wing in 1694. The Treaty of Paris brought the region under British control in 1763; a few years later the British handed it off to the Americans. But the new United States showed little interest until Zebulon Pike passed through in the early 1800s.

The rich lands of the southeastern sector then drew American farmers, with the Red River area populated with newcomers by the mid-1850s. Soon the entire area was flooded with settlers, immigrants from Scandinavia, Germany, and Ireland being most heavily represented. Wheat farming become the major occupation.

If furs and wheat built the area, it is now best known through its literature, for Laura Ingalls Wilder was born on the shores of Lake Pepin. Wilder's family was moved by their restless father to Walnut Grove, Minnesota, as well as to homesteads in Kansas and Iowa, before they finally settled in the Dakotah Territory. Wilder began to write for a local newspaper and gradually expanded her ambitions until, at the age of sixty-three and with the help of daughter Rose Wilder Lane, she achieved fame with the Little House series. A scenic byway near Preston honors the author.

The region's cultural capitol is Winona, site of St. Mary's College and Winona State University. Nearby Red Wing is renowned among those who collect pottery and shoes. Other communities include Caledonia, wild turkey capital of Minnesota; Lanesboro, model city for arts development; Harmony, home to a large Amish community; and Minnesota's first Norse settlement, Spring Grove. With dramatic scenery, historical heritage, and an active arts scene, southeastern Minnesota welcomes the visitor.

ALEXIS BAILLY VINEYARD

To the left of the counter in the serving room at Alexis Bailly hangs a photograph of a stern-featured soldier in a massive, elaborate frame. A flowing inscription reads, *"Á la ville de Minneapolis en souvenir de mon séjour, Nov. 26, 1921."* The signature: Maréchal Foch.

High on the opposite wall, a romantic painting depicts a French-looking fellow quaffing a glass of wine. Painted by winemaker Nan Bailly's husband Sam Haislet, the canvas shows the eponymous Alexis Bailly, Nan's ancestor and a Minnesota settler of the 1820s.

The French influence is obvious at Alexis Bailly, named for a man from eastern France who made Minnesota his home. His descendent, Minneapolis attorney and oenophile David Bailly, was inspired by his heritage to take

his family to France. There he found that, despite Draconian laws against their cultivation in favor of more prestigious *vinifera* grapes, some farmers still cultivated hybrid varieties created to save the French wine industry from that American import, the phylloxera that ate European grape roots into oblivion. Delighted to find these heritage grapes, David Bailly decided to bring them into cultivation back home.

His search for an appropriate piece of land led him to a moraine near Hastings, where in 1973 he planted twelve acres of hybrids, predominantly Maréchal Foch. Other hybrids in that early planting included Léon Millot, Aurore, and Baco Noir—some of which still live in the Alexis Bailly vineyards today. Bailly's determination to raise high-quality wine grapes was soon given a boost by renowned French

Foch in Minnesota

On the front page of the old scrapbook, spidery letters spell out the inscription: "Return to David L. Sutherland, 1819 Dupont Ave. S."

"And we lived at 1812 Dupont for seven years!" Nan Bailly marvels. A friend found the scrapbook at a rummage sale and passed it along to Nan. Its pages crammed with yellowed clippings, the scrapbook had been kept by Sutherland, organizer of a historic Twin Cities event: the visit of Maréchal Foch in 1921, to dedicate a memorial to soldiers from Hennepin County who died in the Great War. As the daughter of the man who brought the grape named for Maréchal Foch into commercial production in the Upper Midwest, Nan Bailly appreciates the historic value of the scrapbook, which she keeps at the winery together with other memorabilia about the World War I hero.

Maréchal Ferdinand Foch was supreme commander of the allied forces at the time of the Ger-

man surrender on November 11, 1918. Before the war, he had been a professor at France's military college, where he carefully examined French defeats in an attempt to learn from them. No armchair general, Foch led the Ninth Army in the Battle of the Marne, during which he is said to have uttered the famous words, "I am hard pressed on my right; my center is giving way; situation excellent; I am attacking." The counterattack, which Foch had studied during his professorial days, stopped the German advance and assured his fame.

Not long after, as joint commander in chief, he led the Battle of the Somme, after which he was removed from command because of the appallingly heavy casualties. But after a series of failures by other generals, Foch was brought back to plan the Grand Offensive that led to the German surrender.

wine critic Baron Phillipe de Rothschild. Dismissing the emerging American wine region of California as unlikely to produce great wines because of its mild climate, the Baron claimed that vines need wind, sleet, snow, and drought to develop subtlety of flavor. Bailly seized upon the Baron's words as the motto for his winery: "where the grapes can suffer." In 1977 Bailly had his first crush, releasing his first wines in 1978. Minnesota did not immediately warm to its first native-son *vigneron*: one local newspaper dubbed him the "freak vintner." But the grapes survived, and the winery thrived.

In 1990, after David Bailly's death of cancer at fifty-seven, his daughter Nan took over the winery, both keeping his original vision and developing her own. She keeps some of her father's original plantings, taking down the less-hardy hybrids from their trellises to bury them in trenches each winter, a labor-intensive process that has kept some vines alive to an advanced age. But as vines have inevitably died, she has replaced them with other, more cold-hardy varieties such as Minnesota-bred Frontenac, which she uses in her signature blends.

Nan Bailly is passionate about wine; she named her beloved husky, pictured on the winery website, Léon Millot after the hybrid vine. Her desire for more oenological knowledge led her to study in both the United States and Europe. She seeks to offer new flavors to the regional market, especially through blending, which she calls "the winemaker's best tool." One of her most striking wines is Ratafia, wine-mixed with spices and citrus fruits. Her most recent: an elegant "big Cab"–style blend called Voyageur in honor of the Upper Midwest's French influence.

Hard on the heels of his victories, Foch was invited to Minneapolis to dedicate a line of elm trees planted on Victory Memorial Drive in the Camden neighborhood, the largest war monument in the area. The Drive makes up part of the Grand Rounds, a fifty-mile circle of parkways that surrounds the city. Cities everywhere were planting parks and erecting monuments inspired by the City Beautiful movement, so park board president Charles Loring and designer Theodore Wirth created a magnificent tree-lined boulevard. Nearly a thousand Moline elms, paid for by Loring himself, stretched along the 3.8-mile Victory Memorial Drive, their branches arching above the boulevard. At the dedication on June 11, 1921, tens of thousands lined the street to honor the 516 men who had died, whose absence was marked by wooden crosses.

But the celebration went on without Foch, who stayed in Europe to suppress a miners' revolt in Prussia. Six months later, he did make a triumphal visit to Minneapolis, where he was greeted with the receptions and parades documented in Nan Bailly's scrapbook. After that visit, Foch never set foot in Minnesota again.

But the grape named for him thrives. Bred in Alsace by the renowned Eugene Kuhlmann, Maréchal Foch includes genes from *vinifera* and an American native, probably *Vitis riparia* (riverbank grape). Foch vines produce better fruit with age; the grape can be vinified in many ways, from a light red to an intense port. The Alexis Bailly vineyard has some of the oldest plantings in the Upper Midwest, but all the grand elms on Memorial Drive were lost to disease and replaced with hackberry trees.

Open on weekends, Alexis Bailly offers a friendly setting for a day in the country. Bocce-ball courts stretch out under huge grape arbors. Picnic tables dot the sweeping lawns surrounded by berms planted with wildflowers and shrubs. Minnesota's oldest commercial winery, Alexis Bailly stays in the forefront of the industry with classy, complex wines served in a charming French-influenced winery.

Alexis Bailly Vineyard

18200 Kirby Avenue • Hastings, MN 55033 • 651-437-1413 • www.abvwines.com

Location: Highway 61 one mile south from Hastings; turn right on 170th Street; follow the road two miles as it curves left and becomes Kirby Avenue; vineyard on the left.

Hours:
May until Thanksgiving:
Friday, Saturday, Sunday, 11:00 am–5:30 pm
Thanksgiving until Christmas:
Saturday, 11:00 am–4:30 pm
Closed Christmas to May except by special arrangement

Tasting: $3 per person

Tours: By arrangement

Signature wines:
Voyageur: big-bodied red
Ice Wine: sweet but crisp dessert wine
Hastings Reserve: jammy port-style fortified wine
Ratafia: orange-infused bold red wine

Events: First two weekends in June, spring open house; first weekend in November, fall open house; December, wine and chocolate tasting.

CANNON RIVER WINERY

"Lots of people start with a piece of land and then decide to grow grapes," Maureen Maloney reflects, "but we started with the idea of growing grapes, then looked for a perfect site." Although their prairie restoration business was thriving, they were ready for a change. Visiting other wineries in the region convinced them that, with the right piece of land, they could succeed as winegrowers.

Their dream drove them to visit more than thirty properties, hoping for the right combination of slope, direction, and soil to develop a fine *terroir*. Finally they found the place, just south of the Twin Cities in the Sogn Valley (the local pronunciation is "so-gun"). John still waxes eloquent about its features: "High south-facing hills, good drainage into the valley, wind-blown soil of silky loam that sits on top of limestone." On this promising site, in a valley so beautiful that "you'd think you were in Napa," according to Maureen, the Maloneys planted twenty acres of vines in 2002.

There were already eleven wineries in the state, many growing cold-hardy grapes from Elmer Swenson and the University of Minnesota. Learning from others, the Maloneys did not plant anything that required extraordinary care. They emphasized varieties known to grow well in Minnesota, including Edelweiss, St. Pepin, La Crescent, Sabrevois, Maréchal Foch, Frontenac, and Prairie Star.

They did not originally envision a winery; they intended to sell to other wineries. But as eight tons of grapes began to ripen in 2004, they decided to make wine themselves. Scouting for properties began afresh, and with urgency. "When we found this historic building, everything fell into place," Maureen recalls.

Everything, that is, except who would actually make the wine. The answer came when, providentially, third-generation Colombian winemaker Vincent Negret called the University enology department inquiring about work in the region, the same week the Maloneys called the enology department looking for a winemaker. Soon thereafter, Negret was in Cannon Falls.

Meanwhile, Maureen began imagining how the spacious display areas of the tasting room would look crammed with antiques. Serendipity struck again when, a few weeks before opening, a deliveryman learned of her interest and mentioned that "he had a whole barn filled with stuff," Maureen marvels. He brought some over, and consignment antique sales have been part of Cannon Creek's operation ever since.

Wine, however, remains the focus. The Maloneys concentrate on estate-grown wines: wines made from their own vineyard. With five thou-sand cases in 2007, the winery is growing and plans to continue doing so. "Twenty acres is a large vineyard," Maureen says, "and I always say, when we hit the fence, that's it. But John is inclined to say, let's move the fences."

Making the vineyard more accessible to visitors is the Maloneys's current effort. They acquired a century-old timber frame barn from relatives of Andrew Volstead, the Prohibition congressman (see Chapter Four). Having carefully marked each of the barn's joints, John disassembled it, moved it, and reassembled it

Tourists Down on the Farm

Agritourism, it's called, or agritainment. Few adults recognize a tractor from its distinctive color any more (hint: a John Deere is not red); few children grow up knowing their way around a barn. With distance comes interest, sometimes based in nostalgia, in knowing how the rural folk live.

Agritourism is one of the fastest-growing sectors of the tourism industry. New to America, such enterprises have flourished in Europe for generations. In France, *gîtes,* or farm holiday residences, are a staple of the rural economy, providing fresh-cooked produce as well as inexpensive accommodations. More recently, wine-harvest or olive-picking holidays provide direct experience of the farming life.

Vineyards and wineries occupy the mainstream of agritourism. With almost two-thirds of American tourists taking short breaks to the countryside, agritourism has a major impact on the rural economy. Once out in the country, the visitor is likely to visit an antique shop, a fruit stand, or some other appealing business. Thus wineries serve as "anchor tenants" for agritouristic development in a region.

John Maloney is delighted to be a magnet for the tourist dollar. "Studies show," he says, "that for every dollar spent in a local winery, another eighty-two cents enters the local economy." The gains are unlikely to be in heavy equipment sales, but the local John Deere agent (hint: the big green tractors) can expect spillover.

Some farms or orchards conduct tours or allow tourists to help with chores; others provide day camps or rental accommodations; many have corn mazes or hayrides. Self-harvest operations, including pick-your-own and Christmas tree cutting, add to farm income. So do rural weddings, where a beautiful setting provides a backdrop for romance and celebration.

In addition to bringing needed income into rural areas, wineries also offer a tax advantage to the state without being heavily subsidized. "Because alcohol is such a heavily regulated and taxed commodity," John Maloney explains, "it creates more in the way of income than, say, corn. An acre of wine grapes generates just under three thousand dollars to the state." Self-sustaining and generating excellent returns to the state, wineries form the vanguard of agritourism in the Upper Midwest.

beside the vineyard, where it immediately became a sought-after site for events.

The Maloneys share a vision of bringing people to small towns for entertainment and education. "Oh, gosh, the future is so bright," John Maloney says, "for viticulture and for locally produced wine. This area is going to be regionally significant in the wine industry, and we're on the cusp of that. Obviously we believe in it—heart and soul."

Cannon River Winery

421 Mill Street West • Cannon Falls, MN 55009 • 507-263-7400 • www.cannonriverwinery.com

Location: Downtown Cannon Falls.

Hours:
May–October:
Monday–Thursday, 11:00 am–7:00 pm
Friday and Saturday, 11:00 am–9:00 pm
Sunday, noon–6:00 pm
November–April:
Monday and Tuesday, closed
Wednesday and Thursday, noon–7:00 pm
Friday and Saturday, noon–8:00 pm
Sunday, noon–5:00 pm

Tasting: Complimentary for first 3 wines; $3 full tasting

Tours: Self-guided during tasting room hours; guided tours Saturdays 1:00 and 3:00 pm year-round; Sundays 3:00 pm May–October

Signature wines:
St. Pepin: off-dry style, light bodied and crisp
Sogn Blanc: slightly sweet, from Edelweiss grapes
Minnesota Meritage: blend of Foch, Frontenac, Cabernet Sauvignon, and Zinfandel

Events: Wine release parties; year-round music calendar; art and antique shows; wine appreciation classes.

FALCONER VINEYARDS

Some people imagine retirement as endless days of golf; others dream of travel to exotic lands; others long to learn watercolor painting. John Falconer's retirement? He started a winery.

He had just sold Red Wing Stoneware, the company he had run for several decades. "I grew up farming," he says, "raising cattle and horses. We like to be outdoors, we like wine, we like to travel to wineries. When we heard about the winter-hardy grape varieties, that was it."

With his wife, Ann Lowe, a family-practice doctor, John began to plant grapes on their land near the Mississippi. "We had grown eight acres of raspberries, so we knew what we were doing with small fruits. We knew it would be a lot of work. But we also knew it was a high-value crop for limited acreage." From the start, Falconer avoided costly experimentation, planting University of Minnesota and Elmer Swenson varieties. He also grows the sturdy Maréchal Foch and, through his nursery, supplies hundreds of other Upper Midwest growers and hobbyists.

While the grapes grew toward maturity, Falconer studied wine-making, launching hundreds of trials with cold-hardy grapes. These new grapes have no enological history. "You can talk to all the experts, get all the ideas in the world, but basically you have to make adjustments as you go," Falconer says of his experiments. In addition to Minnesota wines, Falconer crafts small releases of popular *viniferas* like Riesling and Gewürztraminer, because he has not yet found enough high-quality cold-hardy whites to satisfy his market.

He also began planning the tasting room, which opened in 2004 above the vineyard. Within four years, the business had grown to the point that he commissioned plans for a new winery to include seating for up to five hundred at banquets and other events. The building, which Falconer hopes to have open to the public in 2009, will supplement rather than replace the current tasting room.

An officer of the Minnesota Grape Growers Association (MGGA), Falconer has seen an "amazing reception" for Minnesota wines—proof of which he also finds in steadily growing sales. When he first opened, visitors would exclaim, "I didn't know you could grow grapes in Minnesota!" Such visitors would gingerly take a sip and then start back in surprise at its quality. "Things are different now," Falconer says, "people know names of northern grapes, they want to see what we're doing with them."

Part of the reason for heightened interest, Falconer believes, is interest in buying local products. But Midwestern friendliness helps too. "We aren't wine snobs here," he shakes his head, "we want to help people find out what they like, and help them enjoy that." And, he adds, "Midwesterners know how to have a good time." Falconer sees the Minnesota wine indus-

try undergoing explosive growth, with new wineries opening each year and hundreds of farmers planting vineyards to supply commercial and home wine-making demands. "It's the maturing of an industry," he says. "It isn't in its infancy anymore."

As for his own maturing, Falconer doesn't see a second retirement ahead anytime soon. "If I drink a glass of red wine every day," he laughs, "I hope to have thirty years in this industry too."

Falconer Vineyards

3572 Old Tyler Road • Red Wing, MN 55066 • 651-388-8849 • www.FalconerVineyards.com

Location: From Highway 61 in Red Wing, turn away from river at Tyler Road, then shortly right on Kosec, immediate left on Old Tyler Road, follow to end.

Pottery and Wine

It was 1967, and Red Wing Pottery had shut its doors. A hundred years earlier, John Paul had moved from Germany to Red Wing. A potter, Paul immediately recognized the high quality of the local clay, which he began using to produce a durable stoneware. His salt-glazed pottery was fashioned into utilitarian bowls, crocks, and jugs. Later, under the guidance of William M. Philleo and David Hallum, the process was mechanized and, by 1906, Red Wing was one of America's biggest potteries—for a time, the largest in the world.

Today, collectors covet the light-gray vessels with a stenciled red wing trademark. But fifty years ago, imported pottery and domestic plastic dinnerware undercut Red Wing. In 1967, the company

closed, creating economic turmoil in a town where it was the major employer. But John Falconer believed in the Red Wing tradition and, in 1984, bought the rights to the name as well as technical records from the factory.

In 1987, twenty years after the original factory closed, Falconer reopened it. Making replica Bristol-glazed stoneware on potters' wheels and, in some cases, from molds using the slip-casting technique, Red Wing Stoneware re-established the town as a center for high-quality pottery. John Falconer sold Red Wing Stoneware in 1998, but his name lives on in the quality stoneware being made once again along the banks of the Mississippi and stamped with a distinctive small red wing.

Hours:
Weekends, May–Thanksgiving:
Friday, Sunday: noon–5:00 pm
Saturday, 10:00 am–6:00 pm
Also by arrangement

Tasting: Complimentary

Tours: Free vineyard walks

Signature wines:
Frontenac Reserve: barrel aged, rich, late-harvest red
Potter John's: slightly sweet blend of five northern white varieties
Prairie Star: Swenson variety, lightly oaked

Events: Music in the Vines monthly summer concert series.

GARVIN HEIGHTS VINEYARDS

When Marvin Seppanen thinks back to the beginnings of Garvin Heights, his eyes crinkle in a self-deprecating squint. "I think we had twenty-four vines," he smiles, "in four varieties. We picked them out of a seed catalogue." He laughs at the memory of that tiny step that led to other small steps, then to the big one.

The sheep were gone from the pasture, the children were grown, and it was time for something new. Linda Seppanen was immersed in her career as professor of nursing at Winona State, and Marvin's own career in factory computer simulation was similarly demanding. But Marvin and Linda had been visiting family wineries for years, always asking questions about how such an enterprise could work. They heard the news from the University of Minnesota about new cold-hardy grapes. And . . . well, there was that sheep pasture. . . .

Fifteen years later, the Seppanens stand on the deck of their winery and look out at three acres of vines, including St. Pepin, La Crosse, and Edelweiss as well as Marquette and Louise

Swenson. Behind them stretches a luxurious Scandinavian-style tasting room. Beneath them, the winery production facility holds stainless steel tanks filled with fermenting wine from their grapes. Those early small steps led to a leap of faith.

The Seppanens, both from farming families, love working the land. They always knew they'd do something with their twenty ridgetop acres above Winona. They had a big garden, and then there was the period of the sheep—"4-H projects that lived," Linda recalls—and the small orchard. They made wine from wild grapes that Linda remembers as "sometimes drinkable," so they understood wine-making basics.

After the wine bug bit, they joined the Minnesota Grape Growers Association, where they found advice on varieties to plant. They also linked up with growers in the nearby Wisconsin region of Vernon County for workshops and training sessions. It was with the Vernon County growers that the Seppanens traveled to Michigan's wine country, a trip they credit with giving them the confidence to design their own winery. By 2006 they were ready for the big step. About to outgrow the federal limit on wine-making for personal use, they applied for bonding and planned their tasting room and production facility. A year later, Garvin Heights opened.

The wines are based on cold-hardy varieties, witness to the Seppanens's belief in local produce; they buy from other local vineyards and do not plan to base their wines on *vinifera* varietals. Their own vineyard produces grapes for their signature blends. Raspberries from their farm and cranberries from Wisconsin are used in crafting fruit wines as well. As the only winery in Winona, Garvin Heights has attracted both locals and visitors. Future plans include hosting art openings and other cultural events. The Seppanens have taken one small step at a time, from planting a few vines to opening a winery, and they expect to keep going.

Garvin Heights Vineyard

2255 Garvin Heights Road • Winona, MN 55987 •
507-454-7179 • www.ghvwine.com

Hours:

Last weekend in April until Christmas:
Friday, Saturday, and Sunday, 1:00–5:00 pm
Other times by appointment

Tasting: $3 per adult, up to five wines

Tours: Complimentary; request when
visiting

Signature wines:

GHV Frontenac: premium dry red
GHV St. Pepin: premium semidry white

St. Urho Red, Rose, and White: blends, slightly
sweetened, of northern grapes

Events: Occasional; check website.

SALEM GLEN WINERY

Dustin Ebert started building an observatory
and ended up with a winery. The observatory
still stands, still looking like the silo it once was,
beside the winery building. Inside, the only clue
to Ebert's original plan is the starry theme on
the wine labels. For now, the observatory is
back-burnered. Wine is on the front burner.

Saint Ur Who?

Because of Marvin Seppanen's Finnish heritage, Garvin Heights house blends are named for St. Urho, the Finnish saint who drove the grasshoppers away from the vineyards by chanting, "Grasshoppers, grasshoppers, get the heck outta here!" (The actual chant is somewhat less polite.) The grasshoppers left, so St. Urho is considered the patron saint of Finnish winemakers.

Okay, the legend has a few holes in it. There is no evidence in Finland of a St. Urho, and no wild grapes grow there, although legend says that archeologists have found grape leaves incised on bones of prehistoric giant bears (right). Nonetheless, St. Urho has a feast day on March 16, conveniently close to St. Patrick's Day. That may be appropriate, because legend says they were one and the same: after his success with the grasshoppers (or maybe frogs), Urho took off for Ireland, where there was a plague of snakes. He took care of them right enough, but the Irish couldn't pronounce his name so called him the Patriarch, which they couldn't pronounce either, so the word became Patrick.

On Urho's feast, Finns reputedly wear green and purple, representing banished grasshoppers and saved grapes. Women and children sing the Urho chant at sunrise while men, attired in grasshopper-green, descend the hills kicking grasshoppers while changing into purple costumes in honor of the grapes. But there is no evidence of any such festival in Finland.

Claims have been put forth that the holiday started in Virginia, Minnesota, in 1956, when a Finnish miner got tired of endless retellings of the "St. Patrick drove the snakes out of Ireland" story by Irish coworkers. (Folklorists have disproved that one: first, there never were snakes in Ireland; and second, the original legend was a pre-Christian story of a hero driving away winter to free springtime.) The legend has also been credited to psychologist Sulo Havumaki of Bemidji State, where "St. Urho" (possibly Havumaki himself) annually chased a grasshopper-costumed student through the hallways. Whoever, wherever: it's good fun.

Like many other winemakers in the region, Ebert first made wine as a hobby, with his father Anthony and other members of the Purple Foot Winemakers Club. He started with imported juice, then graduated to grapes from major wine-growing regions. As his wine knowledge grew, so did his curiosity. No longer content to follow traditional wine recipes, Ebert began to make wines with local varieties.

Soon, Ebert became even more ambitious and decided to plant a vineyard on his land in the open valley of the Zumbro River. Rather than take out business loans to pay others, Ebert enlisted his family for the arduous work— father, brother Anthony, and mother Dottie. The first year, they planted sixty vines. The next year, twelve hundred. By the time Salem Glen opened its tasting room in 2007, Ebert had planted five acres with three thousand vines.

"That is a lot of work," he says modestly. "But we plan to plant another two acres soon."

Like other growers in the region, Ebert enthusiastically experiments with cold-hardy grapes. "There is a certain leap of faith aspect to this," he admits, because the grapes are so new that winemakers are still learning vinification techniques. In Beaujolais, a couple of centuries of experimenting with cultivation techniques, harvest sugar levels, yeast strains, blending, and aging led to knowledge of how to create the best wines. Even California has a hundred years of experience. Minnesota, by contrast, has worked with its new grape varieties for only a decade.

But the regional wine industry is developing quickly, and new growers like Ebert have the advantage of speedy communication, the Internet having replaced the ox-cart for information sharing. Ebert is grateful for the connection and

Wine and Health

Salem Glen Winery sits on the outskirts of one of America's largest medical communities. Which brings up the question: Will wine ever again be medically prescribed, as it was during Prohibition with instructions to "take as a stimulant until stimulated"?

A best-selling 1991 book, *The French Paradox* by Lewis Perdue, claimed that the French have a low rate of coronary disease. They eat four times as much butter as Americans (*sauce béarnaise, s'il vous plais*) as well as more pork and cheese, so they should be falling over dead of clogged arteries outside their charming patisseries. But they don't. Meanwhile Americans eat lots of soybean and other vegetable oil in such delicacies as French fries, and we expire regularly near our fast-food stands. Something in red wine, the author contended, offsets the effects of all that fat. Sales of red wine

soared. (No health benefits are claimed for white wine, which is not fermented on the skins.)

The French paradox theory contends that resveratrol in grape skins protects against cancer as well as heart disease. But other studies deny the link or show other damage caused by frequent alcohol consumption. The healthfulness of the French diet has been questioned by researchers who claim that heart disease is underreported in France. Some studies even suggest that relaxation brought on by drinking wine, rather than any specific substance in it, provides health benefits.

Science has not yet spoken definitively about the question of wine and health, except to prove that excessive imbibing linked with driving can be fatal. *Comment vous dire* "designated driver" *en Français?*

advice. "There is a long time range with grapes," Ebert says. "You plant, then you're looking four or five years ahead to when you have grapes, and then you start working with them to make wine. There is a lot of risk in this enterprise."

Response to the winery has been enthusiastic. Rochester, a sophisticated community centered on medical facilities, welcomed having its own winery. Ebert believes that "people are interested now in local products," including wine made from local grape varieties. Once the winery is established, Ebert will finish that silo-observatory so that he can host wine tastings and gatherings of stargazers there. The renowned Dom Pérignon described sipping champagne as "drinking stars." At Salem Glen, visitors will someday be able to drink in the stars on clear Minnesota nights.

Salem Glen Winery

5211 60th Avenue SW • Rochester, MN 55902 • 507-365-8758 • www.salemglenvineyard.com

Location: From downtown Rochester, take Broadway (Hwy 63) south to 40th Street. Turn right on 40th and travel 4.5 miles to Hwy 117. Turn left and travel one-half mile, then left on 60th Avenue for one mile.

Hours:
Thursday–Saturday, noon–8:00 pm
Sunday, noon–5:00 pm

Tasting: $3 per person

Tours: By arrangement

Signature wines:
Edelweiss: semisweet Swenson hybrid
Pulsar Red: blended northern varieties, some estate-grown
Dark Skies: a fortified chokeberry dessert wine

Events: Occasional; check website.

SCENIC VALLEY WINERY

This winery's name could not be more appropriate: it is located in Lanesboro, a small town nestled beneath a 320-foot bluff beside the Root River in a beautifully scenic valley. Lanesboro was established as a resort community by a New York company that dammed the river to create a two-mile-long lake for boating, where high-priced lakefront summer homes could then rise like the fortunes of the speculators. It didn't take off, so the developers did.

A resort was not in the town's future, but Lanesboro almost immediately prospered as a railroad hub, with grain elevators storing the abundant crops of prairie farms. Flour mills such as Carrolton and White-Nash opened during the 1870s. By the middle of that decade, the town even had its own doctor, renowned bird-watcher Johan Christen, a harbinger of many birders to come.

The town thrived until an economic decline began in the 1930s and continued for a half century. Buildings fell into ruin, leaving little to draw visitors to the town—or to keep locals there. But when the historic railroad depot was torn down in the mid-1980s, the town was galvanized. A volunteer group dedicated itself to commercial revitalization, a process that began with the removal of sixty miles of railroad track and its replacement with a paved bicycle path, now one of the nation's most popular. With a vision encompassing outdoor and cultural tourism, the people of Lanesboro rebuilt a thriving small town, which has been honored with the Great American Main Street Award, named one of *Outdoors* magazine's American dream towns, and cited in books for the innovative use of culture as a basis for economic development.

Right about the time that Lanesboro began its renaissance, Richard Brehn launched Scenic Valley Winery, believing that a winery would be popular among the new visitors. And so it has proven, under the guidance of winemaker Karrie Riestau, who with her mother Lucretia and her daughter Brittany now runs the establishment in a historic building, once the town's creamery.

Using only local produce, Scenic Valley makes wines that range from sweet to dry. "Now that's Lanesboro dry, not Napa Valley dry," announces long-time "pour guy" Bucky Rogers to visitors as he dispenses wines from behind an antique counter. An employee since the start of the enterprise, Bucky shares his obvious enjoyment of the products with visitors. "Guess," he urges, "what this is . . . now isn't that tasty . . . that's right, cranberry, perfect for holidays." Every wine is as good as the last to this ebullient raconteur. If you're lucky, you might get him to tell the secret to his prizewinning beet pickles (hint: it includes wine).

You might not make pickles with Napa Valley Cabernet, but Scenic Valley's vegetable wines are just the thing. While it is rare to find onion, garlic, and green pepper wines, these cooking wines are among the winery's specialties and are made, not by adding flavoring to a grape wine, but by fermenting the vegetables themselves. Like an herbed vinegar, the wines add a splash of flavor to stir-fries, salads, and other recipes. No other winery in the Upper Midwest offers such wines.

In addition to pleasing the tourists, Scenic Valley has a following among locals as well, especially for their rhubarb wine, which is made from dozens of gardeners' crops. "Our rhubarb comes locally every year," Kerrie says, "by putting ads in the papers. Everyone's a bit involved in that wine. We hear them saying, 'Of course I'm going to buy a bottle, I know my rhubarb's in there somewhere.'"

Cooking with Wine

Many famous dishes rely upon wine: *Bœuf bourguignon, coq au vin,* lamb in port sauce. But beyond splashing some Chianti into spaghetti sauce, many home cooks are unsure about how to use wine. Rules offered by cognoscenti that suggest using only high-priced wines serve to further dismay the typical cook, but recent studies have shown little difference between extraordinary and average wines in cooking. (Cooking does not improve really bad wines, however, so if you wouldn't put it in your mouth to drink—don't put it in your mouth at all.)

The addition of wine to a dish adds flavor. Most, although not all, of the alcohol will burn off during cooking, but if any guest is a teetotaler, it's best to leave the wine out of the stew. Beyond that, the rules are few:

- Avoid "cooking sherry," a heavily salted product that bears little resemblance to wine.
- Do not add red wine where you don't want color; use white instead for such things as sauces for fish.
- Do not plan a meal with competing wine flavors.
- Add wine early in the cooking process so the flavors have time to meld.
- Wine can be used in marinades, sauces, soups, stews, even desserts (a bit of ice wine in sherbet is heaven, but too much alcohol makes freezing impossible).

Scenic Valley Winery

101 Coffee St. W. • Lanesboro, MN 55949 •
1-888-965-0250 • www.scenicvalleywinery.com

Hours:

April–October only:
Monday–Saturday, 10:00 am–5:00 pm
Sunday, 1:00 pm–5:00 pm

Tasting: Complimentary

Tours: No tours

Signature wines:

Rhubarb: light white wine, off-dry
Purple Passion: jammy, sweet Concord grape wine
Cherry Chill: blend of white grapes and fresh cherry juice
Cooking wines: onion, garlic, and green pepper

Events: Winery participates in all town special events.

Central Minnesota

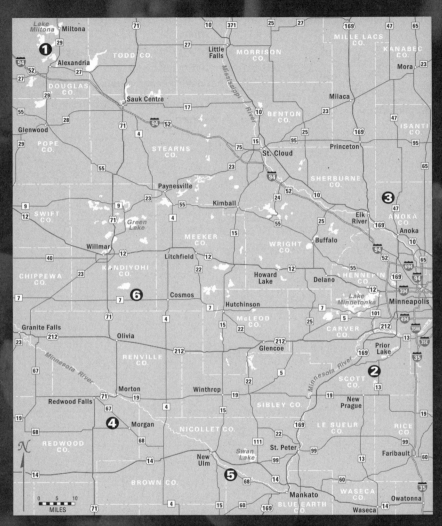

1. Carlos Creek Winery 2. Crofut Winery 3. Goose Lake Farm and Winery
4. Fieldstone Vineyards 5. Morgan Creek Vineyards 6. Olde Country Winery

CALL IT MAIN STREET. Call it Lake Wobegon. Central Minnesota has received more than its share of spiteful or parodic commentary over the years. But to those who love its flat fertile plains and gentle river valleys, this land is as good as it gets.

Yes, there are lakes, as might be expected in an area that was heavily glaciated. In addition to the surface lakes, vast underground aquifers underlie the area. Such an abundance of water, together with rich soil, made this an agricultural paradise when the prairies were first broken more than a hundred and fifty years ago. But prairie has not traditionally been considered a fine wine-growing region. Grapes prefer lean, rocky soil to deep rich topsoil.

More importantly, wine grapes have not previously survived the region's challenging winters. Intense storms sweep the plains, and between storms the land bakes in drought-like sunny spells. Grapes can take the heat, but they die in the cold. The fussy *vinifera* grape, well bred for Europe's climate, suffers especially in such conditions. But new hybrids have permitted the development of wineries in central Minnesota, primarily along the crescent-shaped bed of the Minnesota River. There, amid historic towns and bucolic farms, Minnesota's wine country has successfully extended itself. Winegrowers, like pioneers of earlier years, plant vineyards in prairie soil, often using the climate-buffering qualities of nearby lakes in selecting vineyard sites.

The glaciers that formed this land are not easily envisioned as one views the fine farms and blue lakes that stretch across Minnesota's middle today. During ages of ice, glaciers flowed like excruciatingly slow rivers across the land. Where the glaciers were stopped by mountain ranges and other geologic features, vast lakes formed. The largest—Lake Agassiz, which contained as much water as all of today's Great Lakes combined—drained through the glacial River Warren, whose route can be traced in the Minnesota and Mississippi rivers. In the interglacial periods, giants ranged the land: beavers as big as bears, mastodons the size of elephants. (One wonders if the tendency toward gigantism is a permanent feature; see Big Ole, page 81.) With the final retreat of the glaciers, the huge animals died away, to be replaced by small modern cousins.

One result of the constant ironing-down action of the glaciers is that much of Minnesota is relatively flat, with only 1,699 feet separating its lowest and highest elevations. Only the areas along the Minnesota River show much variation in elevation. In addition to the plains, other glacial landforms are apparent. Ridges called moraines outline ancient ice masses. Drumlins and eskers, little hills and rows of hills, were formed as rock was carried along and ultimately deposited by the ice-rivers. Where a glacial river once poured forth, an outwash plain remains, with sandy soil from the pounding erosion of the river's water; the Anoka Sand Plain is one of the largest. These areas of glacial-born rock offer sites for vineyards.

Neither cosmopolitan nor sophisticated, the towns of central Minnesota became iconographic of the limited social options of small-town America with the publication of Sinclair Lewis's *Main Street* in 1920. The novel tells of a bright Minneapolis girl, Carol Milford, who falls in love with the doctor from Gopher Prairie (a barely disguised version of Lewis's hometown of Sauk Centre), Will Kennicott. Carol attempts to bring modern values to the town but is rebuffed until, in the end, she accepts its limitations. Initially awarded the Pulitzer Prize for literature in 1921, the award was withdrawn by the Board of Trustees for the book's negative portrayal of Middle America; when later awarded the Pulitzer for *Arrowsmith,* Lewis bitterly turned it down.

More recently, central Minnesota has been satirized by Garrison Keillor as home to Lake Wobegon, where "all the men are strong, all the women are good-looking, and all the children are above average," a phrase that echoes Lewis's mockery of boosterism. The imaginary town's most significant public monument is the statue of the Unknown Norwegian; the Catholic Church is Our Lady of Perpetual Responsibility. The fictional stores and sports teams, to say nothing of the annual Blessing of the Snowmobiles, have become part of contemporary Minnesota culture.

Central Minnesotans deal with such mockery by accepting and even celebrating the stereotypes. The Lake Wobegon Regional Trail stretches scores of miles from Sauk Centre. Sinclair Lewis's boyhood home has been restored, and the Sinclair Lewis Interpretive Center offers a candid insight into the author's mind. The third weekend in July sees the celebration of the annual Sinclair Lewis Days, and an October writers conference is dedicated to him.

In a region where all the people are friendly and all the lakes are blue, wineries add a new dimension to agricultural and cultural life. Although viticulture encounters challenges on prairie land, the region's wineries bring the pioneer Minnesota spirit to bear in creating a new wine region where the vines, like the people, are immigrants from milder climes.

CARLOS CREEK WINERY

In the heart of Minnesota's lake country, the lavishly appointed Carlos Creek Winery is a destination winery, offering a Siberian elm maze, an orchard of eight thousand apple trees, and an entertainment program that includes music on the patio outside its wine-tasting room.

The area around Carlos Creek was settled in the mid-nineteenth century by Scandinavians, who are honored in the nearby city of Alexandria with a twenty-eight-foot-tall statue of a Viking bearing a shield proclaiming the town the Birthplace of America (the shield's slogan has never been adequately explained). Built in 1964 for the New York World's Fair, where the theme of the Minnesota pavilion was Minnesota: Birthplace of America (also unexplained), Big Ole was later donated to Alexandria. There he was provided with a biography: he was born in Norway, immigrated with Viking Paul Knutson, fell in love with a girl named Lena, and carved the Kensington Runestone. Ole has suffered ignominious attacks from small envious humans, like the one who shot fiery arrows at Santa-attired Ole one Christmas, causing the statue to burst into flames. But generally, Ole is viewed with affectionate bemusement by the town.

Ole's imaginary biography precedes Alexandria's actual history, which began in 1858, when brothers Alexander and William Kinkead settled on a tract of land where, their surveyor brother had tipped them off, the state road would soon pass. They established a post office, and Alexander named the new town after himself. Other settlers arrived, including Alexander's young sister-in-law Clara, whose diaries form a major source of information about the settlement of the area.

The early years did not bode well for the town; by 1860, Alexandria was deserted. But with the opening of a Government Land Office in 1868, a settlement rush began and, within seven years, homesteaders had claimed most of the land around the town. With the coming of the railroad, the area attracted urban dwellers looking for a pleasant escape. Resorts began to spring up, taking advantage of the recreational opportunities afforded by the area's lakes. Today, condominium estates replace the grand old resort hotels of earlier years. Golf courses, shopping malls, and amusement parks offer entertainment, but the biggest draw remains the water sports and fishing available on lakes Carlos, Ida, and Darling.

At Carlos Creek Winery, a large shop and tasting room is fully staffed, as are a Starbucks outlet and Panera Bread. A crafts barn offers artisan-made goods. Musicians play daily during the summer and every weekend year-round. Tours take visitors through the orchards, from which fruit is picked for the apple and other fruit wines. Regular tours provide insights into the experience of growing grapes in the brutal winters of central Minnesota.

Carlos Creek Winery

6693 County Road 34 NW • Alexandria, MN 56308 • 320-846-5443 • www.carloscreekwinery.com

Location: North on State Highway 29 from Alexandria, right to County Road 42, then left to County Road 34.

Hours:
Monday–Saturday, 11:00 am–6:00 pm
Sunday, noon–6:00 pm
Closed Easter, Thanksgiving, Christmas, and New Year's Day

Tasting: Complimentary

Tours: Daily

Signature wines:
Apple Peach: made with local fruit
Peach Chardonnay: fruit-filled, aged in oak
Red Zinfandel: hearty, food-friendly

Events: Early September Grape Stomp.

A Viking Visitation?

To the Vikings, the North American continent seemed so overrun with grapevines they called the place Vinland, or "vine-land." They were probably seeing *riparia*, or riverbank grape, which sprawls along waterways far into Canada. In its natural state, *riparia* does not make very good wines—not that the Vikings were big grape-wine drinkers anyway, preferring mead.

The Upper Midwest is thickly populated with descendents of Vikings and their stay-at-home relatives. The term "viking" denotes an activity rather than an identity. In the brief northern summertime, ancient Scandinavians worked their small farms. When winter arrived, they set out to make additional income raiding coastal European towns. These renowned seafarers reached North America, but it is unclear how far they traveled. As the Great Lakes provide a waterway into the heart of the continent, it is possible that the Vikings got to Minnesota. Note: possible. Probable? That is not, as archaeologists say, well attested.

An alleged piece of evidence stands in central Minnesota. Called the Viking Altar Rock, the natural boulder rests on a hill near Sauk Centre. On it, several triangular holes seem to have been drilled. Together with several other apparent Viking artifacts, this holed stone has been used to create a narrative that brings the ancient Scandinavians to central Minnesota long before any other Europeans.

According to the reconstruction, Norwegian records show that, in 1354, King Magnus Ericson heard that a colony in Greenland had been abandoned. Even more disturbing, the settlers had reverted to Norse paganism, then escaped to North America. The king sent the nobleman Paul Knutson in search of the colonists. His expedition departed in 1356, returning without success in 1363 or 1364. This expedition supposedly left runestones, engraved with Viking letters, throughout North America. One was the famous Kensington Runestone, allegedly found on a farm in central Minnesota in 1898 by farmer Olof Öhman and describing a visit by Vikings to the area. The stone has been the center of controversy for more than a century, with enthusiasts finding linguistic evidence of a fourteenth-century origin while academics find evidence of nineteenth-century fraud. The stone rests in the Runestone Museum at 206 Broadway Street, Alexandria.

Less controversial, less well known, but still questionable, the Viking Altar Stone might not unify local boosters and academics, but it has had one salutary effect: it was dedicated in August 1975 by an ecumenical group. The Vikings became Christians long before the Reformation, so they were neither Catholic nor Protestant, but simply Christian, and Lutherans prayed with Catholics in their honor.

CROFUT WINERY

To Don Crofut, wine connects family, heritage, and the land. He remembers his grandfather Willis making wine during the Depression. After visiting relatives every summer in California, the family brought back grapes to Oklahoma to become that year's wine. Sights and scents of family wine-making remain vivid in Don's memory.

His father Bill made wine, too, making Don the third generation to practice the craft. When he moved from Oklahoma to Minnesota, Crofut planted six acres of cold-hardy grapes near Prior Lake. The first planting included La Crescent, Frontenac, Frontenac Gris, Prairie Star,

Sabrevois, and St. Croix, with the new University of Minnesota release Marquette joining the party later. An experimental vineyard was established at the entrance for Crofut's own work in plant breeding. The first tiny crop came in several years later, in 2005 ("Just enough for a party," Crofut smiles), with the first real crush of 2006 yielding eight hundred cases. The winery itself opened in 2007 over the Memorial Day weekend.

Crofut keeps in touch with friends and customers through his wine blog, where he reported on the opening party: "The thirsty throng of people overwhelmed us and even the cash register. We burned the thermal printer out of the cash register on Sunday." The rush of happy customers convinced Crofut that others shared his vision of creating a friendly winery on the rural outskirts of the Twin Cities area.

Unlike wineries that separate bottling from sales, Crofut Winery uses a historic barn for both. When visitors enter the renovated 1886 dairy barn, they are greeted by staff offering wine samples, but they may also see Crofut sterilizing, bottling, or labeling. This fluidity continues throughout the farm, where no fences keep visitors from wandering through the vineyards to appreciate the varieties and their different growth habits.

If family heritage was what originally drew Crofut to wine-making, he is also drawn to the concept of *terroir* and believes that south-central Minnesota can develop a unique taste in its wines. Minnesota wines should "taste of the lakes and the crisp blue sky of Minnesota summer" he says, dismissing the idea of relying on imported grapes to attain a "premium level"

Sips of History

The wine trail is a convention of the wine industry, but south-central Minnesota has come up with a variant that showcases its unique qualities: the Minnesota River Sips of History Trail. Visitors can follow the trail to breweries and historical sites as well as to wineries.

Starting near Minneapolis at Crofut, the trail continues south to August Schell Brewing Company, the nation's second-oldest family owned brewery. Founded in the mid-nineteenth century by a German immigrant who figured that his fellows missed their homeland beer, the New Ulm brewery survived Prohibition by making soft drinks. The fifth generation of the Schell family now runs the brewery.

While in New Ulm, the Sips tourist can take in the historic John Lind home, an elegant Queen Anne built by the first Swedish-born U.S. congressman; Lind also served as governor of Minnesota.

Listed on the National Register of Historic Places, the Lind House dates to 1887. Nearby, the tour takes in Morgan Creek Vineyards, run by a descendent of August Schell, then moves on to the small town of Lucan, where the new Brau Brothers brewpub offers craft beers; then to Fieldstone Vineyards, located on a heritage farm near Morgan.

Two Mankato historic sites conclude the tour. The R. D. Hubbard House was the home of the founder of a linseed oil processing plant (1870) who also established grain elevators across the state after traveling through the wildernesses of British Columbia and Nicaragua with his wife, a daring adventure at the time. Also on the Sips Trail is the handsome Blue Earth County Heritage Center, which houses exhibits and archives of the local historical society. Information is at www.mnriverwine beerhistorytrail.com.

wine. "Our wines should clearly come from our part of the world."

Both because of that philosophy and the Minnesota law that requires 51 percent Minnesota-grown fruit for a product to be labeled as "Minnesota" wine, Crofut has reached out to encourage others to grow grapes. Several new vineyards have been planted to provide the winery's growing needs. He is especially excited about one whose gravelly soil holds out the promise of a sharp, flinty wine.

Crofut's two sons Sam and Jake join him in the vineyard and the winery, helping with tasks ranging from weeding to bottling. As the fourth generation to be involved in wine-making, they represent the continuity of heritage that Don Crofut cherishes and nurtures.

Crofut Family Winery and Vineyard

21646 Langford Avenue South • Jordan, MN 55352 • 952-492-3227 • www.crofutwinery.com

Location: 185th Street (exits off I-35W or I-35E) from Prior Lake to State Highway 13; turn left; go 7.5 miles.

Hours:
Memorial Day weekend–November 1:
Saturday and Sunday, 10:00 am–5:00 pm

Tasting: $3 fee

Tours: Upon request

Signature wines:
La Crescent White: estate-grown, off-dry, crisp
Frontenac Rosé: estate-grown Frontenac, softly tannic
Crow's Nest White: sweet white dessert wine

Events: Occasional; check website.

GOOSE LAKE FARM AND WINERY

The first thing you notice at Goose Lake is the bustling activity of the hundred employees who rush about, sometimes screaming at each other in their eagerness to do their jobs. Mostly they ignore visitors, but if crossed, a glare shoots forth at the interloper from a beady little black eye.

The scores of peacocks and their peahen companions, bantam chickens, and guinea fowl are not pets, like the llamas, donkeys, and horses that also live at Goose Lake Farm. "Those birds earn their keep," says winemaker Cindy Ohman. In a six-acre orchard kept productive with minimal spraying, the birds keep the fruit insect free. "Anyone can take a walk out there today," Ohman says with pride, "pick an apple, and bite into it, without it being an insect trap."

Ohman helps too. "I take a walk twice a day and pick off any bugs they miss." Her chickens and other fowl are part of the balanced farm she and her husband, Leon, have developed in Anoka County over the last two decades. Although only a few miles from a suburban-sprawl landscape of box stores and fast-food joints, Goose Lake Farm seems to exist in a parallel universe, generations removed from the hectic modern world.

That is the feeling Ohman seeks to create. She grew up on a farm near Monticello, in western Minnesota, and worked in horticulture professionally. With over sixty acres of farmland, the Ohmans planted an orchard of apples, plums, and pears.

Ohman had learned to make wine from her great-grandmother, Eva Wilson of Maple Lake. Eva made wine the way she made jellies and jams—another skill set she passed along to her great-granddaughter, who offers preserves for sale at the farm. However, the jam market is more limited than the orchard's production capacity. "You can't eat as much jam as you can make," Ohman says. "But you can drink all the wine."

Having made wine since childhood, Ohman paid close attention when wineries around Minnesota started opening. She and Leon talked to other winegrowers before deciding that their location was suitable. Suitable, but not ideal, because Anoka soil is "sand, sand, and then some clay with your sand," Ohman laughs. "At least we have a pocket of sandy loam, which holds water better than straight sand." In 2003, they planted University of Minnesota bred cold-hardy grapes. In 2007, they had their first crush, enough for 330 gallons of wine. Young grapes bear scantily. In the future, the vines will produce considerably more.

But the Ohmans did not wait until their grapes matured to start making wine. There were all those fruit trees, just begging to be harvested and pressed: Prairie Spy and Honeycrisp apples, Reliance and Contender peaches. Ohman began to develop a line of fruit-based wines, ranging from blueberry and cranberry to peach and plum, with several apple blends. She hopes to double her production capability every year until she produces around two thousand gallons of wine. "That will be enough," she says. "I don't want to be in every liquor store and discount store." Instead, she wants to create drinkable, affordable wines that sustain the family's rural lifestyle a chicken's flight away from suburbia. "We don't have a big acreage. But I hope we can show that this is viable on a small farm."

Minnesota's Farm Winery Law

Minnesota, unlike its next-door neighbor Wisconsin, licenses "farm wineries" that must make their wines from 51 percent Minnesota-grown fruit. In Wisconsin, a winery can purchase fruit or juice from another grape-producing state. (An obscure provision of federal law makes it possible for a winery to buy bulk wine and bottle it, or even to buy bottled wine and slap on labels; such wine must be labeled as "vinted" at the winery. The word tips off the buyer that the wine is not produced by the winery.)

Minnesota defines a winery as "operated by the owner of a Minnesota farm and producing table, or sparkling, or fortified wines from grapes, grape juice, other fruit bases, or honey with a majority of the ingredients grown or produced in Minnesota." There is a bit of leeway, because the law does allow purchase of out-of-state fruit "if Minnesota produced or grown grapes, grape juice, other fruit bases, or honey is not available in quantities sufficient to constitute a majority of the table, or sparkling, or fortified wine produced by a farm winery." At the rate that vineyards are being planted,

wineries will be increasingly hard-pressed to show that insufficient Minnesota fruit is available.

The law further limits the wine produced on a farm to "table, or sparkling, or fortified wines produced by that farm winery at on-sale or off-sale, in retail, or wholesale lots in total quantities not in excess of 50,000 gallons in a calendar year.... Sales at on-sale and off-sale may be made on Sundays between 12:00 noon and 12:00 midnight. Labels for each type or brand produced must be registered with the commissioner."

Winery owners must listen to the state. They also must listen to the federal government, which sets all sorts of standards to ensure health, safety, sanitation, tax code adherence, and so forth. Some municipalities and/or counties have their own regulations as well, so a farm winery owner can spend as much time filling out forms as enjoying wine.

Why do it? Cindy Ohman is typical. "I like to grow things," she says simply. "And I like making wine out of them."

Goose Lake Farm and Winery

6760 213th Avenue NW • Elk River, MN 55330 • 763-753-9632 • www.gooselakefarm.com

Location: From Elk River, take U.S. 169 north to County Road 33; turn east to County Road 13; turn north to County Road 24; turn east to Pinnacker Road, which becomes 213th Avenue NW.

Hours:
May 31–January 1:
Thursday–Saturday, 10:00 am–6:00 pm
Sunday, noon–6:00 pm

Tasting: Complimentary

Tours: By arrangement

Signature wines:
Chapel: semisweet cherry and apple
Summer Blend: strawberries, pears, and Honeycrisp apples
Razzy Apple: semisweet blend of apples with raspberries

Events: Occasional, including Rhubarb Fest, Ladies' Night, wine-making classes; check website.

FIELDSTONE VINEYARDS

Winery names share recurrent themes. Words indicating height, like "ridge" and "hillside" appear often, because elevations protect vines from frost pockets. Words connected to running water, like "creek" and "river," refer to slopes above a stream, often fine vineyard sites. But "stone" is perhaps the most commonly recurring word. The Upper Midwest has several wineries with stony names, pointing to the importance of lean soil with good drainage in creating a wine with tangible *terroir*, the taste of place.

Often such vineyards are located on rocky ridges, but the nearly two thousand vines at Fieldstone march in orderly procession across three acres of old farmland in the flattest part of central Minnesota. Surrounded by conventional farmland, the farm was once indistinguishable from its neighbors. Since 1901, when Henry and Katherine Reding purchased the three hundred-acre farm, it has remained in the family.

At one point, today's vineyard was a barnyard, but a few years ago Charlie Quast began digging to establish a vineyard. It was not long before he struck solid stone. Charlie remembers it well: "The original planting was in an old hog lot. It was—probably still is—the practice to add rock to the yard to cut down on the mud. Once the livestock left and the vines were planted, the rock just kept on sprouting up in the vineyard." The name sprouted there as well.

From the start, Quast and his partners wanted to create wines from Minnesota-grown grapes. Two hundred plants went in, then hundreds more, then even more, until today a vineyard stands where hogs once lounged, and tourists drink wine in a sparkling new tasting room within a renovated dairy barn. From the start, Fieldstone has been a team effort—indeed, it has created its own community of partners, growers, and friends. With the help of the University of Minnesota's viticulture program, Fieldstone received a small grant from the Minnesota Department of Agriculture that provided funds for training workshops for local growers interested in establishing vineyards. Later Mark Wedge, already an avid amateur winemaker, joined the team to oversee production.

As with all of the early Upper Midwest wineries, the first years at Fieldstone included some bitter learning experiences. Most of the French-American hybrids planted that first year died; the space has been filled with cold-hardy grapes. But by 2003, the vineyard was producing enough for a first vintage. Renovation of the barn was an imperative, and tourists began arriving immediately. Despite the winery's location off the main tourist trail, traffic remains steady, boosted in recent times by cooperation with other wineries in the Sips of History Trail (see page 83).

Charlie Quast, whose wife Michele's parents still live on the farm, remains one of Fieldstone's most vital partners. He is pleased with the winery's success in building a network of growers and suppliers. Some twenty-five to thirty other farmers are putting in vines to provide the grapes that Fieldstone will need as it reaches full production. With production doubling each year since opening, that day may not be far away.

Fieldstone Vineyards, Inc.

38577 State Highway 68 • Morgan, MN 56266 •
507-249-9463 • www.fieldstonevineyards.com
Location: 4.5 miles west of Morgan, Minnesota, on State Highway 68.

Hours:
May–December:
Saturday, 11:00 am–6:00 pm
Sunday, noon–5:00 pm
Other times by appointment

Tasting: Nominal fee

Tours: By request

Signature wines:
Minnesota Glacial Rock Red: dry, medium-bodied Frontenac
Prairie Stone: semisweet blend of Frontenac and Minnesota strawberries
Wine-ing Farmer: novelty rosé from Bluebell grapes

Events: Occasional; see website.

Everybody Likes Grapes

Mark Wedge comes out of the vineyard armed with a shotgun. He looks dangerous—as he is to the crows, wild turkeys, and other birds that are trying to sneak into the vineyard on a sunny summer morning to devour the grapes just as they become sweet enough for wine.

Wine sugar is measured in Brix, which roughly equates to twice the percentage of alcohol in the finished wine. A low-alcohol wine of 11 percent requires at least twenty Brix. And at that level, birds descend like a Biblical plague, stripping the grapes from their vines in a sugary frenzy.

Around the world, vineyard owners know that everybody likes grapes. Not only birds, but raccoons, deer, foxes—even bears. At the continent's farthest-north vineyard, Royarnois, located north of Québec, bears steal part of every crop. What does the vineyard owner do when they come? "We go inside," says Roland Arnois.

Vintners may give up against bears, but wild turkeys and other birds are worth fighting. Some vineyards are equipped with noise machines that emit blasts at irregular intervals. At Fieldstone, a recording of what seems to be a crow being tortured warns away marauders. Nets are also necessary, especially on fragrant grapes like La Crescent. One Upper Midwest grower lost an entire year's crop to wild turkeys who tore down the nets and gobbled every grape in sight.

One tiny pest can cause tremendous damage. Invasive Asian beetles cannot puncture grapes themselves. But when wasps sting grapes, beetles crawl into the miniscule hole, gorge themselves, then die. An infestation of beetles might pass into the crusher with the grapes. One grower had to throw away an entire year's worth of Foch. "The smell," she could only say, years later. "Oh, the smell." That vineyard planted late soybeans near the grapes, to attract the beetles away to a more-favored food.

Nets, guns, noise machines, alternative crops—winegrowers try all of them, sometimes at the same time, sometimes in sequence. But everybody likes grapes, and some of every harvest gets away.

MORGAN CREEK VINEYARDS

A long, low building nestles into the side of a hill, surrounded by rock terraces bursting with perennial blooms. On the patio, a wood-fired oven generates gentle warmth. In front, a green lawn sweeps down to the small eponymous creek, beside which the vineyard stretches.

Only the educated eye will notice that this is the Upper Midwest's greenest winery. That cozy tasting room and production center is built into the hillside, using the earth's heat to sustain a fifty-five-degree year-round temperature within its ten-inch-thick walls. The building is constructed of recycled materials, including fir doors salvaged from a shuttered Mankato factory and timbers from an old barn. "We are proud that so much of our building was done sustainably," says Paula Marti who, with her husband Georg, started Morgan Creek in 1993.

That was prehistory when it comes to the Upper Midwest wine industry. There were only four wineries in Minnesota at the time, all near the Twin Cities, where zoning was unproblematic. Morgan Creek was deep in rural south-central Minnesota. "Some people thought we were going to be a liquor store with a big parking lot," Paula remembers today. But Paula and Georg were committed to the project, which had started as a vineyard. "We didn't originally think of having a winery," Paula says, "but Georg had been working at the brewery for many years, so the idea of pumping thousands of gallons of fluid didn't daunt him a bit."

Georg's own great-great-grandfather, August Schell, was the founder of that brewery, so starting an entirely new industry was something of a family tradition. As they explored the idea of opening a winery, the Martis grew passionate about how wine helps people appreciate the earth and its response to seasonal change. That passion helped them "machete through the red

tape" to create the first Minnesota winery devoted to principles of sustainable agriculture.

Sustainability is a buzzword in economic circles today, but a dozen years ago it was a new concept. The Martis see it as a return to traditional values that include caring for the human community as well as the environment. Wine fits into this vision, because "this is not just about coming to a building and buying wine," Paula Marti explains. "Wine is not just a commodity to be purchased, but a product of a certain land at a certain season. And the wine experience itself is not just about drinking, because wine is a creation so closely married to the land."

The connection of wine to land is the most important part of Morgan Creek's vision. "Everything we do is connected to the seasonal cycle, and we want visitors to understand that." From the dormancy of winter through the flourishing of spring, the color change (*veraison*) and ripening of grapes, up to harvest and the fermentation and bottling that takes up the winter months, the vineyard and the winery are tied to the seasonal flow.

In addition to wine, the Martis offer handcrafted flatbreads made in their wood-fired outdoor oven, as well as local and regional cheeses. "We had seen communal ovens of this sort when we were in Germany," Paula remembers, "and we wanted to give the community an authentic experience of how they worked."

Originally planted with ten varieties in 1993, the three-acre vineyard has settled down with five hardy survivors: Frontenac and Frontenac Gris, St. Pepin, Maréchal Foch, and La Crescent. The Riesling, Gewürztraminer, Pinot Gris, and others that did not thrive were gradually torn out and replaced. Ironically, the planting replicated a similar planting a century earlier by August Schell, who also found that the European varieties did not well tolerate the fierce Minnesota winters. But he did not have the University of Minnesota varieties to turn to, as did the Martis. The Martis also nurture a few vines of a rare Russian variety, Minchurnetz, which they use only for wine for their annual wine-makers' dinner, hosted for the fourteen other growers who provide them with grapes. None of those guests were originally winegrowers, but rather are enterprising farmers who saw a new market opening up and developed small vine-yards to meet it.

Not content with having been the first vine-yard far from the Minnesota metropolitan area, the Martis plan to become the first organic win-ery in the region. "We have always been inter-ested in growing with the least amount of toxic chemicals possible," Paula says. They do not, for instance, use heavy doses of herbicide to keep their rows clear. "For weed control . . . well,"

Paula laughs, "I don't think we have control of our weeds." A few weeds are, to her, less dis-turbing than the long-term effects of applying toxic chemicals to vineyard soil.

Using fewer rather than more chemicals is often described as a "best practices" approach to grape-growing. This differs from "organic" not only in the strictness of the ban on chemicals but also in the certification process. Happily for the Martis, their land was never farmed but only used as pasturage, so they do not need to wait for any residue to clear. They have enrolled in training at Angelic Organics farm in Illinois, featured in the popular documentary *The Real Dirt on Farmer John*. They are also learning biodynamic agriculture at the Michael Fields Institute and have begun to learn the intensive composting required of that approach.

Organic and Biodynamic

As more Americans become concerned about their health and the health of the planet, interest grows in organic and biodynamic farming. Of the two, "organic" is more widely recognized, although what constitutes an organic product is the subject of some controversy. The U.S. Department of Agri-culture (USDA) certifies the use of "organic" to describe grapes by requiring that the vineyard be tended without pesticides or artificial fertilizers. For the grape grower, this presents certain chal-lenges. Conventional vineyard practices protect the precious wine-bearing vines from anthracnose, powdery mildew, and other blights through regular application of pesticides. Herbicides are also com-monly used to keep the ground around the vines free of competing weeds. Growing grapes organi-cally is challenging, especially in the Upper Mid-west with its harsh climate.

More challenging is the biodynamic process, which is not federally regulated but certified

through the independent Demeter organization. The approach views a farm as a balanced ecosys-tem, encouraging the building of strong soil through composting and use of cover crops to help build soil. In addition, herbal sprays, mineral addi-tions to compost, and planting in accordance with astronomical observations are part of the process.

Biodynamic agriculture is rooted in the theories of Rudolph Steiner, whose educational ideas form the basis of the renowned Waldorf schools. Many of the applications required by biodynamics have their roots in traditional herbalism, such as appli-cations of stinging nettle (*Urtica dioica*) picked in full bloom. As that plant has been shown to be high in calcium and iron, its use may bring those elements to the treated plant. Biodynamic vine-yard management is practiced in France, Califor-nia, and other traditional wine-growing areas. And, within a decade or so, in the Upper Midwest as well.

The process will be multistage, moving toward organic certification first, then toward the prestigious Demeter certification in biodynamic agriculture. Along the way, the Martis will move the winery as much off-grid as possible. Wind turbines on the roof will provide electricity, and further environmental developments are in the works. For the Martis, growing and making wine is only part of a sustainable lifestyle that they hope to model for their children and their community.

Morgan Creek Vineyards

23707 478th Avenue • New Ulm, MN 56073 • 507-947-3547 • www.morgancreekvineyards.com

Location: Between Mankato and New Ulm; State Highway 68 to County Road 47 to 101 South, first farm on the left.

Hours:
May–October:
Friday and Saturday, 11:00 am–9:00 pm
Sunday, noon–5:00 pm
November and December:
Friday and Saturday, 11:00 am–6:00 pm
Sunday, noon–5:00 pm
Closed January–April

Tasting: Complimentary

Tours: Daily, every hour

Signature wines:
St. Pepin: semisweet Elmer Swenson variety
Zeitgeist: off-dry La Crescent with Muscat aromas
Puck's Pride: red Frontenac named for the vineyard's first dog

Events: Spring Bacchus Festival; German Wine Tasting Festival; harvest-time grape stomp; Christmas Candlelight Wine Tasting; Winedown for the Weekend on Fridays, May–October, 6:30–9:00 p.m.; Jazz Nite on the first Saturday of the month, May–October; also gourmet cooking classes and other events; check website.

OLDE COUNTRY WINERY

People are always walking into Olde Country Winery and exclaiming, "Wow, this was my room!" Not because the winery is built in an old boarding house or a hotel. No—it's in an old elementary school.

When winemaker Irv Moen was in the Marines, or when he was a Twin Cities industrialist, few of the projects he led would be described as "charmingly offbeat." But this schoolhouse-turned-winery certainly is. Take the old multipurpose room, now a wine-themed banquet room. Artificial grapevines twine about old basketball backboards, and tables are neatly set within the old court boundaries. The seventh-grade classroom holds a huge fermenting vat. The hallways are decorated with wine art that recalls yesteryear's in-hallway art displays. At Olde Country Winery, the oddness of a winery in a 1950s public school building soon dissolves, and it all begins to feel utterly appropriate.

The kids go to the consolidated school now, together with students from Bird Island and Olivia, so the old school stood vacant for a few years until Moen saw its potential. He had just sold his company in the Twin Cities and had decided that his next challenge would be to build a Minnesota winery. He had noticed the trend toward regional wineries and as a long-time winemaker, he was eager to turn hobby into profession.

His wine-making hobby began when, as a young Marine in Hawaii, he made a batch of coconut wine. "When you're a Marine and you make wine," he chuckles, "you're a popular guy." He continued to make wine during the four decades that he ran a chemical company in St. Paul. Starting Olde Country was like coming home.

It was like coming home in another way as well, as Moen's family has vacationed in the Lake Lillian area for generations. Although he was brought up near Lodi, California, Moen's family returned every summer to a cabin on Scandinavian Lake in central Minnesota. He grew up knowing the land of lakes and lake peoples, and he was eager to return.

He looked at several other properties before finding the school, with its single-story layout and space to grow. A vineyard occupies part of the schoolyard, but Moen's larger vineyard is at his home, where he grows cold-hardy grapes:

Edelweiss, King of the North, Swenson Red, Frontenac, and others. Moen is not interested in experimenting with *vinifera* varieties, which are not hardy in prairie winters. He wants to make wine, and he wants vines that reliably provide grapes.

His appetite for grapes is large enough that he has convinced almost thirty-five other growers to work with him, bringing the total acreage of available grapes to nearly seventy. Although

Awfully Close to Granite Falls

Irv Moen's favorite family story tells how his father ran afoul of the law during Prohibition. "Dad had made up a bunch of bootlegged beer," Moen recalls, "and had it out at the lake, and he got busted. The sheriff was there, and the judge was there, so they had the trial right there. They fined him five bucks, and then the judge turned to the sheriff and said, 'Good, now let's have a drink.' And they all had a drink of the bootlegged beer."

Whoa, you might be thinking, what was this, a corrupt judge? But what the judge did was perfectly legal. Manufacturing and transporting intoxicating beverages was made illegal by the Eighteenth Amendment. Drinking them was within the law.

Popular culture paints a picture of speakeasies where, when the fuzz busts in, screaming patrons run out the back door in terror. But those flappers just stayed in their seats, sipping away at their illegal hooch. Unless they could be proven to have made or transported the bathtub gin, they were in the clear.

Prohibition has deep roots in central Minnesota, which was already mostly "dry" before local boy Andy Volstead wrote the law that laid out how the new amendment would be enforced. Perhaps the most problematic part of the Volstead Act was that

more than one division of government was charged with enforcement. Federal, state, and local officials were to cooperate to make sure that prohibited substances were not made or carried about. But cooperation among different and sometimes dissonant branches of government is invariably difficult.

All those "cooperating" law enforcement officers made for all that many more potential bribe takers. By the middle of the 1920s, Minnesota politics was notoriously corrupt, with gambling and prostitution accompanying alcohol in the business portfolios of organized crime. When Minneapolis journalist Walter Liggett, publisher of the *Midwest American,* tried to reveal the facts, he was first offered bribes, then threatened. The threat was no idle one: in front of his wife and ten-year-old daughter, Liggett was machine-gunned to death near his home. Despite the identification of his killer as Minnesota's notorious mob boss, Isadore Blumenfeld (Kid Cann), no one was ever convicted in the case.

With all that was going on during the Prohibition years, no wonder the judge and the sheriff had a drink. A young man making home-brewed beer out in central Minnesota was the least of their worries.

only opened in late 2006, Olde Country now offers sixty-two different wines. Some are fruit wines, using Minnesota raspberries, blueberries, and rhubarbs. Minnesota's own Honeycrisp apple finds its way into one wine, but perhaps the most exotic is the Dandelion Mango Citrus.

Not only is the winery open daily, but it is increasingly used as a venue for public and private events. That converted multipurpose room has been put to use for weddings, business meetings, organizational luncheons, and reunions. "We haven't had a reunion of kids who went to school here—yet," Moen says. "But I hope that will happen someday." For now, individuals can visit their old homerooms and see how well they have been adapted to serve the winemaker's art.

Olde Country Winery

301 Olde Country Schoolyard E • Lake Lillian, MN 56253 • 320-664-9463 • www.oldecountrywinery.com

Location: State Highway 7 west from the Twin Cities to Lake Lillian; north on County Road 8 (120th Street), right on Meadow Lane to end.

Hours:
Monday–Saturday, 10:00 am–6:00 pm
Sunday, 10:00 am–6:00 pm

Tasting: $5

Tours: By arrangement

Signature wines:
Pinot Grigio: popular Italian white
Peach Apricot Chardonnay: fruity flavored white
Honey Mead: sweet version of honey wine

Events: Monthly, Ladies' Night Out; January, Hawaiian Luau; February, Valentine's Show; September, Grape Stomp and Harvest Fest; October, Grape Stomp; December, New Year's Eve Party.

The Driftless Area

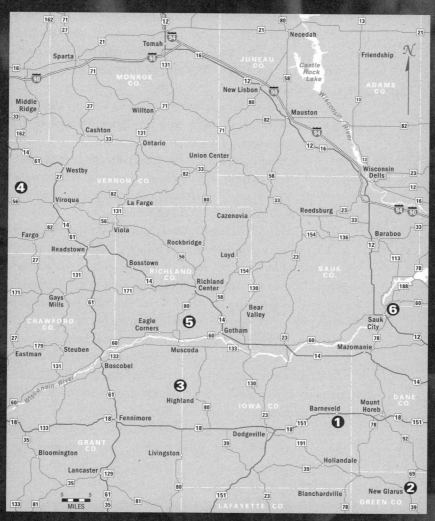

1. Botham Vineyards 2. New Glarus Primrose Winery 3. Spurgeon Winery
4. Vernon Vineyards 5. Weggy Winery 6. Wollersheim Winery

IF WISCONSIN HAS A WINE COUNTRY, it is surely the Driftless Area. In the Upper Midwest, only Minnesota's Great River areas boast more wineries than southwest Wisconsin. Most of Wisconsin's biggest wineries can be found within an hour's drive through scenic hills and shadowed valleys. Another half-dozen smaller enterprises take advantage of the limestone-rich hills to provide the state with close to 90 percent of its wine production.

But the Driftless Area is less well-known among tourists than Wisconsin's Door County or north woods regions. Those who do know it, love it. Imagine a bucolic landscape with cows and red barns, set against darkly forested hills, and you have the Driftless Area. Throw in charming towns, great antique stores, cheese factories, microbreweries, outdoor theaters, museums (weird and other) and galleries, and you have some folks' definition of vacation heaven.

Also called the Western Uplands and the Coulee Region, the Driftless Area has a unique geological history. Throughout the rest of the region, slow-moving ice rivers deposited ridges (moraines), hills of detritus (drumlins) and odd boulders (erratics) during the Quaternary ice ages. Not so in the Driftless Area. The now-small hills called the Baraboo Range stopped the glacial advance. Some ages saw the ice end north of the Driftless Area, while in others, the area was a small green island in a sea of ice, surrounded even on its southern border.

As a result, the region's topography is distinct from the lake-studded flatlands that surround it. Surprisingly steep hills shade narrow valleys. Small streams run to the Sugar, Pecatonica, Kickapoo, and Wisconsin rivers, forming a maze of waterways, many navigable by canoe or kayak. The main east-west roads follow ridges, offering long vistas over the land, but to truly appreciate the Driftless Area, you must venture onto the spiderweb of smaller north-south roads that bring you into hidden valleys whose rich bottomland offers dairy grazing and corn and soybean fields.

Dotted along the valleys are small towns, each with special attractions. Mount Horeb is the world capital of trolls (yes, trolls, who line the "Trollway" in all their chainsaw-sculptured glory) and home to the Mustard Museum with its "Poupon U" T-shirts. Barneveld is the gateway to one of Wisconsin's best-known attractions, the Cave of the Mounds, as well as being adjacent to Blue Mounds State Park, which the Ho-Chunk people said was the home of Earthmaker, the creator-god. Mazomanie's historic downtown has been revitalized with new galleries and a public park, while in Boscobel you can visit the room where two traveling salesmen, trying to avoid sin, formed the Gideon Bible Society.

Spring Green is home to Taliesin, home of architect Frank Lloyd Wright, who took his inspiration from the beautiful Wyoming Valley where he grew up. In Mineral Point, Cornish lead miners lived on Shake-Rag Alley, so called because the miners were called home for dinner by their wives shaking rags in the air like inaudible dinner bells. Today the town is filled with galleries and artists' studios, and the old Pendarven and Shake-Rag Alley houses are arts centers offering tours and programs.

Located between these two towns is Wisconsin's most-visited tourist attraction, the bizarre House on the Rock, built by the eccentric Alex Jordan. In the early 1940s, drawn to a 450-foot rock outcropping near Dodgeville, Jordan decided to build a house from local limestone. Soon the one-room house grew too small, so he began to add rooms, for Jordan was a world-class collector: of stained glass and antique guns, of dolls and suits of armor, of Titanic memorabilia and music machines. He kept building more rooms to hold his collections until, when he died in 1989, the House was a warren of display areas. Now part of a tourism complex that includes golf courses and resort hotels, the House on the Rock is not to everyone's taste, but for tens of thousands of people a year, it's just right.

There is much else to see in the Driftless Area: the historic stave church at Little Norway, the Ringling Brothers Circus Museum and the Crane Center at Baraboo, the train museum in Fenimore, the Historic Cheesemaking Center in Monroe. You can attend a folkdance encampment at Folklore Village, a pagan solstice at Circle Sanctuary, a Buddhist retreat at Global Vision, or a Catholic environmental celebration at Sinsinawa. You can learn gourmet cooking at Carr Valley Cheese factory in Sauk City or attend a Robert Burns Day celebration at Luckenbooths Café in Arena. You can go antiquing, canoeing, or biking; stay at a B and B with local organic breakfasts; or just hang out at the General Store in Spring Green, as John Kerry did while he was on the campaign trail in 2004.

All this, and wine too.

BOTHAM VINEYARDS

A quarter century ago, in the gentle hills south of Barneveld, Richard Botham raised Herefords. Then his son Peter came home to make wine, having abandoned an artistic career on the east coast. "Why that change?" he ponders today. "Because I really like wine. And I love farming. This is an ideal job for me, a marriage of two things I love."

He had done some apprentice wine-making in Virginia, so Botham already knew the industry. In 1989, he planted his first vineyard, which was immediately destroyed by severe weather.

Botham replanted; today's vineyard of Maréchal Foch, with a sprinkling of DeChaunac and Léon Millot, dates to 1990–92. While he tended his vines in those early years, Botham continued to learn his craft with Philippe Coquard at nearby Wollersheim. "Wisconsin wine was a small world at the time," Botham remembers, "there were some folks making fruit wine, and Glenn Spurgeon and Bob Wollersheim. And me."

When his first crop came in, in 1992, it was so scanty that Botham sold it to Wollersheim. But the next year the crop was large enough to bottle, and Botham Vineyards opened with four wines, three of which are still being made. One,

Packers vs. Parker

Some people call it the Parker Effect, for wine critic Robert Parker Jr., who made his name when, at the age of thirty-five, he predicted the 1982 Bordeaux vintage as the most impressive in years—before the wine was in the bottle. No one disputes that the man has an incredible palate. Where Parker becomes controversial is the way that palate has become an international force in the wine business.

Parker favors "big reds," wines like those made in Bordeaux: tannic, even astringent when young but mellowing as they age. He established the 100-point scale to judge wine quality—a scale used, for better or worse, even by small retailers in Wisconsin, where buyers who might prefer a sweeter, less-alcoholic wine find themselves buying an unfamiliar Cabernet Sauvignon from Australia just because it rates a 91.

Not only that, but Parker likes the new crop of "hot" wines, wines with a higher-than-usual percentage of alcohol. Alcohol comes from yeast-eating sugar, so to get more alcohol in wine requires more sugar to start. California has recently pushed the sugar content of wine grapes to what some consider outrageous levels. "Hang time," the time after ripening that a grape stays on the vine and develops additional sugars, has moved to previously unheard-of lengths. With all that additional sugar, yeast can create a wine of 14–16 percent, a considerable step up (or, in some opinions, down) from the 11–12 percent found in most wine.

How do Midwestern wines rate on a Parker scale? Poorly. This is no region for hot, fruity, tannic wines. For one thing, they must be made from *vinifera* grapes, which do not thrive here. For another, the climate would have to offer longer growing seasons to develop that extra sugar. So chances are poor to none that a Parker-pleasing wine will come from the Upper Midwest. That's a good thing for the region's wine drinkers who are anti-Parker by taste. Light, quaffable reds and clean off-dry whites are not only the region's best wines, but also its most popular. Parker might sneer, but he also might sneer at brats with sauerkraut. To say nothing of lutefisk and lefse. *De gustibus,* you betcha!

Uplands Reserve, is one of Botham's most popular wines. Cupola Gold and Seyval Blanc, both made from the latter varietal but vinified differently, are also still on the Botham list, but Amber Light Blush has been replaced by Badger Blush.

Botham intended his winery as a business, not a hobby, so he worked with imported juice from the start. The climate is wrong for raising whites, he believes, so he works with Finger Lakes and California Riesling, Seyval Blanc, and other varietals. His own vineyard, which now covers nine acres, provides a good portion of his estate-grown reds. "Truth is, the Upper Midwest will never produce a Cabernet-style red," he says, "but we can do well with Beaujolais-like lighter reds."

His own favorite grape does not grow in his vineyard. "I love Riesling," he says. "There is something about that grape—it's so versatile, takes well to so many different wine styles. I have an affinity for it." Although it can be made bone-dry, as it often is in its Rhine homeland, Riesling in Botham's hands becomes the basis for an off-dry wine.

During the first years, Botham sold most wines directly from his tasting room, but as awareness of regional wines has grown, his business has boomed. By late 2006, more than 60 percent of his wines left the winery in wholesale trucks. "The business has grown astonishingly in the last several years," he muses, "and at a steady rate. Wine has become the beverage of choice for more drinkers now, and taste has become more sophisticated."

Keeping up with that increasing sophistication has led Botham to add new wines. With oceans of well-crafted wine available at under ten dollars a bottle, Botham feels that only those who can make a quality product will thrive in the emerging Midwestern wine industry. "It's like microbrews a few years ago. More people are entering the market, and there's a huge upwelling of interest in the product." But to be competitive, the Midwest must encourage excellence as well as enhanced production.

So what does one of the state's premier winemakers drink himself? "Not my own wine, I've had plenty of that!" he laughs. "I can't learn anything by drinking my own wine. And I rarely drink any wine a second time. I'm always trying things, from a supermarket or a liquor store. Right now, I like Riojas, and reds from Chile. But I'm not drinking much California wine now—the high alcohol doesn't appeal to me."

Despite producing nearly thirty thousand gallons of wine each year, Peter Botham is almost a one-man band. With a little seasonal help, especially at harvest, he manages the vineyard and personally prunes every one of his over five thousand vines. He's also the winemaker, working in a production facility between the tasting room and the home he shares with his wife, Sarah, who serves as the company's marketing director.

Employees in the tasting room free Botham to concentrate on vines and wines, but he does lecture at the annual open house each spring. "Every year I talk about something different. This year, I focused on the work of the winemaker. I gave them each two wines and challenged them to determine the similarity. I had five tours of about a hundred people each before someone figured out that they were made from the same grape." The annual two-day event brings thousands to the winery each year, many of them return visitors.

From art school to wine-making may seem a big step, but to Peter Botham, wine-making is an art, one that begins in the vineyard. "It's hard work, but when it comes right down to it, there's nothing I'd rather do." A slow smile crosses his face as his eyes wander over the six huge steel vats in which the next wine is fermenting. "Like I said, I really like wine."

Botham Vineyards

County Road K • Barneveld, Wisconsin 53507 •
1-888-GR8-WINE • www.bothamvineyards.com

Location: Just east of Barneveld and west of
Mount Horeb; turn onto County Road K, south off
Highway 18-151, and follow signs.

Hours:
May 1–December 31:
Monday–Saturday, 9:00 am–5:00 pm
January 2–May 1:
Monday–Saturday, 10:00 am–5:00 pm
*Closed Easter, Thanksgiving, Christmas, and New
Year's Day*

Tasting: Complimentary

Tours: By appointment for groups of 15 or more if
requested 2 weeks in advance, $3 per person

Signature wines:
Uplands Reserve: dry, light red, especially for meals
Field III: estate-grown Léon Millot, dry and fruity
Riesling: semidry style, quite fruity

Events: Memorial Day weekend open house.

NEW GLARUS PRIMROSE WINERY

A long southern slope, called a cuesta, descends
from Military Ridge west of Madison. In Green
County, fields are wide and long, roads hug
sweeping hills, and farmers raise dairy cattle
rather than corn and soybeans. Classic red barns
dot the gentle countryside, as do cheese factories
like Silver-Lewis, Prairie Hill, and the Amish
cheese-makers Hill and Valley. Just an hour's
drive southwest from Madison, this region draws
bicyclists and antique hunters as well as those
looking for a pleasant country drive.

Among communities of the Driftless Area,
New Glarus stands out: it is the only Swiss village, named for one of the oldest cantons in the
home country, a conservative place where citi-

zens still gather on the first of May to enact
communal business. The 108 immigrants who
arrived in 1845 and grew successful in the new
land never lost touch with the old, so delega-
tions of Swiss tourists annually make their way
to New Glarus.

New Glarus loves being Swiss. Swiss flags fly
from Alpine chalets and, in summer, geraniums
burst from hanging flower boxes. The downtown, lined with ornately decorated chalets,
offers Swiss food (sausage and schnitzel). Nearby
is the Swiss Historical Village, whose fourteen
buildings, including a firehouse and school, have
been preserved since 1942. Cows parade through
town; the painted sculptures are manufactured
in Zurich, which hosted the first "cow parade" in
1998, followed shortly thereafter by Chicago. But
where Chicago flirted with cows, New Glarus
brought them home to Mom—more than a
dozen cows, including one dressed in traditional
Alpine garb, line the streets.

Summer solstice brings the Heidi Festival,
complete with outdoor dramatization of the
classic story of a Swiss girlhood. Late summer
sees Swiss Independence Day, or Volksfest, with
folk music and dancing. In early September, the
Wilhelm Tell Festival centers on a community
production of the play by Friedrich Schiller celebrating Swiss independence, performed outdoors with goats and cows playing their parts in
the cast. Yodeling is featured at every event.

Although Swiss wine is not as well-known
as that of their neighbors to the north and
south, Switzerland has a distinguished wine
heritage. Red as well as white wines are produced from unusual varietals such as Chasselas
and Sylvaner, as well as the better-known
Gewürztraminer and Pinot Noir. America's
largest importer of Swiss wines, Swiss Cellars, is
located near New Glarus and hosts regular tastings throughout Wisconsin. They carry Heida,
from grapes grown at an astonishing 3,770 feet
above sea level in Europe's highest vineyard, as

well as Swiss grappa, an aperitif made from fermented skins and stems.

New Glarus's winery, begun in Mineral Point by Bob and Peg Borucki, has been offering wines made predominantly from Wisconsin grapes and other fruit since 1990. A move to New Glarus brought them closer to the state's population centers. In a heritage building just a block off the main street, the winery offers wines made from Wisconsin-grown grapes such as Foch, Concord, and DeChaunac. The winery is causal

and low-key, offering newcomers to the wine world an introduction to the tasting experience and advanced tasters an opportunity to savor less-known varietals. Yodeling is optional.

New Glarus Primrose Winery

500 First Street • New Glarus, WI 53574 • 608-527-5053 • no website

Location: From Madison, take State Road 18-151 toward Mineral Point, turn south on County Road 69 to New Glarus; winery is downtown.

That Wine-and-Cheese Thing

It's enough to drive a cheesehead crazy: a $21-million a year national commercial campaign showing smiling California cows suffering post-traumatic stress disorder from their horrifying heiferhoods back in the cold Wisconsin winters.

While it is true that California overtook Wisconsin as the nation's largest milk producer in the 1990s, proud dairy folk from the Midwest point out that their competitors represent agribusiness run amok, while back in cold Wisconsin, small producers still produce a significant proportion of the product. Almost a third of Wisconsin cheese comes not from soulless fermentation factories but from small operations, some of which date back to the cheese heyday of the early twentieth century, when nearly three thousand tiny cheese factories stood at crossroads throughout the state. Their distinctive boxy outline can still be detected today, incorporated into a house or garage or farm outbuilding.

Bad enough that California has stolen the milk crown. Even worse, the cheese championship may slip away. In 2005, Wisconsin made 2.4 billion pounds of cheese, to California's 2.14 billion pounds. A couple billion pounds is all that stands between the secure knowledge that squeaky curds rule and a state agricultural identity crisis.

Not for nothing are Wisconsinites called cheeseheads. Would Californians bring Brown Swiss and Holsteins to the capital every year, as do Wisconsinites on Cows on Parade day? Not likely. Would foam cheese hats be embraced as Rodeo Drive couture? Laughable. Cheese is to Wisconsin as yodeling is to Switzerland. As earthquakes are to California. Where is Squeaky Fromage when Wisconsin needs her?

Cheese and wine seems an inevitable coupling, but recent studies from the University of (sorry!) California, Davis show that the mouth-coating quality of cheese cuts into the taster's ability to distinguish the subtle flavors of wine. The study, conducted by Berenice Madrigal, shows that cheese mutes deficiencies in wines, but takes away fruity and oaky flavors. Blue cheeses are the worst offenders, essentially erasing a wine's qualities. This surprising finding has been controversial but suggests that it's not necessary to wed extraordinary wine to a cheese tray.

What about cheese and beer? Such tastings are now growing in popularity. Might be a good thing. California is still way behind Wisconsin in beer production.

Hours:

January–April:
Thursday and Friday, noon to 5:00 pm
Saturday, 10:00 am to 5:00 pm
Sunday and Monday, noon–5:00 pm
May–December:
Monday–Saturday, 10:00 am to 6:00 pm
Sunday, noon to 6:00 pm

Tasting: Complimentary

Tours: None

Signature wines:

Fridolin White: Swiss-style white from Wisconsin-grown Elvira grapes
Apfelmost Wine: mulled spiced apple wine
Classic American Red: hearty Concord

Events: Winery open house during Heidi Festival and other community events.

SPURGEON WINERY

"Know what I'd do if I were starting over?" Glenn Spurgeon says with a twinkle in his eye. Recalling the old instructions on how to make a small fortune in wine, he jokes, "I'd start with a large fortune."

That might be the only thing he would do differently. Spurgeon, founder of the eponymous winery near Highland, knew his ambition in high school: to raise grapes and make wine. He did not come from a wine-making family or a wine-making region. But somehow a small-town Missouri teenager dreamed of a life in wine.

First he earned a master's in agronomy at the University of Missouri, then headed north to teach in Green Bay. There he met Mary, a young woman from the Driftless hills. Soon they moved back to her hometown and, in 1978, started planting vines on a hilltop next to her family farm. Grapes are not a crop for impa-

tient people; it would be years before they released their first wine.

Spurgeon, one of the region's oldest wineries, recently celebrated the twenty-fifth anniversary of their first vintage in 1982. Turning out forty thousand gallons of wine annually, Spurgeon distributes through Sam's Club and other major stores. But much of its wine goes home with visitors to the winery's pleasant, no-frills tasting room. Some are annual customers from Illinois or Minnesota. Others are once-off passersby, taking a bike tour across the Wisconsin hills or exploring the heritage of the Cornish lead miners who came to the area in the early 1800s.

When Spurgeon planted his first grape, only the late Bob Wollersheim had a commercial vineyard in Wisconsin, and Wollersheim relied on French-American hybrids. Spurgeon went in a different direction: he planted native Americans, ones he felt would survive Wisconsin's winter deep freezes and its baking summers. His vines include Elvira, a grape he knew back home in Missouri that makes a fragrant white wine, and Delaware, an early hybrid still employed for wine.

Almost two dozen varieties share Spurgeon's sixteen-acre hilltop vineyard. Some, like Maréchal Foch, are common in the area, but others like Aurore and Chambourcin are less so. Indeed, less-experienced growers believe some Spurgeon varieties should not grow here. "You can't listen to what they say in New York, you can't just go to the hardiness charts," Spurgeon says. "We don't have warm winter nights—even when it warms up during the day, the temperature goes back down at night—so vines that don't wake up just from daytime temperatures can grow here."

His vineyard is proof of his theories. He planted four acres the first year and five the second; the rest of the vineyard soon followed. Making the right grape choice was significant to Spurgeon's success, for he has replanted little.

As a result, Spurgeon harvests grapes from old vines whose fruit is more deeply flavored than less mature ones.

While most of Spurgeon's grapes are estate-grown, the winery's size demands importation of grapes from New York and Washington state. Other wines are made from Wisconsin-grown fruit, including the state's signature cranberry, which sells by the semi-load come Thanksgiving.

Customers may like fruit wines, but Glenn Spurgeon loves his grapes. Get him started talking about his vineyard, and the scientist-teacher appears. "We've got Rosette, an unusual variety that does well for us. And Foch, of course, which has to be cluster-thinned or it gets too productive. We look for grapes that can take thirty-five below. We've got 'em: some of our Concords are four inches in diameter."

But if he loves his vines and his wines, Glenn Spurgeon is also a businessman. "I like dry wines," he says, "but the Midwest has a sweet tooth. So we make wines that people like to drink." He is quick to acknowledge the part that politics and marketing play in the emergence of the regional wine industry, pointing to the surge in sales when the State Fair opened a building—into which local winemakers poured more than sixty thousand dollars in renovations—as a wine-tasting facility. "That's when things really took off" for Wisconsin wine, he recalls. With increasing public awareness of regional wines, he sees a bright future ahead.

But still, "if I had it to do over, I'd start with a lot more money," Glenn Spurgeon grins as he looks out from the deck of the winery he dreamed of owning when he was a boy in Missouri.

Spurgeon Vineyards and Winery

16008 Pine Tree Road • Highland, WI 53543 • 1-800-236-5555 • www.SpurgeonVineyards.com

Location: Just off County Road Q west of Highland. Reach Highland from the south on State Road 80 from Cobb on Highway 18, or from the north on 80 from Muscoda.

Hours:
January 2–December 24:
10:00 am–5:00 pm

Talk Dry, Drink Sweet

Visit an American wine shop, and you'll hear it: "Oh, I only drink dry wine. I don't like sweet." Dry wines have cachet. They bespeak sophistication and class. Sweet wines? Teenagers drink them after the prom, when they want to get tipsy on something that tastes like pop.

But winemakers know the truth: Americans "talk dry, drink sweet." Confronted with a flight of wines, Americans buy the sweeter ones. The sharpness of a true dry wine does not please their palate, no matter how much they protest. Some theorize that Americans, growing up on sodas, are accustomed to sweetness in beverages; others, that the flavor of the native American grapes in juice and jelly creates an expectation that anything made from grapes will be sweet.

Yet Americans persist in believing that they like dry wines. For this reason, the old term "semi-sweet" is increasingly being changed to "off-dry." Same wines, same taste. But customers snap up an off-dry wine who would not be seen drinking one labeled semisweet. Dryness can be in the eye, not on the tongue.

Tasting: Complimentary

Tours: Guided tours of the winery at noon daily April–October, or by appointment. Self-guided vineyard tours available year-round.

Signature wines:

Ruby Lady: light, sweet red with berry overtones

The Loreley: fruity white made in German Rhine style

Harvest Red: semisweet, full-bodied red with soft tannins

Events: Memorial Day weekend, Great Chocolate Trail; mid-June, Cheese Extravaganza; early October, Harvest Festival; early December, Christmas open house.

VERNON VINEYARDS

It may be the most beautiful vineyard view in Wisconsin. The small patio outside Vernon Vineyards looks down hundreds of feet into narrow Newton Valley, one of southwestern Wisconsin's coulees. Named from the French *couler,* meaning "to flow," these coulees are steep-sided valleys formed by stream erosion. A half century ago, this was classic Midwestern dairy land where most farmers grew a little tobacco on the side. When the tobacco industry died, grapes emerged to take its place.

That's how Bob Starks and Loren Cade began—as farmers getting out of tobacco and into grapes. In late 2000, they were among the farmers who signed up with the local Agricultural Extension Service for a series of educational programs to help farmers who wished to make that transition. Starks gives extension agent Tim Reiburn credit for kick-starting the local wine industry. "He wrote grants and brought in people like Peter Hemstad from the University of Minnesota. By the end of the workshops, about twenty-five of us had signed up to grow grapes." Most, like Starks, started

small: he put in an acre that first year. "I was anticipating retirement in a few years and had planned to grow tobacco. But I thought this would be less physical." Starks laughs, the laugh of a man who has since learned better.

Within the year, he was hooked. He joined Northern Vineyards, the wine cooperative, on whose board of directors he served. Starks retired from farm equipment sales, followed by his neighbor and fellow hobby-winemaker Cade. In 2004, Starks and Cade converted a building used for cooling grapes and storing equipment, and in 2005 opened for business. Cade, with twenty-five years of wine-making experience, became the winemaker, using grapes from both properties.

More than most regional wineries, Vernon Vineyards has a variety of grapes to blend—seventeen whites and eight reds, as well as nine varieties of table grapes on almost twenty acres. The whites include regional standby varieties like La Crosse and St. Pepin, but also less common varieties like Swenson's Kay Gray and the customers' favorite, Edelweiss. Vernon Vineyards grows the *vinifera* Gewürztraminer directly in front of the tasting room, trained on low trellises for winter burial. The reliable Foch and Frontenac take up the greater part of the vineyard, together with Swenson's Sabrevois and the native American Catawba. Starks and Cade plan to plant the new Marquette, released in 2007 by the University of Minnesota. "They have a history of being honest with us growers," Starks says, "so we believe them when they say this will be a good one."

They are also thinking of replacing some Pinot Noir, torn out because the variety is so labor-intensive in the north. "We made a great Pinot at Northern Vineyards, three years running." But the delicate *vinifera* had to be buried every year, and with large acreage under cultivation, that was inefficient. But Vernon Vineyards has decided to focus on entirely Wisconsin-grown wines and "we need a premium red. There will always be that person who comes into the tasting room who overlooks any wine but *vinifera*." Pinot Noir is a vine that can do well, with coddling, in the coulee region, so Starks plans to plant a thousand vines in a half acre—dense spacing for vines—then take them off trellises and bury them each year to protect them from severe weather.

Their greatest challenge? "To get people to cross the river. We get more people from Green Bay than from Minneapolis," although the drive from the former is almost two hours longer than from the latter. With trout fishing, horseback riding, antiquing, and wine, even the mighty Mississippi should not be a barrier.

Vernon Vineyards

S3457 A Dahl Road • Viroqua, WI 54665 •
608-634-6734 • www.vernonvineyards.com

Location: Between Viroqua and Westby; turn on County Road Y and follow the signs to Irish Ridge Road, then Dahl Road. From the north, take County Road B just past Coon Valley to the intersection of County Road Y and follow the signs.

Hours:
May 15–December 22:
Friday and Saturday, 10:00 am–6:00 pm
Sunday, noon–6:00 pm
Closed winters and weekdays except Friday

Tastings: Free

Tours: Self-guided vineyard walks

The Tobacco Connection

You might not think of Wisconsin as tobacco country, if you imagine Southern plantations with vast acreages devoted to cigarette production. Not all tobacco grows well in the Midwest, but the kind that makes cigar wrappers and chewing tobacco does fine. From the turn of the twentieth century through the First World War, tobacco acreage increased in Wisconsin, until by the early 1920s, forty thousand acres were in cultivation. Until twenty years ago, farmers in southwestern Wisconsin relied upon tobacco for that thin financial edge that kept them farming.

Tobacco needs heat during the growing season, which Wisconsin's prairie climate provides. But it also needs late winter humidity, so that plants don't crumble into dust when stripped. The tobacco belt excludes such areas as Florida, where the leaves never dry sufficiently and disease spreads easily in the fields.

Bob Starks was a championship tobacco grower in his day. "What was nice is that you could have another job. Tobacco kind of takes care of itself," Starks says, a bit ruefully, looking out over his higher-maintenance vineyards. "It's not time-sensitive. You didn't have to be there at the exact moment of ripeness, like baling the hay. It was a nice sideline." And profitable. "Time was, you could buy a farm, work your tail off, pay it off in two years with the tobacco. Most people raised an acre to five acres, but then if the kid was going to college, maybe go up to ten acres." But when tough times hit the farmers ("I remember those days of paying 14 percent interest") and the market for tobacco dropped out of sight, Vernon County began to look for something to replace tobacco.

There was a short spell of interest in echinacea, but "an acre of echinacea would kill the market, there just isn't that much demand," says Starks. Besides, western Montana has a lock on the market. Grapes, however, like hot summers and dry falls, and so those extra acres are slowly turning into vineyards.

Signature wines:

Edelweiss: soft, food-friendly semisweet white

Ridge Red: high-flavored Frontenac blend

Three Chimneys: full-bodied, oaked Frontenac blend

Events: Mid-May, Syttende Mai Norwegian celebration.

WEGGY WINERY

Marion Weglarz remembers when he first saw the Driftless Area. It was 1988, and he was working in his hometown of Chicago. His brother read a newspaper interview with Bob Wollersheim about a cold climate wine-growing class the famous winemaker was teaching. This was the first Weglarz had heard of cold-hardy grapes. Although raised in the city, Weglarz harbored a quiet dream of making his living tending the land. His interest piqued by the news that grapes can grow in Wisconsin, Weglarz signed up for the class.

A few months later, Weglarz found himself headed to La Crosse for a business meeting. On a whim, instead of taking the interstate, he drove up Highway 14. There he had another revelation: he had never known that such lovely

Northern Wines

Wine drinkers who think in terms of "southern reds" and "northern whites" (think Rioja and Gewürztraminer) might expect lots of crisp white wines in Minnesota and Wisconsin. After all, California produces Cabernet, while one looks to Washington state for Riesling. The average wine drinker readily assumes that cold climates create good white wines.

Such drinkers would be wrong. The most consistently good wines made in the Upper Midwest are light, easy drinking red wines, often resembling a classic Beaujolais. Whether bone-dry or slightly sweet, such wines are readily made from grapes that grow hardily here. Maréchal Foch is the workhorse grape for such wines (though it also makes an excellent port), with its sibling Léon Millot and the Minnesota variety Frontenac making good table wines of similar style.

The "big Cab" taste may be the winemaker's holy grail, but plenty of drinkers like to sip a white wine on the deck in summer or serve it with salmon on Friday night. For them, finding a good white wine made from locally grown grapes is harder than finding a drinkable local red. Germany's Riesling does not do well here, because the cold is too intense and prolonged. Ditto Gewürztraminer. What's a white winer to do?

One northern white is Frontenac Gris, a natural mutation of the Minnesota-bred Frontenac that began as a single bud in the University vineyard and produces a distinctly peachy white wine. Several other Minnesota varieties are used to produce white wine, especially the twins La Crescent and La Crosse—named for twin cities on the Mississippi—which produce flavorful sweet wines.

Those who like the spicy quality of Gewürztraminer harbor a passion for its New York-bred descendent, Traminette. A pretty vine with pale green leaves and greenish-mauve grapes, Traminette makes a light zingy wine much like its ancestor. A similar white that occasionally harbors the botrytis ("noble rot") that sweetens wines, the French-American hybrid Vignoles (also known as Ravat 51) is more flowery than spicy. Both are marginal in southern Wisconsin and Minnesota and not hardy farther north. Estate-grown white wines are uncommon in the Upper Midwest, so fanciers should stock up when they find one.

hill country could be found in the Midwest. "I just couldn't believe it," Weglarz recalls. His fate was sealed, but it took two years more and many trips north to look at land—over 150 properties, none with potential for grape growing. Then he saw an eighty-acre hilltop farm between Richland Center and Muscoda, and Weglarz knew he had found his site.

"I wanted a hilltop with south-southwest exposure," Weglarz recalls. His study of vine cultivation led him to the classic wisdom that vines want hills. At the time, Weglarz had no plans for a winery. He just wanted to grow grapes, which Wollersheim had promised to buy. The acres of Maréchal Foch were planted by hand by Marion and his wife, Marlys. Then the bug really bit, and the couple started planting in earnest. Those first few acres have grown into fifteen acres planted with ten thousand vines of thirty varieties.

Weglarz remembers the excitement of the first season. "Every weekend, we'd go up and see the growth. The first week, they'd grown a few inches. Then the next week, they were four to five inches long, and following week, up to twelve inches. Then they were gone—eaten by deer. That was when I learned about grow tubes," the clear blue plastic tubes that protect young vines from predation. The deer still nip in the vineyard, but healthy older vines withstand being fodder. "They just eat the tips," Weglarz shrugs.

Weglarz is an experimentalist. At the beginning, that was inevitable: he started his vineyard when few others existed in the area. With no conventional wisdom to discourage him from planting one variety or to encourage another, Weglarz tried vines destined for a short lifespan. He tried and eliminated the native American Niagara, whose intense foxy taste was not popular among his customers. Also destined for the scrap heap was Chambourcin, a French-American hybrid that was not productive enough. In their place went some unusual varieties like the native Americans Stueben and Worden, as well as Traminette, a cold-hardy offspring of spicy Gewürztraminer grown extensively in Illinois.

Although now a winemaker as well as a winegrower, Weglarz finds his heart remains in the vineyard. In addition to grapes, Weglarz also grows a seven-acre orchard of apples, peaches, Asian pears, and cherries, some grown for fruit wine, others for the fresh market. Every Saturday and Sunday, as well as on holidays, Weglarz conducts tram tours of orchards and vineyards, enthusiastically showing grape varieties and cultivars as well as discussing the techniques he uses to help them flourish.

Marion Weglarz says that he's slowing down and will only be adding a new tasting room in the near future. But if the past is any predictor, some new revelation might be just around the corner.

Weggy Winery

30940 Oak Ridge Drive • Muscoda, WI 53573 • 608-647-6600 • www.WeggyWinery.com

Location: From Madison, take Highway 14 west to County Road O, then north, the winery is at the intersection of County Road O and Oak Ridge Drive.

Hours:
Daily, 10:00 am–5:00 pm
Closed Thanksgiving, Christmas, and New Year's Day

Tasting: Complimentary

Tours: Hour-long tram tours Saturdays, Sundays, and holidays (except as above) and by appointment; $6.50 per person; limited seating, book ahead via website

Signature wines:
Hilltop Red: full-bodied dry red from St. Croix
Marlys Blush: semisweet blush from Maréchal Foch
Autumn Crisp: fruity, dry white, estate-grown

Events: Occasional; check website.

WOLLERSHEIM WINERY

If you see a wine-colored car zipping by with PINOT on the Wisconsin license plate, smile to yourself and think, "There go Philippe and Julie." If the plate reads TERROIR, you'll know it's Julie's mom JoAnn Wollersheim, widow of one of the greats of Upper Midwestern wine; if it says BON VIN, it's the company car.

Whimsical as the vanity plates are, there is no way to overstate the importance of Wollersheim in the history of Midwestern wines. Wollersheim occupies the first vineyard in the region and was named as the region's first AVA (American Viticultural Area), in recognition of a unique *terroir*. In 2005 Wollersheim, together with its sister winery Cedar Creek, produced one million bottles of wine, a regional record. Finally, although many Upper Midwest wineries win awards, Wollersheim is in a class by itself, having steadily won competitions for over thirty years and receiving the Blockbuster Wine of the Year award in 1995 for its best-selling Prairie Fumé.

The winery's history goes back to the 1840s, the era of "count" Agoston Haraszthy (see Chapter Three), who planted the first vines on the steep limestone hillside with its picturesque vistas over the Wisconsin River valley. The Count did not last long in Wisconsin and the vines soon died, but the idea of a winery did not. German immigrant Peter Kehl took over the vineyards and replanted with native American varieties as well as the famous German Riesling, which he nurtured using the same technique employed today: burying the vines to keep them from freezing. In the 1850s and 1860s Kehl built two magnificent stone buildings, today on the National Register of Historic Buildings, and the Wollersheim family home and winery.

The winery continued for another generation. Under the leadership of Peter's son Jacob, the Kehl family expanded the operation to include a still (then legal) to produce brandies to fortify wines. The winery had customers as far away as Maine, but with the historically terrible winter of 1899, both the vines and Jacob died. At that point, the Kehl family turned to dairy farming. From 1900 to 1971, no wine was made on the Count's old land.

Then, in 1972, came Bob Wollersheim. A hobby winemaker, he dreamed of building a local wine industry. He bought the historic winery and began the process of replanting its vineyards. Wollersheim was an adventurous planter, putting in French-American hybrids as well as the occasional *vinifera*, which had to be buried each year. Although the vines he planted were not as cold-hardy as today's, a few Foch survive.

Enter Philippe Coquard. Here is where an already romantic wine story hits dramatic high notes. Scion of a wine family in Beaujolais, Coquard held degrees in wine-making, viticulture, and wine marketing from one of the premiere wine universities in France, as well as having experience in his uncles' wineries. Coquard came to Wisconsin courtesy of the Future Farmers of America exchange program. His 1984 internship brought him to the Wollersheim winery—where he fell in love with young Julie Wollersheim. Two wine-making families were soon joined in a historic vineyard.

Wollersheim continues to grow and expand, despite losing its founder to cancer in 2005. Coquard has served as winemaker since 1985; he is responsible for the winery's most famous wine, Prairie Fumé, a light blend of predominantly Seyval Blanc grapes. Julie Coquard concentrates on marketing and management.

Tastings in the old heritage building go on daily, as do narrated tours of the winery facility. The dance-hall above the tasting room is used for private parties and special events. A nine-thousand-square-foot extension holds fermentation and bottling rooms. Outside, a tented platform provides a spot to enjoy wine and picnics in fair weather. Nearby is the old Haraszthy wine cave, now converted into another event space.

Events bring thousands of guests to the winery each season. Indeed, the fall grape-stomping grew so popular that the winery was forced to cancel it; the Coquards are considering alternatives. But there are still many activities, including the winter Port release party and the fall Nouveau release, timed to coincide with the release of Beaujolais Nouveau in Philippe Coquard's homeland.

A small vineyard between the parking lot and the tasting room allows visitors to see grapes being grown on T-trellises, but the rest of the twenty-five vineyard acres are off-limits. The majority of vines are Maréchal Foch; other French-American hybrids and some Minnesota varieties also grow there. But Wollersheim's production outstrips its vineyards. Like other major wineries in the area, Wollersheim buys from local as well as New York and Washington State growers.

The Coquards travel constantly, promoting the wines of the Upper Midwest. Do they face doubts about the quality of the region's wines? Julie Coquard is unfazed. "We tell the doubters: just taste them," she says.

A Pioneer in Regional Wine-Making

When sixty-six-year-old Bob Wollersheim died of cancer in 2005, the Upper Midwest lost one of its pioneers in wine-growing and wine-making. The winery he left stands as a testimony to the spirit of a man who believed that good wine could be made from grapes grown in Wisconsin.

In 1972, that was not a widely held view. That was the year that Bob and his wife, JoAnn, purchased the region's most historic vineyard. No vines were left from the days of Agoston Haraszthy, but the arched stone entrance to the wine cellar dated from his Wisconsin sojourn. And the steep limestone-rich hill above the Wisconsin River held promise as a site for the redeveloped vineyard.

When he started his vineyard, Wollersheim was already successful in a different field. Wollersheim began and ended his academic life at the University of Wisconsin in Madison, where he earned degrees in engineering, then worked as an engineer at the Space Science Center. Simultanously, he acquired the skills that would lead to his second career. Making "basement brew" wine, he found a need for supplies and equipment that led first to his open-

ing a mail-order business, and later to a wine-making shop on State Street, which still exists as the Wine and Hop Shop under Dave Mitchell's management.

When the old Haraszthy property came up for sale, the Wollersheims stepped away from steady job and suburban home to wood-heated limestone farmhouse and heritage vineyard. Some of the first vines Wollersheim planted still thrive, but other vines did not survive the experimental stage. Undeterred, Wollersheim kept planting; hundreds of varieties were tested, only a few proving good candidates for Wisconsin wine-making. As he experimented, Wollersheim shared his findings. Glenn Spurgeon and Peter Botham both remember early conversations with Wollersheim as they planted and tended their own vineyards. Wollersheim's willingness to share his hard-earned wisdom about wine-growing and wine-making is legendary.

Where Haraszthy failed, Wollersheim succeeded. But as much as Haraszthy gave to California, Wollersheim gave to the Upper Midwest.

Wollersheim Winery

PO Box 87 • Prairie du Sac, WI 53578 •
1-800-VIP-WINE • www.Wollersheim.com

Location: Between Madison and the Wisconsin
Dells; State Highway 12 or State Highway 60 to
State Highway 188, directly across the Wisconsin
River from Prairie du Sac.

Hours:
Daily, 10:00 am–5:00 pm

Tasting: Complimentary

Tours: Daily at a quarter after each hour, 10:15 am
to 4:15 pm; $3.50 fee

Signature wines:

Domaine du Sac: estate-grown, medium-bodied,
Beaujolais-like red
Domaine Reserve: oak-aged wine from old vines
on the steepest slopes
Prairie Fumé: named fifth of the Top 100 Wines
East of the Rockies

Events: Mid-November, Ruby Nouveau release
and tasting; late January, Port Release Celebration; early March, winery open house.

Southeastern Wisconsin

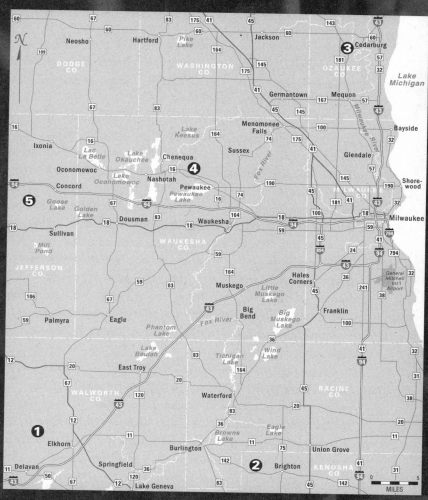

1. **Apple Barn Orchard & Winery** 2. **AeppelTreow Winery**
3. **Cedar Creek Winery** 4. **Mason Creek Winery** 5. **Vetro Winery**

THE SOUTHEASTERN PART OF WISCONSIN is glacial terrain, marked by ice sheets that pressed down upon the land four times in recent geologic history—"recent" in geologic terms being unimaginably long in human years. Over and over, the glaciers pushed across the land, dragging rock debris beneath them and pushing mountains of soil and gravel before them. Melting, these mile-high glaciers left behind them lakes and ponds that dot the land, including the most impressive of the area's glacial features, the Great Lakes.

Beside Lake Michigan, second-largest after Superior, the land rolls gently along the lines of moraines, those dustbins of glaciers, and along rivers that have further eroded the land into graceful dips and swells. There is still some farming in southeast Wisconsin, but the region is more noted as an outdoor playground for nearby metropolitan areas. Milwaukee is dwarfed by its southern neighbor, Chicago, America's Second City. Between them stretches a band of smaller cities, like Kenosha and Racine, each having a rich industrial and social history.

Although proud of its cheesehead identity, southeast Wisconsin leans southward to Chicago. Many Chicagoans have second or vacation homes in the area, only a few hours' drive away. And despite occasional grumblings about FIBs (freakin' Illinois bums, or a more vulgar version of that phrase), fulltime residents know their economy relies on Chicago.

Second city to the Second City, Milwaukee occupies a stunning natural setting where three rivers (Menominee, Kinnickinnic, and Milwaukee) flow into Lake Michigan. Long a town of immigrant neighborhoods that defined the blue-collar lifestyle, Milwaukee fought its way through hard economic times in the mid-twentieth century to reinvent itself as a regional cultural capital. In addition to museums and historic sites, the city has a lakeside festival park, the setting for summer ethnic festivals.

The triangle from Milwaukee to Madison and down to Chicago offers visitors many leisure opportunities. Old World Wisconsin in Eagle is composed of frontier buildings where costumed staff show how life was lived in early Wisconsin, while the landmark Ten Chimneys mansion of Broadway stars Lynn Fontaine and Alfred Lunt gives a glimpse of high life in Genesee Depot. Fort Atkinson provides professional theater and the chance to explore the terrain of esteemed author Lorine Niedecker.

Less intellectual pastimes also abound, with racing, boating, and other water sports available throughout the region. Renowned spas cater to visitors in need of pampering. Increasingly, winter tourism makes the region a year-round playground for the urban resident in need of a countryside break. And both FIBs and Wisconsinites enjoy visiting the wineries that are springing up in the region.

APPLE BARN ORCHARD & WINERY

Not far from Lake Geneva and Delavan, near a stretch of undulating cropland and the protected wetlands of Turtle Valley Wildlife Area, the Apple Barn's orchards stretch out. Inside a converted barn, crowded shelves offer jams and jellies, cider and cider donuts, crafts and books, and seasonal fruit: strawberries and apples primarily, but also pears and pumpkins.

The Jacobson family has worked the farm since 1848, making it one of Wisconsin's oldest continuously operating family farms. Today's farmers are Steve and Judy Jacobson, who have been planting and tending the forty-acre orchard since 1976. Visitors are likely to see pick-your-own customers bringing in fruit, or a school tour being conducted through the orchard. Sharing the earthy beauties of their heritage farm is part of the Apple Barn's yearly cycle. Like other farm families, the Jacobsons looked for "value-added products," and wine is the latest to be offered in the comfortable converted barn. Crafted in small batches to preserve fresh fruit flavor, the wines include apples, mulberry, blackberry, pear, and strawberry.

The region around the Apple Barn is popular among urban visitors hoping for a taste of rural life. Nearby Lake Geneva, long a holiday haven for Chicagoans, rests in a depression left after the retreat of the latest two ice sheets. The region around the lake is called Kettle Moraine for its glacial kettles, depressions formed when blocks of ice buried in glacial debris melted into ponds and lakes.

Scenic Lake Geneva was settled in early historic times by the Potawatomi people under Chief Big Foot (Muc-Kis-Sou). Big Foot, who had his main residence in what is now Fontana, had a center as well on Williams Bay, from which his people were removed later to Kansas. The name of the lake was changed in 1836 from Big Foot Lake to Geneva by surveyor John Brink because of a fancied resemblance to its famous namesake in Switzerland.

Within four years, the town on its shores had both a distillery and a temperance society. When the railroad reached the town, Geneva grew into a prosperous settlement. Geneva boasts a twenty-one-mile lakeside walking path through deciduous groves that is especially beautiful in fall, when the apples are ripe. Century-old mansions set back from the shore offer a glimpse into the area's history. But throughout this period of expansion, farming remained a mainstay of the local economy and, maintaining that tradition, the Jacobson family still works the land.

Apple Barn Orchard and Winery

W6384 Sugar Creek Road • Elkhorn, WI 53121 • 262-728-3266 •
www.applebarnorchardandwinery.com

Location: From Elkhorn, north on State Highway 12, west on County Road A, south on County Road O.

Hours:
June:
Daily, 9:00 am–6:00 pm
July–August:
Thursday–Saturday, 10:00 am–4:00 pm
September–October:
Tuesday–Saturday, 10:00 am–6:00 pm
Sunday, 11:00 am–5:00 pm
November–December 15:
Wednesday–Saturday, 10:00 am–4:00 pm
Also by appointment

Tasting: Complimentary

Tours: None

Signature wines:
Strawberry Jewel: semisweet rich strawberry
Mulberry Lane: unusual fruit wine, off-dry
Wild Blackberry: fruit-filled and crisp

Events: Late September, Apple Festival.

AEPPELTREOW WINERY

The name only looks hard to pronounce. It's "apple-true," spelled in the Anglo-Saxon way to evoke the heritage of one of the oldest traditional beverages: cider, the intoxicating fermented juice of the apple.

"In America, we call it hard cider, but in Europe, it's just cider," says Charles McGonigle of AeppelTreow. The name literally means "apple tree," with the second part also evoking other words derived from *treow*, including "truth" and "troth" and "truce." McGonigle and his wife, Milissa, chose the name to suggest the connection between traditionally crafted ciders and the values of country life.

Located on the huge Brightonwoods Orchard near Burlington, AeppelTreow is a family enterprise, right down to young Alex, who eagerly leads visitors to his lemonade stand, where hand-drawn labels reflect what he learned from watching his mother paint watercolors for the winery's labels. Charles and Milissa pick, ferment, bottle, label, and sell the wines themselves. They use fruit from over a hundred apple varieties grown by Brightonwoods, including cider breeds as well as crabapples and modern apples. They also use fruit from heritage trees in the area, including a rare cider-pear tree of untraceable lineage.

The McGonigles are enthusiastic about cider's rich heritage and delight in sharing it

Keeping the Harvest

Refrigeration is relatively new in America. Development began in 1748 in Scotland, but more than fifty years passed before the technology was predictable and safe. Even then, refrigeration was expensive. At the beginning of the twentieth century, only half of American households had "iceboxes," insulated boxes in which a block of ice was placed. Within the next twenty years, households began to purchase "fridges," but only after World War II were they common in American homes.

Before that, preserving took many forms. Saving ice by burying it was commonplace from early times. American colonial farmers who had fresh water near their homes often had a spring house, a small stone building built into the side of the bank. Root cellars were common, using the earth's natural fifty-five-degree temperature to keep foods cool.

Fruits presented a special problem for the householder. Anyone who has left a peach in the sun knows the sorry results: spoilage caused by microorganisms eager to devour plant sugar. Pre-

serves kept fruits from decaying: adding sugar produced jams (from whole fruit) or jellies (from juice), while vinegar made chutneys and pickles. But sugar is expensive, and vinegar produces condiments rather than actual food.

Making wine is an easy way to preserve food. Left to its own devices, fruit juice ferments as wild yeasts devour fruit sugars. The digestive processes of those yeasts releases carbon dioxide as gas, but the other digestive product—alcohol—remains in the liquid until the yeast produces enough to poison itself. At that point, fermentation stops and wine can be stored indefinitely.

This natural process was a boon to those who wished to store or ship produce. Not only does wine retain the fruit's calories and nutrients, it is tasty (and intoxicating). Farm wives made wine as well as pickles, jellies, and other preserves that graced the table on winter evenings. As a means of preserving the fruit harvest, wine was part of the yearly cycle on America's farms, as it remains at the Jacobsons today.

with visitors. Common throughout Europe, *cidre* entirely replaces wine on tables in Brittany and Normandy. But Britain is by far the world's largest consumer of cider as well as its biggest producer. In recent years in the West Counties, cider, or "scrumpy" as the locals call it, has enjoyed a renaissance as artisanal cidermakers revive and modernize traditional methods.

Before cheap, fast transportation, cider was common in the United States, especially in northerly regions where apples outperform grapes as juice-producing crops. Before refrigeration, apples could be stored only for a limited time, while juice never went rotten, instead naturally fermenting into cider. However natural, cider was vilified by teetotalers. "Just as groups went into saloons with axes," Charles McGonigle says mournfully, "some people burned orchards to make sure there was no fruit for cider." Some of these orchards were never replanted, leading to the loss of heritage varieties.

Apples for cider may not be good for eating or cooking, McGonigle says. Indeed, some of the best cider apples are small and, to the modern eye, rather unattractive. Size and shapeliness are not an issue, because the apples are crushed before fermentation. Thus the number of apple types useful for cider is larger than those good for fresh eating.

Johnny Apple Cider

American schoolchildren are introduced to John Chapman as a frontiersman who planted seeds that grew into productive orchards—over a hundred thousand square miles of orchards in Pennsylvania, Ohio, and Indiana, some of which still produce apples. But few schoolchildren meet Johnny Appleseed as a man who planted fruit for getting high.

Children also do not learn apple botany; if they did, they would realize Johnny's apples were never intended for eating. Apples cross-pollinate, so a productive and tasty tree might bear fruit whose seeds, once planted, produce small, unpleasantly flavored apples. (The same is true of grapes.) Eating-apples are grown from scions of a favored tree planted on a hardy rootstock. But Johnny planted "seedling apples": small, sour, and tart, useful only for cider-making.

Born in 1774 in Massachusetts, Chapman moved to western Pennsylvania around 1797. From there he traveled by canoe ahead of settlement, carrying apple seeds to likely spots. He had a good eye for real estate: when settlers invariably arrived, he had apple trees to sell them, priced reasonably at five to six cents each. Then he moved on, returning each winter to Pennsylvania to gather more seeds. He never married and died in Indiana in 1845 at the age of seventy—a wealthy man.

American schoolchildren also learn little about the spiritual beliefs of their cartoonish hero. Nominally Christian, Chapman followed the philosophy of Emmanuel Swedenborg, who described a "doctrine of signatures" that connected the visible world and the spiritual one; to Swedenborgians, the apple tree was a symbol of spiritual truth. A vegetarian, Chapman traveled barefoot rather than wear shoes made of animal hides. He was too kind to animals to ride horses and sometimes bought animals destined for slaughter and freed them. If he did not eat meat or wear leather, Chapman did drink. Indeed, part of his legend grew up because as he traveled, he stopped to share a few pints of cider with settlers, who later told and retold the tales of the barefoot orchardist called Johnny Appleseed.

Heritage apple names call up visions of other times and other lands: Kingston Black, Golden Harvey, Pomme Gris, Hughes Virginia Crab. There is also poetry in cider names, like Pommeaux, traditional Norman sweet cider; Cyser, tart apple mead; and Perry, the cider made from small juice-rich pears. McGonigle makes sparkling cider in both brut (dry, made with September-ripening heirloom apples) and doux (semisweet) styles. He offers single-barrel wines, using whatever is most abundant. An August apple wine called Apple High Summer uses Gravensteins finished in oak, while Fencerow Perry is crafted from the fruit of that old cider-pear tree mixed with Bosc.

Although dedicated to his cider enterprise, McGonigle harbors another ambition as well: to help change state laws so that artisanal distilleries can create brandies from Midwestern orchards and vineyards. "I tasted a brandy made from La Crescent," he marvels, "all that fragrance . . . marvelous." Today breweries and wineries can sell direct to customers through tasting rooms, but distilleries cannot—a vestige of Prohibition. A pending law in Wisconsin would change that and permit the production of uniquely northern spirits. Should that happen, AeppelTreow would expand their line to include handcrafted brandies.

AeppelTreow Winery

1072 288th Avenue/County Road B • Burlington, WI 53105 • 262-878-5345 • www.aeppeltreow.com

Location: I-94 to State Highway 142, 10 miles west to County Road B (Rustic Road 43), .5 mile north.

Hours:

May–August:
Saturday, 10:00 am–5:00 pm
September–October:
Friday, noon–5:00 pm
Saturday, 10:00 am–5:00 pm

Sunday, noon–5:00 pm
November–December:
Saturday, 11:00 am–4:00 pm
Sunday, noon–4:00 pm
Closed January–April

Tasting: Complimentary

Tours: By arrangement

Signature wines:

Appely Brut and Doux: sparkling apple wines in dry and semisweet styles
Perry: sparkling pear wine of mixed varieties
Apple Sharp English: traditional cider from gourmet English varieties

Events: Occasional; check website.

CEDAR CREEK WINERY

Step through the big wooden doors at Cedar Creek Winery and step into history. In 1845, European immigrants were delighted to find a strong-running creek just north of the emerging metropolis of Milwaukee. Soon five mills used Cedar Creek to grind flour, spin wool, and saw lumber. One was an enormous limestone structure built in 1860 by Diedrich Wittenberg. A millrace guided rushing waters into waterwheels that, turning with the pressure, generated electricity. Once the largest woolen mill west of the Alleghenies, the fifty-horsepower turbine powered twenty-one looms and knitting machines. The mill operated for almost a century, at one point knitting socks for the Chicago White Sox.

The mill closed in 1969 and began to fall into disrepair, and the mill was slated for demolition. Enter Jim Pape, a hobby winemaker from Milwaukee. He had been making wine in his garage and knew the mill's massive stone walls would make an ideal wine cellar. He bought the building and started Newberry (later Stone Mill) Winery, specializing in fruit wines.

After fifteen years, Pape was ready to move on, but in the late 1980s there was little interest in Wisconsin wineries. At the newly formed Wisconsin Winery Association, he struck up a conversation with Bob Wollersheim and Philippe Coquard whose winery (see Driftless Area) was thriving. A deal was struck, and the Wollersheims had a second winery.

From the start, they envisioned a different line at Cedar Creek than at their original winery. Coquard had more ideas than one winery could manage. "You can't dilute a brand," explains Coquard's brother-in-law, Cedar Creek manager Steve Danner. A winery cannot offer six different versions of a Maréchal Foch without confusing the customer, although that flexible grape could be made into that many wines or more.

Cedar Creek draws visitors who appreciate the charm of a historic town. Like Stillwater or Lanesboro in Minnesota, Cedarburg is a destination for weekenders looking for a taste of history and for small-town ambience with sophisticated shopping and dining. In the mill building, more than two dozen small artists' and antique shops makes it a "shopping heaven," says Danner.

Under Danner's management, the winery remains distinct from its originating company, while benefiting from Wollersheim expertise. As for Danner, he says he got into the wine business "the old-fashioned way: I married a Wollersheim." His wife, Eva, grew up in the wine business and remains involved in Cedar Creek's production. With a background in management

Mills and Industry

The five mills along Cedar Creek were among hundreds in the Upper Midwest that harnessed energy from fast-flowing streams for industrial applications. Some mills ran machines directly; others generated electricity to run machinery. In either case, mills provided an economic boon wherever they were located. In some cases, mills were so significant that they are memorialized in town names, as in the western Wisconsin town of Gays Mills, named for the mills along the Kickapoo River; or Lake Mills, named for the gristmills and sawmills along the lakeshore.

Water was not the only means of powering a mill. Mills could also be powered by wind or, in ancient times, by human or animal strength. Water had advantages. Unlike a horse, water needs no food; unlike wind, water runs relatively regularly. In Upper Midwestern winters, water mills took winter holidays; when the stream froze, the mill ceased operations until thaw.

The efficiency and cleanliness of waterpower made it attractive to early settlers. In addition to making wool and flour, mills were common in the lumber and paper industries. In Milwaukee in 1848, a huge mill made newsprint from rags, supplying all the paper that the *Milwaukee Gazette* needed—ninety reams a week. Other mills made paper from wood pulp, often generated as a byproduct of lumber milling. As the lumber industry thrived on and later destroyed the virgin forests of northern Wisconsin, the milling industry similarly boomed and went bust.

Some of these mills stand empty, ghosts of an industrial past. Others, like Cedar Creek Winery, were converted to commercial purposes. Some are historic sites, including Cedarburg Woolen Mill, which offers classes as well as exhibiting spinning wheels. A few became comfortable family homes while yet others, sadly, were torn down.

and finance, Danner worked for an investment company for many years, helping out around the winery as needed. Then in the early 2000s, as Cedar Creek experienced significant growth, he joined the family firm. "But first," he laughs, "I had to convert." It wasn't a matter of religion for this Wisconsin native. "I used to drink beer."

Cedar Creek Winery

N70 W6340 Bridge Road • Cedarburg, WI 53012 • 262-377-8020 • www.CedarCreekWinery.com

Location: 20 miles north of Milwaukee in downtown Cedarburg.

Hours:

Monday–Wednesday, 10:00 am–5:00 pm

Thursday and Friday, 10:00 am–8:00 pm

Saturday, 10:00 am–6:00 pm

Sunday, 11:00 am–5:00 pm

Closed Easter, Thanksgiving, Christmas, and New Year's Day

Tasting: Complimentary

Tours: $3; offered daily at 11:30 am, 1:30 pm, 3:30 pm

Signature wines:

Waterfall Riesling: semidry version of classic German grape.

Beaujolais Uncle Pierre: dry and fruity, named for the winemaker's uncle

Settlement Gold: sweet white blend

Events: Second weekend in February, Winter Festival; third weekend in March, winery open house; fourth weekend in June, Cedarburg Strawberry Festival; third weekend in September, Wine and Harvest Festival.

MASON CREEK WINERY

The Milwaukee suburbs are at the door; indeed, one of them bears the name of the old Lynndale farm. But the farm itself sits by the side of the road in Pewaukee as it did a century ago, now home to a collection of shops offering Americana-style décor—and wine. In an old barn, Mason Creek Winery uses imported juice to create small-lot wines. The winery began over a decade ago in Delafield, when Bobbi Goman gave her husband Kyle a wine kit as a present. He enjoyed the hobby so much that he became a fulltime winemaker. In 2005, the winery moved to Lynndale Farm.

A winery so close to Milwaukee, once America's brewing capital? During the 1840s, German immigrants flocked to Wisconsin's premiere city, so many that it became known as Deutsches Athen, or "the German Athens." Into the twentieth century, there were more native speakers of German in Milwaukee than native English speakers. That German heritage was the most significant factor in Milwaukee's emergence as America's beer capital, because the city offered no advantages in price of raw materials or labor, quality of water, or ease of transport. The presence of beer-drinking Germans, as well as proximity to Chicago, helped make Milwaukee's brews famous for many years to come.

At the height of its beery fame, Milwaukee was home to four of the world's largest breweries. Later, consolidation among the big brewers and a move towards purchasing brand names, while terminating the factories that made the brews, together destroyed Milwaukee's status as the nation's premier beer center. But on the heels of the decline in fortunes of its famous old breweries, wineries have begun to spring up in the towns around Milwaukee. Time will tell whether Milwaukee will take them to its heart as it did, for almost a century and a half, the town's historic breweries.

It's All in the Name

There's Naked Grapes. Cardinal Zin. And Fat Bastard.

Once, wine names were geographical, referring to the location of a vineyard or chateau. Many carry great prestige: Chateau Lafitte, Chateau Margaux. Even outside France, geographical names are popular, as with Australia's Jacob's Creek and California's Stag's/s' Leap (that last so popular that there are two brands, with the apostrophe in different places). Other wines are named for their owners, like Robert Sinsky, Mondavi, Gallo, Sebastiani. There are varietals: Chardonnay, Vidal Blanc, Frontenac, named for the principal variety of grape used to make them. Yet others offer poetic names, like Turning Leaf and Clos du Bois.

But Donner Party Red? Marilyn Merlot?

It's the hottest fad in wine marketing, wines that are unromantic, silly, or even coarse. Especially hot are "critter names," with the ubiquitous Yellowtail (decorated with kangaroo art) leading the pack. Some French winemakers have followed the herd, with Elephant on a Tightrope and Arrogant Frog (in Ribet Red and Ribet White). Animal puns, as in Goats Do Roam (think Côtes du Rhône) and Bored Doe (Bordeaux), are risibly popular. Names of people, whether real (Richard the Lionheart, Benito Mussolini) or imaginary (Vampire Merlot) are acceptable. And surprisingly, vulgar names sell, as in Cats Pee on a Gooseberry Bush, a Sauvignon Blanc, or Cleavage Creek, a nonexistent voluptuous estate.

Naming wines in this way has a surprisingly respectable heritage. If you know Italian, you can translate Cacamosca as "fly dung" (the grape is black-speckled when ripe). Then there's Arneis ("pain in the butt"), a fussy grape from the Piedmont area of Italy. Such names have been around for a long time, and it's no surprise to find them appearing again. So lift a glass of Dogs Bollocks, Frogs Piss, or Hair of Dingo, and enjoy.

Mason Creek Winery

N47 W28270 Lynndale Road • Pewaukee, WI 53072 • 262-367-6494 • www.MasonCreekWinery.com

Hours:
Daily, 11:00 am–5:00 pm

Tasting: Complimentary

Tours: By arrangement

Signature wines:
'47 Pick-Up: a dry blend of Merlot, Cabernet, and Zinfandel
Riesling: vinified in semidry style
Cranberry: sweet version of the state's ubiquitous fruit wine

Events: Occasional; check website.

VETRO WINERY

In a town named for America's most famous grape, a traditional Italian winery has taken root. Concord, Wisconsin, is a world away from Sicily, but only an hour from the Italian neighborhoods of Milwaukee. When Michael Vetrano arrived there a century ago from a land where making wine was part of every householder's annual activities, he brought tradition with him. His son Joseph trained grandson Bill to make wine from fresh wine grapes brought in from California by an Italian company that now provisions a third generation of Vetranos.

Before opening the winery, Bill Vetrano made wine for twenty-five years, starting by helping his father fill the cellar. He moved into commercial wine-making with the encouragement of a priest who, in 2004, urged Vetrano to sell wine at a parish fund-raiser. It's one thing when friends like your wine, another when strangers come back for more. Vetro Wines was born.

Their winery stands beside the Vetrano home where it all started. LaVerne Vetrano remembers how visitors entered through the front door and went downstairs to taste and buy. Not a lot of privacy in those days: LaVerne recalls a customer who snapped photos of her bathroom in order to copy its decor. "Some people! You never know!" she laughs.

Vetro grew quickly. In ten months, the business had met five-year predictions. A year later, it had outgrown the basement, so a new winery with a tasting room was built. Its big windows reveal a gentle slope down to the vineyard where Delaware and La Crescent vines stretch out. The winery occupies already tight quarters behind the tasting room. There, LaVerne hand-sterilizes each bottle, and Bill corks them.

Larger wineries have automated filling stations, but Bill and LaVerne fill each bottle using a small pump. A room stacked with boxes of completed wines hints at the energy the couple puts into their winery.

Vetro wines include some classics made from California grapes, including Chardonnay, Zinfandel, and Merlot. Other wines are made from local and regional fruits, including the de rigueur Wisconsin cranberry blended with Concord, and Winter Spirit Hill, made with cranberries, strawberries, and grapes. Local farmers provide much of the fruit for Vetro's wines, but the raspberries are grown on the Vetrano hillside.

A few years after opening, the Vetranos bottle thirty-five hundred gallons a year; local groceries and restaurants sell their wine; they have had customers from as far away as Europe. Bill Vetrano thinks his grandfather would be proud: "He always believed in sharing a good glass of wine with friends."

The Italian Connection

Michael Vetrano wasn't much bothered by Prohibition. Sure, it was illegal to buy wine in America. But he wasn't in the habit of buying wine. He made his own, just as he had in Sicily.

"In the bathtub, of course," Bill Vetrano remembers. "He'd go down to the third ward with his horse and buggy, buy enough grapes to sell some up in Cudahy, then bring the rest home to press and ferment." Michael used California grapes to made wine worthy of serving at family meals and holidays. "Red, it was always red wine," Bill recalls. "Dad crushed and pressed. Later I got to do that—I remember the way we pressed to get every last drop of juice out of the grapes."

It was a tradition shared with other Midwestern Italians, whose families in the old country made wine from grapes grown on backyard trellises or purchased from a vineyard. In the Midwest, finding no locally grown wine grapes, some turned to importing grapes from New York or California; the regional Italian market was so strong that the Mondavi family from Minnesota moved to California and began planting grapes there to sell back home. Other Italian immigrants to the Upper Midwest adapted their craft to local fruit, creating the basis for the long-standing fruit wine industry of the region, which has many vintners of Italian heritage.

Vetro Winery

N5817 Hillside Drive · Concord, WI 53178 · 262-593-5123 · www.VetroWine.com

Location: Between Milwaukee and Madison; exit 275 (County Road F) off I-94, turn west on County Road B; turn left on Hillside Drive, follow signs 1.5 miles.

Hours:
Tuesday–Friday, 10:00 am–6:00 pm
Saturday, 10:00 am–4:00 pm
Sunday, 10:00 am–6:00 pm
Closed Mondays and holidays

Tasting: Complimentary

Tours: $2, with $1 donated to Wisconsin Down Syndrome Association

Signature wines:
Concordia Rossa: semidry red made from Concord grapes
Vetro Bianco: sweet dessert wine from Italian Muscat grapes
Watermelon: semisweet, rich melon wine

Events: First Saturday in June, Wine Festival.

1. Captain's Walk Winery 2. Kerrigan Brothers Winery 3. LedgeStone Winery
4. Parallel 44 Winery 5. Trout Springs Winery 6. von Stiehl Winery

YOU MIGHT NOT REALIZE, navigating through traffic in Appleton— or Green Bay, Oshkosh, or Fond du Lac—that a short drive leads to a bucolic setting where you can spend an afternoon tasting wine. But more than half of Wisconsin's population lives within an hour's drive of a thriving wine region.

A geologic feature called the ledge makes it possible. Farther east, the ledge forms a cliff over which the Niagara River tumbles. The dolomite sweeps across Ontario to the islands of Lake Huron, then into Wisconsin. This dramatic seven-hundred-mile-long landform must, surely, have resulted from an ancient cataclysm. But no: the vistas of the Niagara Escarpment were caused by erosion over millions of years. Dolomite resists erosion, so as softer rocks melted away, the great ledge was exposed.

Grapes thrive on the Escarpment's soils, creating one of the Upper Midwest's prime wine regions. The Escarpment stretches from Door Peninsula, where it forms dramatic lakeside bluffs, to the Illinois border, where it is almost entirely submerged under glacial soil. Its dip slope rises gently, then descends on the steeper bluff side to two enormous glacial vestiges, Green Bay and Lake Winnebago.

The Escarpment brings grape-pleasing limestone into east-central Wisconsin, a wine region with a workaday feel, with old industrial cities and a still-thriving lumber business. The area is best-known as Packerland, home to the only community-owned nonprofit franchise in the National Football League. Originally formed as a sandlot team on August 11, 1919, by Curly Lambeau and George Calhoun, the Packers took their name from the meat-packing company that sponsored them. Only two years later, the Packers became one of the first teams in the NFL. Nearby teams, like the Duluth Kelleys/Eskimos, failed, but the Packers thrived. They are the last remaining team from the small-town era, with over 110,000 stockholders who receive no dividends—except the satisfaction of being an owner of the team that holds the record for league championships.

For visitors who imagine Lombardi to be an Italian restaurant chain and Lambeau Field to be an airport, east-central Wisconsin offers other treasures. Among notable museum collections are the tramp and hobo art at the Historical Society in Ashwaubenon, Norman Rockwell paintings at the Old School in Mishicot, vintage trains at the National Railroad Museum in Green Bay, and paperweights at the Bergstrom-Mahler Museum in Neenah. Aircraft enthusiasts know Oshkosh as the location of the annual fly-in sponsored by the Experimental Aircraft Association (EAA), where unique hand-built aircraft fill the skies. And the region's Indian heritage is celebrated in several large annual powwows, including that of the Oneida Nation each July.

History buffs delight in this region. You can explore Algoma's fishing history at the Art Dettman Fish Shanty, try to figure out how he did it at the Harry Houdini exhibit in Appleton, or learn about the life of a bridge-tender at Tayco Street Bridge Tower Museum in Menasha. In Green Bay, the Heritage Hill State Historical Park offers reenactments of voyageur and frontier life on forty-eight acres of farmland and forest. Progressive poetic types can reenact that great moment on February 20, 1968, when beat poet Allen Ginsburg made a pilgrimage to Appleton with the rock band the Fugs and seventy-five of their closest friends to exorcise the demons of paranoid conservatism haunting Joseph McCarthy's grave. The altar constructed on the grave for the ceremony included antiwar pamphlets, marijuana seeds, flowers, and a "Get Fugged" button.

CAPTAIN'S WALK WINERY

Downtown Green Bay is being transformed. Like other industrial cities, it has seen shopping districts shrink as malls drained business away. But the city core, home to significant institutions, is now becoming an entertainment and dining destination. That transformation can be seen in a downtown Italianate house with a captain's walk on the top floor. No sea captains ever lived there, however. The 1857 house was built by Elisha Morrow and occupied by the family for the next sixty years. Later the home was converted to a law office—an appropriate transformation, as Morrow was one of Wisconsin's first lawyers. His home's interior, lavish even by modern standards, has been meticulously restored, from plaster crown molding to a curving hardwood staircase. Few wineries can boast such elegant historic premises.

In the living room, which serves as a tasting bar, a window cut into the hardwood floor lets visitors gaze down on oak barrels of aging wine. Some is made at the sister winery, von Stiehl (see page 132). But a production room located at Captain's Walk permits visitors to observe the wine-making process. "A winery always has an educational aspect," says general manager Jim Koehler. "It's important to take the snobbery out of wine tasting, to show people how to appreciate wine." A small wine sensory garden outside is planted with flowers and herbs whose names are used to describe wine tastes. Violet, anyone?

Koehler and his brother Paul, also part of the winery's management, grew up around wine. Their father, a wine distributor, appreciated wine with meals. Koehler joined the family business and then moved to the region's newest winery. The match goes beyond wine: Koehler is an enthusiast about local history, and history is an important feature of Captain's Walk Winery.

The town's history is a long one. Originally occupied by the agricultural Ho-Chunk (Winnebago) people, Green Bay was visited in 1634 by Jean Nicolet, whose arrival frightened the people because he immediately fired rifles into the air. After calm had been restored, Nicolet was welcomed with a rich feast. Nicolet stayed for a year; several decades passed before other voyageurs followed. Despite its strategic location, the Green Bay area was not settled by the French. In 1816 America claimed it by placing a military post at Fort Howard. By the time of Wisconsin statehood, lumbering and shipping had become Green Bay's major industries, followed, in the 1920s, by meat-packing.

In a town so drenched with history, the Captain's Walk Winery combines old and new. While the house is old, the approach to wine is contemporary. Focusing on *vinifera* varietals, Captain's Walk sources grapes and juice from across the country, including the Pacific Northwest as well as California. Presentation in oversized glasses allows the taster to breathe deeply of the wine's fragrance, or nose, before drinking. But it's still Green Bay; Minnesota Vikings or Chicago Bears sports attire should never be worn, and the words "Brett who?" never spoken.

Captain's Walk Winery

345 South Adams Street • Green Bay, WI 54301 • 920-431-9255 • www.captainswalkwinery.com

Location: Downtown Green Bay, corner of Adams and Crooks, one block east of Fox River.

Hours:
Tuesday–Saturday, 11:00 am–7:00 pm
Sunday, noon–4:00 pm
Closed Mondays

Tastings: $3 for up to seven samples

Tours: Production room viewing, but no regular tours.

Signature wines:

Captain's Red: low-tannic, off-dry red blend of Foch and Frontenac

Chardonnay: lightly oaked and aged *sur lies* for deep flavor

Disappearing Treasure: sweet dessert blend of Riesling and Gewürztraminer

Events: Wine appreciation classes, other events; check website.

KERRIGAN BROTHERS WINERY

Troy Landwehr has the perfect name for a brewmaster, stoutly Germanic. But he's a winemaker. Landwehr Winery? It just didn't sound right.

Landwehr made wine for several years after finishing art school in Milwaukee. Then he came home to Appleton and met Marv Heippas. "Marv had been making wine for over thirty years and was looking for someone to teach," Landwehr recalls. Using the recipes Heippas handed down, Landwehr developed his own wines.

With a family history of entrepreneurship, the next step seemed inevitable: open a winery. So he began a three-year course of research. He talked to winery owners about business strategies. He also sought out people who had failed during the boomlet in microbreweries. "They knew things I needed to know," he reasons.

His research convinced him that there would be a market for his wines, and by 2000 he was ready to open his winery. What to call it? Landwehr did not sound like a winery. But Kerrigan—his mother's name—had possibilities. Landwehr remembered his five uncles and their merry, celebratory attitudes toward drinking. With his grandmother's permission, he named his winery in memory of his late uncles.

Landwehr's business plan never included working with grapes, because, he says, "I like the freedom of working with other fruit." He buys most of his fruit from Wisconsin, including pears, plums, and cranberries, as well as cherries from nearby Door County. But when he wants to make wines from unusual fruits, like pineapples and lemons, he seeks out small

The Nose Knows

Novice wine drinkers are often baffled when directed to put their noses into wine glasses before taking a taste. But it works: smell and taste are so deeply connected that it is difficult to ascertain where one leaves off and the other begins.

It's an odd thing, the human nose, with its three structures called turbinates—little plates that slow passing air so that the brain can "read" it. For smell really happens in the brain, not in the nose. The sensitive tissue called the olfactory epithelium carries receptor molecules that change odor molecules into electrical stimuli to be decoded in the brain. There we determine whether we are sniffing something pleasant or foul.

How is this connected to taste? We can taste only sweet, sour, bitter, and salty. (Several new candidates for basic tastes have recently been proposed—one is umami, a savory earthy taste like mushrooms.) Wine is rarely salty but possesses the three other main taste sensations. But wine has more flavors than a cup of sweet lemony tea, which includes sugar, acid, and tannin just as wine does. We perceive these subtler tastes through the retronasal passage, a tube in the back of the throat that allows us to distinguish hundreds of tastes beyond the basic ones. So swirl away, to aerate the wine and release its fragrances, then put your nose deep into the glass and breathe.

operations like his own from North or South America.

In addition to offering him a larger palate, fruit wines are a Wisconsin tradition, and Landwehr calls himself "a traditionalist at heart. Around here, people's grandparents made wine in the '20s and '30s. There are lots of recipes that people have dug out of their basements for me. It's neat to see those handwritten notes in that old-fashioned language." The strangest of these Prohibition-era wines? "Tomato jalapeño," Landwehr says immediately. "Tastes like a Bloody Mary."

Having met his original business goals, Landwehr is now set to expand. He purchased ten acres of his grandmother's farm to plant an orchard. "It will be my biggest artwork," says the former art student, who plans "a destination garden," with blueberries, raspberries, and other fruit creating a "a nontraditional orchard, with the plants setting off each other with colors and blossoms." The expansion is a big step, "as big a step as opening was," Landwehr admits, "but when I started this, I wanted something to do for the rest of my life. And this is it."

Kerrigan Brothers Winery

N2269 County Road N • Appleton, WI 54913 • 920-788-1423 • www.KerriganBrothers.com

Location: I-41 to Little Chute exit, County Road N; north 1.5 miles.

Hours:
Monday–Saturday, 9:00 am–5:00 pm
Sunday, 10:00 am–3:00 pm

Tastings: Complimentary

Tours: By arrangement, $3 person

The Apples of Appleton

Drinking apple wine in Appleton seems appropriate, if you assume the town was named for its orchards. But such is not the case. A New Englander named Samuel Appleton, who never visited Wisconsin, donated funds in 1847 to build a library at Lawrence College. In gratitude for the gift, the citizens of the town bestowed his name upon the town.

Although the city's name does not refer to apples, apple orchards do abound in the area. The Wisconsin Apple Growers Association (WAGA) contends that Wisconsin's climate makes it the world's best place to grow apples, which thrive in brisk northerly climates. Specialists believe that contemporary apples derive from a species that survives today in the wild on the borders of Kazakhstan and China. But millennia of cultivation and crossbreeding have developed a plentitude of apples, estimated at some seven thousand five hundred cultivars, bred both for eating and for preserving, the latter including making wine or cider.

Apples are not only suited to such chilly climates; they require cold in order to flower and fruit. Although they demand chilly weather, apples are not helped by late spring frosts, which can freeze the blossoms. Locating orchards near large bodies of water, therefore, has been common throughout history. Appleton's location on Lake Winnebago and near Lake Michigan gives apple growers a climatic advantage. More than two dozen apple orchards thrive near Appleton, some offering pick-your-own options and most having retail operations so that consumers can buy apples direct from the orchardist.

Signature wines:
Blueberry Cherry: sweet blend of Door County cherries and Michigan blueberries
Dutch Apple Pie: fortified, mulled apple-spice wine
Irish Gold: two-year-old aged and numbered honey wine

Events: Occasional; check website.

LEDGESTONE WINERY

Behind the vines rises the ledge, the geological feature that gives LedgeStone Winery its name. In New York, this same cuesta creates the drama of Niagara Falls, but here it is a long earthen ridge. And the rock is identical at both ends: dolomite, beloved of grapes.

Vines stretch out, acres of them, the dream come true of Tim and Sara Abel. In the early 1990s, working in Minneapolis, they imagined moving back to Sara's home. They dreamed as many young couples do: of hard, healthy work in a family-friendly industry, a dream expressed in their winery motto, "How you spend every day is how you live your life."

Wine did not cross their minds. They had never seen a Midwestern vineyard and did not know grapes grew here. Then, at the Minnesota State Fair in 1993, Tim met members of the Minnesota Grape Growers Association and learned about cold-hardy grapes. The future became clear. The Abels would move to Wisconsin and start a winery. It took more than a decade, but the young couple now lives their dreams.

They selected Greenleaf because Sara's family lives there. Only after moving in 1996 did they realize the Escarpment offered excellent vineyard land, "the same soil type," Tim remembers learning, "as Ontario," which has a thriving wine industry. Taking jobs in the area, they looked for land, finding in 2001 a tract of former cropland in the shadow of the dolomite

ledge. LedgeStone opened its doors in late 2007 with fifteen acres of vines planted in Swenson and Minnesota varieties; another ten or more acres are yet to be planted. At approximately five hundred fifty vines to the acre, this vineyard will allow LedgeStone to raise enough grapes to support the family.

Before finding their vineyard, Tim and Sara grew grapes at home, trying out varieties to find which were most productive. At the vineyard, they grow Frontenac and Sabrevois for red wines, with Frontenac Gris, La Crescent, La Crosse, Edelweiss, and St. Pepin for whites. With the 2007 release of the lauded Marquette grape, they planted a large acreage. "This grape could change the face of red wine in the Midwest," Tim Abel says. Most cold-hardy red grapes make a light wine, but Marquette offers a full-bodied wine with the same cold-hardiness as another University of Minnesota red, the workhorse Frontenac.

Learning wine-making at conferences and workshops around the Midwest and the nation, Tim has been especially pleased with some of the wines made from the vineyard's Frontenac, which can develop deep rich flavors in good years. The 2006 harvest was perfect, producing a wine that "even Californians can like," Tim jokes. He also intends to produce ice wines in the traditional way, letting the grapes freeze on the vines and harvesting in midwinter; although always limited in terms of production, the ice wines made with Frontenac at a stunning forty-five Brix have proven popular with LedgeStone visitors.

With a patio overlooking the vineyard, LedgeStone was built to encourage visitors to stay. Tim plans instructional signs to describe the land's geology and history along walking trails beside the vineyard. Tim and Sara Abel, having seen some dreams come true, are confident that more will follow.

State Fairs and Wine

Throughout rural America, the State Fair is an important avenue for sharing agricultural information. Whether it be gardeners sharing ideas about how to grow the perfect dahlia, Future Farmers studying the steer contest winners, or cooks getting ideas from this year's best jellies, the competitions breed continued improvement in rural crafts and agriculture.

The Wisconsin and Minnesota State Fairs played a major role in the emergence and expansion of the regional wine industry. In Minnesota, the wine division committee works with Minnesota Grape Growers Association to evaluate wines by professional and hobby winemakers and, in 2007, opened the first Minnesota wine-tasting bar at the fair.

In Wisconsin, commercial wineries banded together in the late 1990s to set up a wine garden at the State Fair, which has done more to expose the state's wines to potential customers than any other single effort. A building on the State Fair grounds was rehabbed in 1996 by the Wisconsin Winery Association. There local wines are showcased, displaying the variety and quality of the state's production. Many visitors will be consumers, but among the throngs will also be young people like Tim and Sara Abel who will help move the region's wine industry forward.

LedgeStone Vineyards

6381 Highway 57 • Greenleaf, WI 54126 • www.ledgestonevineyards.com • 920-532-4384

Location: 8 miles south of DePere on Highway 57.

Hours:
Variable; check website

Tasting: $3 charge or credit toward purchase

Tours: With tasting fee

Signature wines:
Frontenac Reserve: hearty, big-tasting red
St. Pepin Ice Wine: traditionally made sweet white

Events: Occasional; check website.

PARALLEL 44 WINERY

In the wine world, Parallel 44 is a magical number. Several of Europe's most significant wine regions, including Tuscany and Bordeaux, lie along that latitude. Draw the line farther west and it goes through the wine regions of Ontario and New York. West of Wisconsin, it moves across Oregon, another prime grape-growing region.

Fighting the commonplace "but can you grow grapes here?" question, Steve Johnson and Maria Milano named their winery with that magical number when they planted a thirty-five-acre gravel pit in Kewaunee County. Abandoned some decades ago, the gravel pit has a thin layer of sandy loam over stones and boulders. "It was a pretty difficult vineyard to establish," Steve remembers. "We busted a lot of equipment putting in the trellises. But now we're set and the grapes are happy."

The grapes were French-American hybrids (Seyval, Vignoles, and Maréchal Foch) and Swenson and Minnesota varietals (Frontenac,

Louise Swenson, St. Pepin, St. Croix, and La Crosse). In 2005, they planted three and a half acres, and another five acres in 2006, for a current total of about five thousand vines. Ultimately, twenty acres will be planted with cold-hardy grapes, as well as four rows of wild grapes. Although such grapes are small and tannic, Steve knows they make good wine. "It's a challenge," he says, "you have to get the sugars up high, to twenty-two to twenty-three Brix. They're mostly seed and skin, so if you crush too hard, you release way too much tannin. Then you have to age it a few years. But I will always have this soft spot in my heart for wild grape wine, because I watched my dad make it every year." Steve's father Carl tends the vineyard today, including those wild grapes.

Maria too has childhood memories of winemaking. Her father Angelo Milano, who immigrated from Reggio Calabria, made the family's wine; the winepress her father used stands in the winery today. That Italian heritage influences the winery's style, which is designed to evoke an Italian villa. An arched entry and a golden interior, together with topiary plants around the patio, provide a hint of the Old Country in the New World.

Inside, a variety of wines made from locally grown and imported fruit is available. Steve has sourced grapes from Washington, California, Ontario, and New York, and will continue to do so until his vineyard reaches full production. But he is uninterested in being yet another producer of Merlot in the long term. "I think people appreciate a connection to the local environment," he says. Steve and Maria are enthusiastic about the work their winery entails. "We were looking for something that would be a way of life rather than just a job," Steve says, "something that the whole family could be involved with for generations." Parallel 44 is the result.

 Under the Wisconsin Sun

Great wine is grown in Spain, New Zealand, South Africa. But when it comes to imported wines, Americans know just two lands: France and Italy. For years, French wines outsold Italian in the United States. But in the last decade, Italian wines grew steadily in popularity until, in 2007, they overtook the French. This increase comes at a time when daily drinking in Italy is slowly fading and more imported wine is sold there. While Italy remains third in European wine consumption—behind France, which is second to an inexplicable front-runner, Luxembourg—these changes have caused consternation in the Italian wine industry.

So the Italians decided to expand the export trade. Several conglomerates now bring Americans a variety of Italian wines. In the past, Americans tended to know a few major brands and a few types of wine—Bolla and Chianti, for example. Yet the breadth and depth of Italian wines is as extensive as that of France. As Americans get to know Barolo and Barberesco, Sangiovese and San Severo, Velletri and Valsusa, they will have the confidence to explore Italy's wine riches even further.

Parallel 44 Vineyard & Winery

N2185 Sleepy Hollow Road • Kewaunee, WI 54216
• 920-338-4400 • www.parallel44.com

Location: From Green Bay, take Highway 29 east 18 miles, then 3 miles south on Sleepy Hollow Road.

Hours:
May–December:
Monday–Saturday, 10:00 am–5:00 pm
Sunday, noon–5:00 pm
January to April:
Friday, Saturday, 10:00 am–4:00 pm
Sunday, noon–4:00 pm

Tasting: Complimentary

Tours: June–October, Saturdays, 3:00 pm

Signature wines:
Bianco Classico: semisweet Geisenheim white
Dolce Blanc: semisweet golden wine from
Cayuga grapes
Nouveau Rouge: medium-bodied red wine from
Rougheon grapes

Events: Third Saturday in April, spring open house; summer Saturdays, live music; second Saturday in October, Harvest Fest; Thanksgiving weekend, holiday open house.

TROUT SPRINGS WINERY

When you have a Class A private trout hatchery running smoothly, what's next? If you're Steve DeBaker, you start planting vines. A self-described "adventuresome sort," Steve's résumé includes founding a theater troupe and running a taxidermy shop. Today Steve continues as an electrical engineer while expanding and developing Branch River Farms at his home in Brown County, on the dip side of the Escarpment where the ledge slopes gently down to the waters of Lake Michigan.

Trout Springs Winery takes its name from the fish hatchery started in 1985 on land that includes the home of Steve and his wife, Andrea. In addition to raising and processing trout, the couple runs a plant nursery specializing in water plants. Perhaps most exotically, they sell cygnets born to swans who tend the largest pond on the farm. "Swans love to eat algae," Steve points out, "so they are great at keeping ponds clear."

Steve has been making wine as a hobby for almost thirty years, having learned it from his parents, who made fruit wines at home "with balloons on top of the jugs." In 1995, he planted vines after an extensive tiling project to make sure that drainage was sufficient for grapes. At first, like many new wineries at the time, Trout Springs was a site for experimentation. Many vines died, were ripped out, and replaced with other varieties. "We tried Chardonnay, Pinot Grigio, Cabernet Franc," Steve grimaces. "We ripped through money." Now the five-acre vineyard is planted with French-American hybrids and Minnesota varieties. The native American grape Niagara thrives as well. A few stray varietals, left over from the experimental days, are used for blending.

Visitors are introduced to Trout Creek wines in a wood-paneled tasting room, where they are also offered a variety of foods: local and imported cheeses, chocolates handmade on the premises, artisan breads, and other specialty foods. The wine list includes estate-grown wines in both varietals and blends, as well as fruit wines including Door County cherry, elderberry-blackberry, and crabapple. Picnickers can enjoy the shaded patio with its views over the vineyard and gardens, where concerts under the stars are held on summer evenings.

Looking ahead to the next adventure, Steve DeBaker has been active in preparing the application for a new AVA (American Viticulture Area) in the Trout Springs region. And when that multi-year task is completed? Something will come up. "The journey is the best part of this life," Steve says philosophically, "not when you get there."

Trout Springs Winery

8150 River Road • Greenleaf, WI 54126 •
1-866-687-9463 • www.TroutSpringsWinery.com

Location: Near the town of Waymor Park; left on
Wayside Road, 1–2 miles to River Road, turn right;
or go west off I-43 to Maribel, turn left on River
Road and go approximately 3 miles.

Hours:

April–December:
Saturday and Sunday, noon–7:00 pm
February–March:
Saturday and Sunday, noon–4:00 pm
Closed in January

Tasting: $5, includes samples of food products

Tours: Free; weekends only.

Signature wines:

Autumn Rouge-Reserve: estate-grown red,
vinified dry
Rainbow Blush: estate-grown light-bodied red
Millennium Cherry: sweet wine from Door
County cherries

Events: July and August, Jazz Under the Stars;
third weekend in September, Harvest Festival;
first weekend in December, Christmas event.

AVA: Wisconsin Escarpment

The most prized designation that an emerging
wine region can get is to be named an American
Viticultural Area (AVA) by the U.S. Bureau of Alcohol, Tobacco, and Firearms. Rather like an appella-
tion in France, the AVA designates an area unique in
its grape-growing climate and geology.

Until the middle of the twentieth century, the
United States had no wine regions; and California
made "chablis" and "champagne" with no regard
for the French idea that those names meant something geographically. As the wine industry emerged
from post-Prohibition torpor, both wineries and the
government realized the benefit of providing clear
regulations about what labels could say and what
language they could use. In 1978, the AVA standard
was established. Henceforth, the "region of origin"
could be noted on wines if they met certain legally
detailed expectations.

As the Upper Midwestern wine industry has
grown, interest in establishing AVAs has grown as

well. The earliest AVA established in the region was
the Wisconsin River AVA, in which Wollersheim is
the biggest producer; wines bearing that label
must come from a limited range of sites adjacent to
the Wisconsin River in the Driftless Area. To become
an AVA, a region must show that it has unique qualities of *terroir* that distinguish it from other areas.

There are some 170 AVAs in America, ranging
from the nationally recognized (Napa Valley) to the
regionally known (Mesilla Valley in Texas and Oklahoma). New applicants must establish that the
area is locally known by a certain name; that historical boundaries can be traced; and that climate, soil,
elevation, and physical features distinguish the
region from surrounding areas. After the application is received, a period of public comment must
be opened. Several AVAs are being proposed in the
Upper Midwest, so expect to see many regional
identities being established as the industry
matures.

VON STIEHL WINERY

In San Francisco, it was the Summer of Love, but in Algoma, it was the Summer of Wine.

It was 1967 when Charles von Stiehl, a local physician and hobby winemaker, took the bold step of setting up what is now Wisconsin's oldest winery. There were no laws permitting such an establishment, so the good doctor had to start by encouraging the enabling legislation. Then von Stiehl licensed and opened his winery, featuring Door County cherry wine.

The historic building in which he housed his winery had originally been Ahnapee Brewery. After the brewery closed, the building found several uses, including a washing machine factory. The defunct brewery had the space and elegance that von Stiehl sought for Wisconsin's first winery. Listed on the National Register of Historic Places, the Civil War–era building offers four floors of magnificently built and decorated rooms. In the basement, arched limestone caves provide cool storage for aging wines.

The Judgment of Paris

To put the establishment of Wisconsin's oldest winery in perspective, consider this: von Stiehl opened nine years before the Judgment of Paris.

Today, no one doubts the quality of California wine. But in the middle of the twentieth century, many connoisseurs scoffed at that now-premiere wine region. French wine was the standard and no California wine, snobs agreed, could touch a great Bordeaux or even a good Burgundy.

Today, it seems extraordinary that great California Chards and Cabs were treated with disdain, but such was the case. It was a different time. Jimmy Carter was running for president. Disco was big. Elton John was recording with Kiki Dee, a woman. Teenagers hung posters of Farrah Fawcett-Majors in their bedrooms. Sophisticated people knew better than to drink California wine.

How do you combat prejudice? The Californians could challenge the French in the marketplace, but not in the homes of the allegedly knowledgeable. To assure a steady demand for the "better" product, an importer of French wines, Steven Spurrier, organized a tasting that has gone down in vinous history as the Judgment of Paris.

The name refers not only to the location of the competition but also to the great myth of how

the Trojan War began. The mischievous goddess Eris threw a golden apple labeled "To the Fairest" into an Olympian gathering. Immediately three goddesses claimed it: Hera, goddess of marriage; Athena, goddess of wisdom; and Aphrodite, goddess of lust and love. The shepherd lad Paris was given the unenviable job of judging which goddess should get the apple. Who was fairest of them all?

Bribery began. Hera offered a solid marriage; Athena offered brilliance and her trademark wisdom; but Aphrodite offered the most beautiful woman in the world. Paris was a lad; Paris chose Aphrodite. Unfortunately the world's most beautiful woman was already married, and to a king at that. But Helen ran off with Paris back to his hometown of Troy. Helen's husband had to get her back, because she was the ruler of her land and he occupied the throne only as her husband. Read *The Iliad* for the rest of the story.

The 1976 wine contest also had lasting consequences. Only Chardonnay and Cabernet Sauvignon, those regal wines, were to be tasted. Spurrier himself was one of the tasters, as was Patricia Gallagher of the American Académie du Vin. But their votes did not count. Only those of the nine French

Algoma is itself a small historic gem. Founded not long after Wisconsin became a state, the town is located at the mouth of the Wolf River. Although its earliest settlers were Irish and English, later immigrants from northern Europe and Belgium left their mark in the timbered architecture of many of the town's major buildings. A significant fishing industry developed and, although commercial fishing has now declined, sport fishing for salmon and trout thrives. Today's primary industry is tourism, as outsiders flock to the charming waterfront and the historic buildings that house galleries and antique stores.

Its founder specialized in fruit wines, but in recent years von Stiehl owners Aric and Brad Schmiling have added production of wines from *vinifera* and hybrid grapes. The Schmilings, who bought the winery in 2003, retained the traditional decor and the fruit wine offerings of their predecessor. But they look to the future as well. "Just ask someone how old they feel when they turn forty," Brad Schmiling says. "And the answer will be: not very. We have grown and

judges—sommeliers, wine critics, restaurateurs, and winemakers—were tallied.

First came the tastings of Chardonnays: a great Mersault and a Freemark Abbey, a Beaunne and a Veedercrest. The French wines were all from Burgundy, the Californias mostly from Napa. The results: all the top scores went to California, for entries from Chalone Vineyard or Chateau Montelena.

But surely the grand reds of France would wipe the floor with those pathetic little imposters from California? Imagine the tension as the tasting began again. The great châteaux were there: Haut-Brion, Mouton-Rothschild, Montrose, represented by vintages supposed to be the best in a half century. And Stag's Leap, Ridge Vineyards, Clos Du Val from America. Ten wines in all, five from each continent, all in identical wineglasses with no identifying features.

The French judges were arrogant. "No nose," sniffed one, "definitely California"—but it was French. Another swooned over a wine showing "the magnificence of France" that turned out to be from Napa Valley. The world's greatest wine tasters, struggling valiantly to assure their country's preeminence, could not tell French from California wines.

While it would be nice to say that the French accepted defeat gracefully, that was far from the case. Squabbling broke out, with judges trying to secretly change their ballots or refusing to give up scorecards. Even a few years ago, some of those judges still refused to discuss the results of the blind tasting due to their enduring trauma over its results.

Those results were, as anticipated, welcomed in California. But in the vineyards of France, they were simply ignored. Only *Time* magazine covered the blind tasting; French periodicals said nothing until months later, when arch comments derided the whole idea. But the tide had turned, especially as further blind tastings confirmed the earlier judgments.

California wines have grown in prestige in the years since the Judgment of Paris, sufficiently so that terms like "revolutionary impact" are used in discussions of the event. The episode shows how deeply held biases influence the subjective view of a wine's value. As more wine lovers drink Upper Midwestern wines, the biases they hold will be revealed and, one hopes, can ultimately be set aside.

changed immensely in the past five years. We constantly change and improve our wines, customer relations, and festival ideas. By keeping what customers love and looking for more ways to enhance their future experience, we are able to delight them each time they walk through our doors."

von Stiehl Winery

115 Navarino Street • Algoma, WI 54201 • 1-800-955-5208 • www.VonStiehl.com

Location: Downtown Algoma, one block from Lake Michigan.

Hours:
January–April:
11:00 am–4:00 pm
May–June:
9:00 am–5:00 pm

July–August:
9:00 am–5:30 pm
September–October:
9:00 am–5:00 pm
November–December:
11:00 am.–5:00 pm

Tastings: Complimentary

Tours: $3.50 adults, $3 seniors

Signature wines:
Johannesburg Riesling: semidry, German-style white
Oktoberfest: semisweet blend of Vignoles, Riesling, and Gewürztraminer

Events: Late September, Wet Whistle Wine Fest; sporadic Ladies of the Vine Luncheons; check website.

Door County

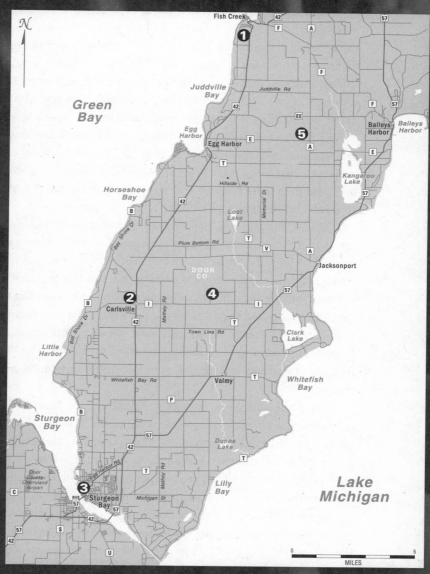

N

Green
Bay

Fish Creek

42
F
A
57

1

Juddville
Bay

Juddville Rd

42

F

F
57

EE

Baileys
Harbor

Baileys
Harbor

Egg
Harbor

E

5

Egg Harbor

E

A

Horseshoe
Bay

T

Kangaroo
Lake

B

Hillside Rd

42

Memorial Dr

57

Lost
Lake

Bay Shore Dr

Plum Bottom Rd

V

A

DOOR
CO.

Jacksonport

B

2

I

57

4

I

Carlsville

Bay Shore Dr

42

Mathey Rd

T

Little
Harbor

Town Line Rd

Clark
Lake

B

Whitefish Bay Rd

Valmy

T

Whitefish
Bay

Sturgeon
Bay

B

P

57

42

Dunes
Lake

T

Door
County
Cherryland
Airport

Mathey Rd

Egg Harbor Rd

C

3

T

Lilly
Bay

Lake
Michigan

BUS
57

Sturgeon
Bay

Michigan St

57

57

S

42

42

U

0   5
MILES

1. Orchard Country Winery 2. Door Peninsula Winery 3. Red Oak Winery
4. Simon Creek Winery 5. Stone's Throw Winery

IF THE MIDWEST HAS A CAPE COD, it is surely Door County, that thumb-shaped peninsula that reaches up from Green Bay into Lake Michigan. For almost a century, the area has been a summertime get-away favorite for resort-goers from Chicago, the Twin Cities, and other urban areas in the region. But its fame also draws tourists from greater distances, who enjoy boating, fishing, and other water sports as well as hiking and golf. Dozens of galleries and chic shops offer indoor enter-tainment. Civic arts organizations, too, make this region a sophisti-cated destination, with plays from American Folklore Theater and Peninsula Players, concerts at Door County Community Auditorium, and art classes at Peninsula Art School. History buffs explore small museums that focus on the region's maritime, pioneer, and Indian his-tory. And then there is always just hanging out at the beach, enjoying the sunrises and sunsets for which the area is famous.

If Door County in summer is crowded, with an estimated two million tourists in three months, in winter shops close up as tight as the little ice-locked bays that line the coast. Some restaurants and bookstores remain open, as well as resorts and B and Bs, so that a visitor in search of peace and pleasant birch-and-pine winter landscapes can delight in both the setting and the off-season rates. When weather cooperates, vis-itors can fish through the ice, ski cross-country, and ride their snow-boards. The year-round residents have more time then to be Wisconsin-friendly to visitors; as a local sign in December sighed, "Now we have time to visit."

Spring and fall are increasingly popular times for visitors who delight in blooming orchards or resplendent fall colors. To serve them, the area offers weekend festivals with quilt shows, pumpkin patches, parades, art fairs and lutefisk dinners. And for those who want to hike the expansive state parks, spring and fall are excellent seasons: no mosquitoes!

Like other area businesses, the region's five wineries are jam-packed in summer, filled with visitors tasting the signature country wines as well as *vinifera* wines crafted from imported grapes. In the off-season, the wineries stay open. The less-crowded conditions mean that visitors receive the full and friendly attention of the staff. You might even get your wine poured by the winemaker or owner.

The wine industry is new in Door County, which holds promise as a wine region because the majestic Niagara Escarpment slices across it. But grapes are not yet replacing cherries, grown in the area's renowned orchards for almost a hundred years. The protective heat-masses of

Green Bay and Lake Michigan modulate the temperature sufficiently to make Door County a unique microclimate. Limestone is close to the surface, so close that in some places the topsoil is a thin sheet over solid rock. Cherries thrive in such rocky soil, and Door County cherries remain a specialty, both for fresh eating and in preserves as well as for wine. Apples, pears, and plums are also grown in the peninsula's orchards. Wild grapes also grow throughout the peninsula, and have been made into some products like jellies. Only in the last ten years have vineyards been developed, most of them planted with French-American hybrids and Minnesota-bred varieties. The winemakers there are betting that Door County wine will someday soon be as famous as Door County cherries.

ORCHARD COUNTRY WINERY

Right beside the main road between two of Door County's most popular tourist destinations, Egg Harbor and Fish Creek, a long stretch of vineyard greets the visitor. In the middle is a complex of red-painted barns clustered around an old farmhouse. The scene could not be more restful, belying the energetic family industry conducted on the premises.

Orchard Country Winery has been in the Lautenbach family for more than a half century, since William and Ruth purchased the hundred acres for dairy farming in 1958. By the mid-sixties, they moved into fruit growing. Like other farmers, they planted the signature Door County cherries, opening a roadside farm market in 1975. It was a good time for cherry growers, who could count on good prices for their crops. But then Michigan became America's bulk cherry provider, although Door County still leads in production of the fruit within the state, providing 95 percent (7.2 million pounds) of the tart cherries grown in Wisconsin.

With the price of cherries at risk, the Lautenbachs looked for a value-added cherry product and, in 1985, son Bob established the winery. Now twenty thousand gallons are produced annually, plus another fifteen thousand gallons of cider, and a third generation of Lautenbachs is involved in the enterprise as daughters Carrie and Erin work the farm started by their grandparents.

Country Wines are Fruit Wines

There are two kinds of wine buyers in Door County, according to Cassie Lautenbach Viste: the kind who come in looking for a souvenir wine from "Cherryland USA," and the kind to whom the mention of cherry wine is received like an insult regarding mama.

The division reaches beyond Door County. Country wines, made from fruit other than grapes, are esteemed for heritage value and taste by some, while others define "wine" as an alcoholic beverage made from grapes. The grape lobby holds sway over the legal definition: apple wine can be called "apple wine," but it cannot be called simply "wine."

The distinction was unimportant in ancient times and outside the Mediterranean. Because prehistoric grapes were small and sour, it is likely that other fruits were the basis of the first wines. The Romans favored violet wine; the English continue the custom of making wines from wildflowers, such as elderberry, to this day. Japan and China have long cherished their plum wines. Northern Europeans made wines from whatever fruit grew in their regions, as well as honey, with both Germany and Poland manufacturing apple wines since early historical times.

If wine snobs will never be convinced that anything worthy of the name comes from fruit other than grapes, other wine drinkers are perfectly happy with wines made from apples, pears, plums, and in the case of Door County, cherries. These need not always be sweet; fruits can make a dry wine. Making wine from pectin-rich fruits such as apples requires the addition of pectinase to keep it from forming a glutinous mass at the base of the fermenter. Aging to soften tannins is often necessary, as some fruit skins can be rich in the sour-tasting substance; extracting the juice from the fruit, then fermenting the juice, can bypass this problem.

The Lautenbachs pride themselves on being a family-friendly location, providing hayrides, cherry-spitting contests, and other events in summer, sleigh rides and musical productions during the winter. The family orientation reveals itself in the names of two recent wines: Audrey Grace and Nathan John, names of the first of a fourth generation connected with the farm and its winery.

The farm continues to sell jams and jellies made from local fruit. Wine tasting is also conducted at a bar custom-built by Jody Viste, Bob's son-in-law. The winery itself occupies the original dairy barn, now a century old. Winemaker James Bowers oversees production there, and informative tours give a glimpse into the wine-making process.

Wine-making has become increasingly central to the Lautenbachs's vision for their farm, and grapes have become increasingly central to the wine-making. Beginning in 1998, new acreage has been planted in grapes rather than fruit trees, despite the difficulty of planting in Door County's thin soil. Trellises required drilling through bedrock just six inches below the surface. But vine roots, like those of cherry trees, love the challenge of twisting through tiny fissures in the rock to gain access to water and nutrients. Putting in the posts may have been difficult, but the Maréchal Foch and Frontenac grapes are doing just fine, yielding three thousand pounds of grapes in 2005, which were used in the Audrey Grace and Nathan John blends. The Lautenbachs have seen the rise and fall of cherry prices, but like other Midwestern farm families, they remain dedicated to keeping their farm a working enterprise.

Orchard Country Winery

9197 Highway 42 • Fish Creek, WI 54202 • 920-868-3479 • www.orchardcountry.com

Location: On Highway 42, between Egg Harbor and Fish Creek.

Hours:
May–November:
Daily, 10:00 am–4:00 pm
December–April:
Limited hours, call for information

Tasting: Complimentary, year-round

Tours: 30-minute guided tours: $3 per person, May–October
No tours November–April

Signature wines:
Cherry Chardonnay: lightly oaked, off-dry blend of Chardonnay and cherries
Audrey Grace: estate-bottled dry red, Foch and Frontenac
Nathan John: estate-bottled semisweet red with Bing cherry

Events: February, Winter Wine and Cherry Fest; July, Summer Harvest Fest; September, Fall Harvest Fest; check website for others.

Door Peninsula Winery

Step inside the front door at Door Peninsula Winery, and you'll find yourself in a cloakroom. Metal double-hooks jut from walls and pencil-marked papers hang from a bulletin board. A few steps up, and you enter what was until 1963 a one-room schoolhouse that served Carlsville for almost a hundred years.

The schoolhouse stood abandoned for a few years, but in 1974 Bob Pollan established a fruit winery there, using locally produced cherries and apples. When his son Rob was in college, he wanted to "do anything else" but work in the family business. After fifteen years of experience elsewhere, Rob was convinced to change his mind about the wine industry. He's never regretted it and now oversees production and distribution of 120,000 gallons of wine annually as well as overseeing a gift shop and restaurant.

Oh, yes, and the vineyard. Like other Door County winemakers, Pollan has seen interest in grape-based wines growing, so he established a vineyard near the winery to grow Minnesota-bred varieties St. Pepin and Frontenac as well as French-American hybrids Léon Millot and Maréchal Foch. He's also worked with University of Wisconsin agricultural extension specialist Dick Widman, who provides Pollan with unusual varieties being tested for cold-hardiness.

With winemaker Paul Santoriello, Pollan develops new wines regularly, employing both imported juice and local fruit. Together, they offer some fifty wines ranging from *vinifera* standards like Merlot to fruit wines including mango, blackberry, and peach. Blends of grape and fruit result in offerings such as Cranbernet (cranberry and Cabernet Sauvignon) and Chardapple (apple and Chardonnay). Some are blended specifically for holidays and special occasions: Hallowine (sweet apple wine with cinnamon and nutmeg) and Red Christmas (cherries and white grapes).

Considering the growth of tourism in the area in the last twenty years, Pollan feels confident that "as a destination, we will continue to grow," and that visitors appreciate having winery visits as part of their tourism opportunities. To that end, he has built observation windows into the wine-making and bottling operation,

Planting in Bedrock

Grapes love rock. The name of the renowned French wine Graves means "gravelly," a descriptive term both for the acerbic taste of the wine and the rocky soil in which it is grown. Too-rich soil encourages grapes to produce lots of leaves but little fruit, for which reason farmers have traditionally saved marginal land for their grape production. Why waste good fertile soil on grapes, when they prefer to work hard for their fruit?

But Door County offers an extreme challenge for grape growers. "Our soil is six inches deep," says Rob Pollan. "Beneath that, bedrock." Planting the grapes is a challenge, but an even greater one is erecting the trellises necessary for supporting the heavy fruited vines. Many local growers have had to hire drillers to put holes in the

limestone bedrock that lies just beneath the light layer of soil.

This challenge is worth meeting, growers say, because the roots of grapes have an uncanny ability to find small cracks and to grow down between them. If they do not root deeply in the first few years, though, they may freeze during hard winters. At the furthest extreme from fertile regions where the grapes do not suffer sufficiently, Door County makes every vine work hard for its living.

On the plus side, Door County offers climate-moderating proximity to large bodies of water, with Lake Michigan to the east and Green Bay to the west. Because climate plus soil produces *terroir* (taste of the territory), Door County wines are likely to provide a unique taste profile.

so that visitors can take self-guided tours. In a sense, the old schoolhouse hasn't moved far from its original purpose.

Door Peninsula Winery

5806 Highway 42 • Sturgeon Bay, WI 54235 • 920-743-7431 • www.dcwine.com

Location: On Highway 42, between Sturgeon Bay and Egg Harbor.

Hours:
Summer:
Daily, 9:00 am–6:00 pm
Winter:
Daily, 9:00 am–5:00 pm

Tasting: Complimentary

Tours: Every 30 minutes or by appointment

Signature wines:
Razzle Dazzle Raspberry: bright fruit taste, mixed with grape
Muscat Alexandria: sweet but crisp from an unusual grape
Cherry Port: fortified grape wine mixed with Door County cherries

Events: Last Saturday in July, Cherry Stomp; check website for other events.

RED OAK WINERY

In the heart of downtown Sturgeon Bay, Red Oak was opened by native son Nicholas "Andy" Wagener, who was inspired by the gardening prowess of his grandfather Frank Weber. Weber grew grapes for decades in Door County; one of his Concord vines still survives. The seed Grandfather Weber planted was slow to germinate but Wagener's interest in wine grew steadily. After college, Wagener moved to California where, on breaks from what he jestingly calls "trying to be a surfer," his wine appreciation grew; he and his wife, Gigi, a native Californian, were married at Wente Brothers, a famous Central Coast winery. Wagener earned a law degree and then, after beginning his practice in Wisconsin, began to study in the famous University of California, Davis program in oenology.

With this preparation under his belt, Wagener launched Red Oak in 2002, producing wines from imported grapes and juices. At the same time, with his father Nicholas R. Wagener, he planted an extensive vineyard, knowing that it would be years before it produced any fruit. "We plan to wait five years," Wagener says, for although the vines might yield some fruit within three or four years, the quality grows as the vine ages. "We want to make wines with local grapes, including ice wines." Until his own vines are producing, Wagener offers a full line of *vinifera* wines sourced from vineyards in California.

The vineyard emphasizes cold-hardy reds, Maréchal Foch and Marquette, with the white wine grapes St. Pepin and La Crescent filling out the vineyard's five acres. Its tending is in the hands of father Wagener, with son Andy serving as winemaker. As with many family-run wineries in the Upper Midwest, the whole family gets involved, with Gretna, Andy's mom, helping in the vineyard and tasting room, which was designed and decorated by Gigi Wagener.

Andy Wagener sees nothing but opportunity in the Door County wine industry. "We have a short growing season and harsh winters," he admits, "but the wine market here is strong." He describes the process of selecting varieties for the vineyards as a matter of "chewing through vines" until he found ones that grew well and hold promise for good-quality wines. "We went through Traminette, Vidal Blanc, Baco Noir. I tried some Pinot Noir, which died instantly. I had some that grew, but with a 40 percent kill-off, which was unacceptable. I did get some Chardonnay and Riesling to grow, but we had to bury them and, really, the growing season is too short to get good fruit." So out came those experimental vines and in went others, until the final four were selected. "Basically the Minnesota program is working the best for us," Wagener says.

While the vineyard grew, Wagener began making wines on a commercial scale. From the start, he knew what he did not want: An "in and out, rushed, what-do-you-want-to-buy" winery. Instead, he envisioned a friendly upscale lounge with food and wine in a serene setting. "We're not a restaurant," he emphasizes, "but wine goes with food, so we have light food with our tastings." His two knowledgeable pourers, Jan and Judy, strive to make visitors feel comfortable, whether they know about wine already or are first-time tasters. The response? "Overwhelming, amazing," Wagener marvels. "People love it."

Red Oak Winery and Vineyard

325 N. Third Avenue • Sturgeon Bay, WI 54235 • 920-743-7729 • www.redoakvineyard.com

Location: Downtown Sturgeon Bay.

Hours:
May–October:
Sunday, 11:00 am–4:00 pm
Monday–Thursday, 11:00 am–5:00 pm
Friday–Saturday, 11:00 am–6:30 pm
November–April:
Tuesday–Saturday, 11:00 am–4:00 pm

Tasting: Nominal fee

Tours: None; will be available in the future

Signature wines:
Cherry Beaujolais: Door County cherries, fermented on skins; light off-dry red

"Death's Door"

If Door County is the thumb of the Wisconsin mitten, Sturgeon Bay is right at its knuckle. Between thumb and hand stretches Green Bay. But like a scissors cutting off the tip of the thumb, engineers cut a canal straight across the peninsula in the 1880s. The Sturgeon Bay Ship Canal effectively made an island out of the upper portion of Door County.

The canal was needed because of the infamous Door of Death—the dangerous strait at its tip that gives the peninsula its name. Called by the French voyageurs Porte des Mortes, "gate of the dead," the passage separates the peninsula's main part from its northern neighbor, Washington Island. For several centuries, the "door" was the main route between the open waters of Lake Michigan and the resource-rich regions around Green Bay; archaeological evidence shows that it was used by Native American sailors too, some of whom lost their lives when their canoes went aground in the stormy waters.

The strait's almost oceanic danger meant that more shipwrecks occurred there than in any other freshwater body in the world. Among the famous shipwrecks were those of the forty-five-ton French *Griffin* in 1679, and three American ships (the *Nichols, Forest,* and *Gilmore*) in 1892; more than a hundred other ships went down in the narrow waters, with the stormy fall months being most dangerous, as they remain today.

The danger led to the proposal for an alternative route in 1881. The most obvious site for a canal was at the end of Sturgeon Bay, where a natural inlet already cut into the peninsula and could be dredged and deepened for cargo boat passage. Less than ten miles of canal needed to be built to create the new, safer passage to Green Bay, which opened in 1890. To ensure the safety of boats using the canal, a series of lighthouses were built that have become iconic images of Door County.

Captain Nick's Port: named for the owner's grandfather, the youngest man to become a Great Lakes shipping captain

Events: Occasional; check website.

SIMON CREEK WINERY

It started with a beautiful piece of land dead-center of Door County. Tim Lawrie, a native of Baileys Harbor stationed in Texas, heard it was for sale from his daughter's boyfriend. The family had been looking for a place in Door County. This one more than fit the bill so, sight unseen, Lawrie arranged the purchase of the 120-acre plot.

Not long after, his daughter called, her voice full of awe. "Dad, this is the most beautiful land in the world," she told him. Soon the whole family agreed. On visits home, Lawrie walked the land with his dogs and relished the rolling moraine landscape. As farmers began selling out as the cherry market tightened, and orchards died as condo developments burgeoned, the Lawries decided to preserve the beauty and peace of the place. The Door County wine industry was just beginning to take off, so the land's future as a vineyard and winery beckoned.

Once retired, Lawrie set out to learn about wine with the perseverance that helped him rise to the rank of colonel during his twenty-six years in the Air Force. He attended seminars, talked to other winemakers, studied the differences between vines, and dug posts for trellises. Within a few years, Simon Creek Winery had opened as the largest and most modern winery in Door County, with thirty-four acres in more than a dozen grape varietals and a lavish deck-lined tasting room above a peaceful pond.

Lawrie faced down a lot of discouragement in the process, including one vineyard owner in the Finger Lakes region who warned him, "Don't do this!" Although he is directly across Lake Michigan from Traverse City, Michigan, where vines thrive, he was told that the weather was different in the two states. So he took a hundred years of weather data and showed that there was only 0.1 degree difference between the two. The result was a $1.5 million loan for a state-of-the-art winery that opened in 2004.

He now produces a dozen wines with Virginia winemaker Tom Payette. How to convince a Virginia winemaker to relocate to Wisconsin? Easy: don't. Payette lives in Virginia and manages the wine on a daily basis as readings on acid and sugar are sent to him by computer; he also travels regularly to Simon Creek, always being there for bottling.

Vines take three to five years to produce sufficient grapes for wine, so Lawrie now imports most of the grapes he presses, but he plans to move toward estate wines as his vineyards mature. Ambitiously, he planted *vinifera* (Gewürztraminer) as well as hybrid (Seyval Blanc, Vidal Blanc, Vignoles, Baco Noir) vines, convinced that the environment can sustain them. Unlike other nearby vineyards, he is blessed with twenty-five feet of topsoil above limestone bedrock. And his location in the center of the peninsula means the vineyard is buffered from cold by two bodies of water.

Yet not all the vines are thriving, as Lawrie is the first to admit. "I'm going to tear up some," he says with more enthusiasm than disappointment, "and replant with others." Because pruning produces huge numbers of woody shoots every spring, he can replant the vineyard with varieties that are thriving. He also encourages expansion of the industry by providing farmers with cuttings; he needs more fruit than he can grow, and he's seeing some dying orchards torn up and replanted as vineyards, a sight that cheers him. Lawrie has also built what he calls a "California and continental wine experience" with local musicians entertaining in season on the deck and winery tours explaining the wine-making process. Visitors can walk the vineyards with a glass of wine, tasting the fruit as they will.

Condos will not soon stretch across this part of the peninsula. Instead, deer will come down to drink at the pond, and the occasional timber wolf will be seen looking for good hunting.

Through Lawrie's enterprise, his beloved portion of Door County's agricultural and forest land has been preserved.

Simon Creek Vineyard and Winery

5896 Bochek Road • Sturgeon Bay, WI 54235 • 920-746-9307 • www.SimonCreekVineyard.com

---

The Capone Connection

Sometime around 1928, local legend claims, Al Capone was looking for a place to hide a moonshine factory. It had to be out-of-the-way, but near transportation to his Chicago base. He found the perfect spot in Door County, on a farm owned by the Simon family.

He did not make them an offer they could not refuse and left the farmhouse in his limousine, never to be heard from again. The story came down through Martha Simon, a child at the time, and led winery owner Tim Lawrie to decide to name a wine for the notorious gangster. But because the Capone name must be licensed by the family, he settled on another name: Untouchable Red (because the Simon family could not be bought off by gangster money), now Simon Creek's best-selling wine.

Lots of small towns in Minnesota brag about their connection to Capone, whose nemesis George Moran was born in St. Paul, Minnesota. Moran, called "Bugsy" because people thought he was crazy, frightened Capone's predecessor into retiring and handing the business over to Capone. Bugsy then tried to have Capone killed, but the plot misfired, and Capone became Bugsy's sworn enemy thereafter. Moran was one of the intended targets of the St. Valentine's Day massacre in 1929, but he arrived at the fateful garage late and missed the

executions. Moran died of lung cancer in an Ohio prison after a botched bank robbery.

Kellogg, Minnesota, brags that a lavish home there was built by a confederate of Capone's, with a secret passageway to allow escape in times of crisis. Duluth was supposedly a favored summering ground for gangster families, evidence for which is offered by the fact that Al's older brother, Ralph James (called "Bottles" because he had a legal water-bottling company in Chicago) was buried there after his death in 1974.

Wisconsin is not left out. Couderay claims to be the site of Capone's summer "cabin" and capitalizes on it with multimedia tours that include the gun tower and "jail cell" used for discouraging potential songbirds. A bar in Onalaska boasts of being Capone's regular watering hole en route to the cabin. Brookfield has a street named Capone, reputedly because a gangland distillery operated there. Some residents of Burlington claim to have located underground tunnels linked to the Capone gang; official denials only reinforce rumors of nefarious doings.

Simon family tradition has it that Capone wanted their land for a distillery. By a nicely ironic twist of fate, the land they refused for that purpose now nurtures one of Wisconsin's biggest vineyards.

Location: Near Jacksonport; turn right going north off WI-42 at Carlsville, follow County Road I to the winery on Bochek Road.

Hours:

May 15–October 31:
Daily, 10:00 am–6:00 pm
November 1–May 14:
Daily, 11:00 am–4:00 pm

Tasting: Complimentary

Tours: 1:00 and 3:00 pm daily in summer

Signature wines:

Untouchable Red: ruby Cabernet in a medium-dry style
American Viognier: an unusual fragrant variety making a rich white wine
American Golden Muscat: light and fruity and somewhat sweet

Events: Memorial Day weekend through October 11, music on the deck, every Sunday and most Saturdays.

STONE'S THROW WINERY

Just for the record, there is no Uncle Gino.

But there might have been. Owner Russell Turco, in honor of his heritage, built a winery that specializes in Italian *vinifera* wines, some well known (Sangiovese, Barbera) but others obscure even to the well-rounded oenophile (Grignolino, Charbono).

Because such Italian *viniferas* don't grow in Wisconsin, Turco arranges for vineyards in California to ship grapes in refrigerated trucks to Egg Harbor, a 2,350-mile trip that takes around thirty-six hours. Once in Wisconsin, the grapes are stemmed and crushed, then vinified using small-batch methods called microvinification.

The winery opened in 1996 in a stone-sided building built as a barn eighty years ago; the same building houses the manufacturing plant and an Italian-themed gold-stucco tasting room. There, staff members view their jobs as informing and educating visitors. If a taster doesn't understand the concept of "fruit-forward wine" upon arrival, that will not be the case upon departure. Don't look for cherry wines, Door County or otherwise; a sign advises, "We use cherries for pie."

Outside the tasting room nestles a small vineyard planted in Pinot Nero, an unusual *vinifera* that may survive Wisconsin winters because its home is at the base of the Alps. No one else has tried to grow Pinot Nero in the Upper Midwest. If the vines bear fruit, they would be the first Italian grapes harvested in the state.

Stone's Throw (as in "just a stone's throw from Napa") prides itself on making California-style wines. Turco subscribes to the winemakers' slogan that "great wine begins in the vineyard," and spends part of the off-season in California meeting with growers, examining vineyards, and tasting wines to locate the best sources for his next year's production.

The winery sponsors regular outdoor events in summer, usually musical evenings with well-known bands of broad appeal. Visitors can bring picnic lunches to enjoy on the patio or can purchase Italian snacks; glasses of wine are available for purchase, or you can buy a bottle and have it opened for immediate consumption. Bocce balls are provided for those who want to try their hand at this Italian bowling-like sport.

Oh, yes, about Uncle Gino. There is no such person, even though one of Stone's Throw's wines bears his name. Every year, the winery joins Peninsula Art School in sponsoring an art contest, with the winning work appearing on a label. In 2003, R. D. Bentley won the contest with an expressively rendered oil painting of an Italian man in overalls enjoying a sandwich, an expression of gusto on his face and a bottle of wine beside him. "Uncle Gino's Daily Red," a hearty blend, was named for the painting, and Uncle Gino also graces some of the wine-based spaghetti sauces available at the winery. Another of Bentley's works, showing a bocce tournament in progress, graces the tasting room.

Uncle Gino would approve. Unless, of course, he was looking for cherry wine.

Stone's Throw Winery

3382 County Road E • Egg Harbor, WI 54209 • 1-877-706-3577 • www.StonesThrowWinery.com

Location: Intersection of County Roads A and E, east of Egg Harbor.

Hours:

Daily, 10:00 am to 5:00 pm

Tasting: $4 per person

Tours: Daily

Signature wines:

Uncle Gino's Daily Red: hearty pasta-compatible red

Field Blend White: inspired by immigrant blends from the early 1900s

Old Vine Zinfandel: spicy, deep-flavored red

Events: Summer concert series, picnic grounds, bocce ball court.

Zinfandel and Wisconsin

"We're all about Zinfandel here," says cellar master Robert Lindsley, and the Stone's Throw wine list shows it. Whether blended with Merlot and Petite Syrah or on its own in four different wines, Zinfandel is the predominant grape at Stone's Throw.

That would warm the heart of "Count" Agoston Haraszthy. In the mid-nineteenth century, he planted a vineyard in Wisconsin but, before he could witness the vines' inevitable deaths (*vinifera* do not thrive in Sauk City), he packed up for California. There, he became the Father of the California Wine Industry (see Chapter Three), planting Chardonnay and thereby launching the tiny-bottle airline wine industry.

He also planted Zinfandel, but whether he was the first to import it into California is a controversial matter. No one in Europe has ever heard of the grape, at least not under that name, which seems to have emerged in California. Recent DNA testing at the University of California, Davis, one of the nation's premiere wine colleges, shows that Zinfandel is the same as the Primitivo grape, a workhorse in Italy's Apulia region, which offers the steady sun and long summers that the grape requires.

Zinfandel produces a tannic wine, full of that tart tea-like flavor that provides immediate structure and good aging potential. The grape makes full-bodied red wines, with the most flavorful coming from old vines. Because Zinfandel has been planted in California for more than a century, and because vines produce less but more intensely flavored fruit as they age, old-vines Zinfandel offers a special spicy taste and heavy body.

The Zinfandel grapes used at Stone's Throw reverse the journey that the Count made between Wisconsin and California in his search for a home for his vines. The grapes might not be Wisconsin-grown, but through Haraszthy, the Zinfandel has a connection to the Midwest wine industry.

Central Wisconsin

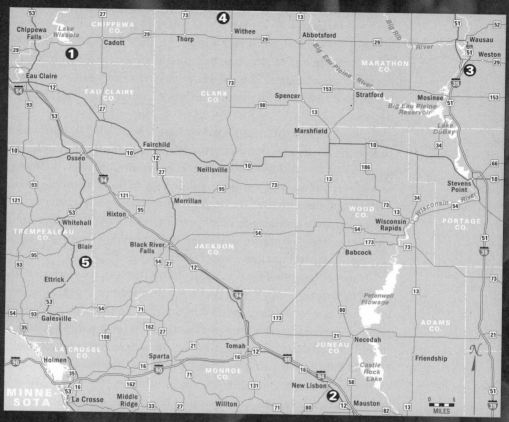

1. **Autumn Harvest Winery** 2. **Burr Oak Winery** 3. **Li'l Ole Winemaker Shoppe**
4. **Munson Bridge Winery** 5. **Tenba Ridge Winery**

THIS IS THE HEART OF THE HEARTLAND. Under an enormous sky, the ancient bed of Glacial Lake Wisconsin undulates gently. The eroded remains of primordial islands offer an occasional vista across industrial-strength farmland. Great sweeps of forest ring with calls of migrating birds in spring and fall, while summer brings flocks of trout seekers. Winter? Suffice it to say that the most common road sign warns of snowmobile crossings. The second-most common: a horse-and-buggy, for large Amish and Mennonite farming communities call the region home.

Central Wisconsin means hardworking land farmed by hardworking people. Its towns are not lined with antique malls and B and Bs but with hardware stores and feed mills. Yes, there are attractions, but the region bases its economy on farming and dairying, so those attractions have a charmingly rural quality. As Upper Midwestern agritourism continues to expand, with predictions of 30 percent growth over the next decade, bucolic central Wisconsin will draw the attention of tourists eager to reconnect to rural life in an unpretentious region.

To meet that emerging market, many farmers have opened their doors to visitors who want to pick their own fruit or vegetables, let the kids play in a corn maze, or learn about traditional farming. Two vital parts of the area's agricultural production—cheese-making (Colby was invented here) and brewing (the regional favorite, Leinenkugel, is brewed in Chippewa Falls)—offer touring opportunities.

For nature lovers, central Wisconsin is one of the Upper Midwest's lesser-known treasures. Vast wetlands provide seasonal shelter for migrating water birds. One of the nation's premiere bird-watching locales, Horicon Marsh, was gouged out by the Green Bay lobe of the Wisconsin ice sheet. The thirty-thousand-acre George W. Mead Wildlife Area is another birders' paradise, with sightings of 268 species recorded. The seven-acre Foxfire Gardens showcases Asian-themed gardens and meditation spaces; Upham Mansion and Rose Garden emphasizes heritage roses, some dating to Roman times. And the ReNew the Earth Institute brings environmental concerns home with demonstrations of solar, wind, and other alternative technologies.

Wisconsin's central plain is cut by two major rivers, the Chippewa and the Wisconsin. Above the scenic Dells, the Wisconsin broadens out into several lakes, while the Chippewa flows over impressive Chippewa Falls. Most larger cities—Marshfield, Wisconsin Rapids, Stevens Point—are located on one of these waterways. The boundaries of the plain are especially rich with geological oddities, including karst outcroppings near Camp Douglas that, on a misty day, look like Chinese scroll paintings. These buttes and mesas, bearing names like Castle Rock and Roche-a-Cri, are remnants of an escarpment long since worn away by wind and water. In the east, the unusual nunataks are found. Once high mountains surrounded by the ice sheets, they remain as hills protruding from the plain.

This land of subtle beauties and rural quiet has many, though widely separated, wineries. For those drawn to the rural outlook and natural resources of the area, the wineries offer yet another way to connect to the land and its people.

AUTUMN HARVEST WINERY

Just after World War II, two Scots-Irish brothers came to the Chippewa River valley. They found a piece of land not far from Chippewa Falls, in a region of rolling hills closer to the Twin Cities than to Wisconsin's metropolitan centers. John and Jim McIlquham planted an apple orchard. All went well, the family story goes, until the brothers married women who needed distance from each other. When the farm was split up, John kept on raising apples. He also raised his son, named for him, on that farm.

John the elder was famous for apple cider. People came from miles around, hauling jugs to fill. But the farm crisis of the 1970s hit central Wisconsin hard. John downsized to twenty acres, and the younger John learned to fly, becoming a pilot for United Airlines.

This could be any of a thousand farm stories from the Midwest, ones that end with a developer buying the heritage farm and subdividing it into "Apple Valley" or "Orchard Heights." But John McIlquham Jr. had married Marykay Kramer, a resourceful woman brought up in a household where preserving had been an important part of every autumn. This meant jams and jellies, but more importantly, it meant wine made from wild fruits and fresh Door County cherries. Frank Kramer taught Marykay

The Wine-Glass Ceiling?

Wine is like fashion: most purchasers are women, and most makers are men. But that long-standing fact may be about to change. In 2007, the first national women's wine competition drew eighteen hundred entries, more than twice the expected number. Not all were made by women; some were designed for women but made by men. But a respectable proportion were the products of women winemakers. The competition's judges were all women—another U.S. first.

Is there a wine-glass ceiling? The question draws defensive comments from some women winemakers, who deny that there is any gender prejudice in the industry. But as late as the 1970s, few women studied viticulture or oenology at universities. Even today, the woman professional winemaker is a rarity. Most women in the industry just try to make excellent wine that cuts across bias. But many remember discouragement from family, friends, and industry associates. One woman vintner recalls that, when she won a scholarship in viticulture, her husband derisively told her she'd never succeed. She traded him in for a vineyard.

A general easing of gender stereotypes over the last thirty years has meant that more women are making wine, and more wine made by women is achieving acclaim. Women winemakers of renown include Maria Martinez in Spain, Paz Espejo in Bordeaux, and Jane Wilson and Louisa Rose in Australia. In California, Zelma Long of Simi is called by her coworkers "Miss Oblivious" because of her ability to turn a deaf ear to sexism. One of the world's premiere wine critics—a woman, Jancis Robinson—has said, "A steady stream of women winemakers over the last twenty years has become quite a torrent."

The Upper Midwest, as an emerging wine region, has relatively few wineries in which a woman can gain experience in the field, but also has fewer entrenched attitudes about women and wine—or, for that matter, about anything and wine. It is almost certain that more women will enter the industry as it matures.

the process, and some of her fondest memories involve crushing fruit and racking wine with her dad.

"Beyond that, I'm self-taught," Marykay says, although her studies included online classes from the prestigious University of California, Davis school of oenology. But that was a few years later, after she had convinced the John McIlquhams, father and son, that starting a winery would be a way to keep the family farm productive for another generation.

She started with apples from the McIlquham orchard. "I had my friends taste the wine. I told them to be honest, because we were going public with the stuff. They told me it was awful." (Marykay has a sharp and self-deprecating sense of humor: her vanity license plate reads YNER.) Marykay set back to work. After three different yeasts and a lot of chemical analysis to get the ethanols under control, she produced a fine, light apple wine.

That was the beginning of Autumn Harvest Winery, whose tasting room opens out on a big pumpkin patch and corn maze so that families can enjoy the farm together. Tables let visitors picnic with wine from the tasting room and local fruit and cheese. There are no tours, however, as the wine-making is done at the McIlquham home.

After introducing her first apple wine, Marykay explored ways to produce wines from local and regional fruit. Blackberry, black raspberry, and elderberry wines offer a range between off-dry and sweet, and Pinot Noir and Pinot Gris from Oregon vineyards offer table wines for those who prefer grape-based wines. But apple wines, including a winter mulled apple, remain the basis of the Autumn Harvest line, still made from apples from the thriving McIlquham orchards.

In the tradition of the elder John McIlquham, Marykay also developed a hard cider. Bottled in beer-sized bottles, the effervescent light drink will surprise those who have tasted heavier European ciders. At 4.5 percent alcohol, somewhat lower than wine, the sparkling cider is likely to go head-to-head with local beers. Marykay bases her cider on apples from the family orchard, which are also available for sale throughout the year. Like any farm enterprise in the Upper Midwest, the McIlquham farm is a work in progress—with a strong emphasis on "work."

Autumn Harvest Winery

19947 County Road J • Chippewa Falls, WI 54729 • 715-720-1663 • www.autumnharvestwinery.com

Location: Off Highway 29 between Wausau and Chippewa Falls; east on County Road J, 5 miles to the corner of County Road K.

Hours:

May–Labor Day:
Wednesday–Saturday, 10:00 am to 5:00 pm
Sunday, 10:00 am–4:00 pm
Labor Day–Halloween:
Daily, 9:00 am to 6:00 pm

Tasting: Complimentary

Tours: None

Signature wines:

Fall Folly: from wild black raspberries (blackcaps), light and crisp
Northern Lights: apple and grapes co-fermented for fruity taste
Grandpa's Best: 100 percent elderberry, a heritage wine

Events: Mid-May, Mother's Day celebration; early June, open house; early September, Fall Festival; mid-September, Oktoberfest.

BURR OAK WINERY

In the middle 1990s, the farmers around New Lisbon were taking a wait-and-see attitude.

Judy and Steve Kennedy, both from area farming families, were planting grapes on their land. Grapes? This is corn and soybean country, a place where things don't happen fast or dramatically. Last time they did was about ten thousand years ago, when an ice-dam broke and the torrents from Glacial Lake Wisconsin carved out weird limestone towers and basins. Things that happen in a hurry don't necessarily bode well, in these parts.

The Kennedys didn't rush into planting their vineyard. They had been thinking about it for years, since Steve tried making wine. An odd chance launched that hobby: he had seen a neighbor picking dandelions. Remembering his grandfather's recipe for dandelion wine, Steve found it and made what the Kennedys recall as a best-forgotten beverage. But the wine-making process fascinated Steve, so he tried grape-based wines. Coming into contact with Elmer Swenson, the near-neighbor from up in Osceola who had bred so many cold-hardy grapes, convinced them to give over a few acres to the new venture.

The first part of the vineyard was planted in 1997. The varieties were mostly Swenson's, although a significant number of Maréchal Foch vines were put in as well. Over the next few years, as the vineyard expanded to nine acres, talk at the local café remained interested, if a bit doubtful. When ground was broken in 2003 for a stone winery that incorporated a cache of century-old stained-glass windows, people took note. When the winery opened two years later, not only was it almost an immediate success with tourists up from the Dells, but local people began booking the attractive function-room for weddings, reunions, and the like. After only a

Baco and His Friends

Although the French have been in the New World for four hundred years, serious hybridization of native American grapes with French *viniferas* did not begin until approximately a hundred fifty years ago, after phylloxera struck the French vineyards.

Phylloxera is a tiny louse that feasts upon grape roots. Soils all over America play host to the louse, but grape varieties native to this continent have lived with phylloxera for so many millennia that they have evolved strategies to protect themselves. American vines harden off parts of their roots where phylloxera thrive. Thus the two species live in balance, a balance impossible to European varieties that lack the adaptive strategies of their American cousins.

This would not have been a problem if the vines had stayed put. At first, the commerce was one-way: *vinifera* vines traveled across the ocean to America, where they were planted and quietly died. But in the early 1800s, impressed by the vigor of the American varieties, French vineyardists brought back some American vines. Even worse, they brought American soil on the roots of the imported vines.

What followed was a fifty-year horror story. Acre after acre of flourishing vines gave up the ghost. Regions were economically ruined. Prizes were offered for anyone who could come up with a solution, with the resulting bizarre inventions eating up time and money. While others were trying sulfur and flooding treatments, a few intrepid hybridizers few years of operation, Burr Oak Winery is regularly crowded with visitors.

The vineyards stretch out from the winery to the enormous old burr oak tree, second-largest in the state, that gives the place its name. In addition to the tasting room and winery, the complex includes a gallery where local artists show their works. The Kennedys have made room for Hickory Hill Artists, a cooperative that holds open-studio day the last Saturday of each month during the summer. During winery hours, the gallery is open for exhibitions. To further encourage community connections, the winery plays host to a variety of classes in arts and crafts.

Judy Kennedy can usually be found in the tasting room, pouring wine under the luminescent colors of the antique stained glass, while Steve works in the winery and vineyards. Varietals include some that are unusual in the area, like the intense Baco Noir and the white Vignoles, a variety typically found in Missouri and other more southern locations. Léon Millot and its relative, Maréchal Foch, are part of the offerings, as are a few Swenson whites used in blends. Steve also keeps his hand in farming, so that on a sunny midweek spring day, the winery may be closed while he plows and plants.

Burr Oak has built an active schedule of special events focusing on the arts and community needs. The unique combination of the art of wine with the wine of art has made Burr Oak a destination for visitors and locals as well. It took more than a decade, but the landscape around New Lisbon has been changed.

Burr Oak Winery

Kennedy Vineyards • N5873 Highway 12&16 • New Lisbon, WI 53948 • 608-562-5271 • www.burroakwinery.com

Location: I-94 to Mauston, then 4 miles west on 12/16.

---

embarked upon a different quest: to crossbreed hardy Americans with tasty Europeans. Thus a new class of wine grapes was created, the French-American hybrids.

Ultimately, it was grafting French varieties on American rootstock that revived the French wine industry. Now almost all European vines are grown on phylloxera-resistant American rootstock. Strangely, the roots do not affect the taste. A Chardonnay grafted onto a *Vitis labrusca* shows no sign of the telltale foxy American flavor. Once the grafting solution was found, hybrids were outlawed because their vigor put them in competition with traditional varieties. They remain illegal in France.

On this side of the pond, hybrids suffer from the same rejection of anything not *vinifera* that affects native American grapes, but with less reason. Some of the hybrids make excellent wine, and most were bred to eliminate the notorious *labrusca* flavor. Some of the important early hybridizers were François Baco, whose Baco Noir (red) and Baco Blanc (white) are still known; the Alsatian Eugene Kuhlmann, who bred Maréchal Foch and Léon Millot; J. F. Ravat, breeder of Vignoles (Ravat 51); Bertille Seyve of Seyval Blanc; and the most famous, Albert Seibel, whose many hybrids include Aurore, DeChaunac, Chancellor, and Rosette. French-American hybrids can create commendable wines due to their *vinifera* parentage. They may never have the status of *vinifera* varieties, but they remain important to the emerging Upper Midwestern wine industry.

Hours:
Wednesday–Sunday, 11:00 am–5:00 pm
Closed Mondays and Tuesdays

Tasting: Complimentary

Tours: Free, year-round

Signature wines:
Castle Rock Red: semisweet white blend
Cranberry: popular dry, fruity holiday wine
Baco Noir: intense, rich red

Events: Last weekend in April, Spring Festival;
weekend following Labor Day, Harvest Festival.

LI'L OLE WINEMAKER SHOPPE

Gail and Mike Closser were hobby winemakers before they moved to central Wisconsin. They bought equipment and supplies in Milwaukee, which has a long tradition of home wine-making. But when they quit their jobs at General Motors to move to Merrill in 1986, keeping up their hobby became difficult. So, to supply themselves and other central Wisconsin hobbyists, in 2001 they started a little shop. A little old winemaker's shop.

Home Wine-Making

In California or Bordeaux, winemakers learn their trade by working in a vineyard or a winery. But in the Upper Midwest, few area winemakers have been brought up in the craft. Rather, they learned their skills as hobbyists before turning pro. Or, in a few cases, they learned wine-making from a hobby winemaker parent, then went on to develop their skills into a profession.

Home wine-making has a long history in the Upper Midwest, a tradition that extends across the sea to the European homelands of ethnic immigrants. Slavs, Germans, and Italians came from regions where every family made its own wine, and despite moving to a region where *vinifera* grapes did not grow well, they continued to practice their harvest traditions. Some wine-makers simply transferred their skills to the local fruits, but others used *vinifera* grapes shipped by rail from California or New York, then crushed and fermented in the Midwest.

Prohibition did not to stop the hobbyists. Indeed, it gave them a reason to refine their practice, because the law allowed each family to make two hundred gallons of wine annually for their own use. At approximately four bottles per gallon, each family could annually cellar eight hundred bottles of wine which, in turn, meant a daily consumption of a bit over two bottles. Such was temperance.

Some home winemakers produced excellent wine; some produced memorably bad wine, often from grapes chosen because they traveled well rather than because they tasted good. And before the ready availability of today's sophisticated tools, there was always the possibility of fermenting wine blowing up or going bad. By the middle of the twentieth century, with commercially made wine readily available again, the hobby wine-making market was small indeed.

Then the downward trend reversed itself. In part, this was due to the new availability of vacuum-packed juice. Instead of personally crushing a ton of second-rate grapes that had traveled leakily in a railroad car, the hobby winemaker could now buy a carboy's worth of Italian Barolo or New Zealand Sauvignon Blanc. As a result, home winemaking surged. There are now estimated to be four million home winemakers in the nation—four times the number of home beer brewers.

Five years later, that little shop has grown to be a restaurant and wine bar, a wine education service, and a winery. But the shop still serves its primary purpose, providing wine and beer supplies to hobbyists in central Wisconsin. The simple but homey shop in a mall just off the freeway offers books, gear ranging from yeast to carboys, and that most important component of wine, grape juice. Boxes of concentrate from important wine-making regions offer the hobbyist a range of choices. To help new hobbyists learn, the Clossers offer regular classes at the store and around the region. And if you get stuck, you can always call the shop, where Mike, Gail, or one of the skilled employees will troubleshoot for you.

If the customer hasn't got room for the fermentation process, or wants more assistance than the class allows, the Clossers offer a wine-babysitting service. Through windows just behind the shop, visitors can peer at carboys labeled with their owner's names. In addition to making their own wine, the Clossers will watch and, when appropriate, rack wine mixed by their customers. For the brand-new winemaker, this service provides an additional level of security about whether the wine will come out well. For more advanced winemakers, the shop provides temperature-controlled space that might not be otherwise available, as well as assistance should it be needed.

Beyond the winery, the Vine and Dine restaurant and the Wine Cellar bar offer light snacks or dinners as well as the Clossers's wine and microbrewed Wisconsin beers. The couple still does small-batch fermentation, as they did when they began as hobbyists, in six-gallon carboys and, occasionally, in a thirty-gallon vat. Some thirty varieties are available in the tasting room at any time, ranging from Australian Shiraz to California Old Vines Zinfandel. By making wines using the concentrates and juice that they sell, the couple offers hob-

byists a chance to sample the kinds of wine they could make.

In addition to wine made with imported juice, the Clossers make specialty wines from local fruits. Their dandelion wine is made from flowers collected by children under sixteen. "This gives them a way to earn some money," Gail Closser says. "We won't buy dandelions from adults for that wine." They buy local berries and wild fruits, crafting wine in small batches, just as they do with expensive imported juice.

The next stage of their development will be production of their own grapes from cold-hardy varieties. The Clossers have planted and are tending a vineyard with Marquette, Frontenac, and other University of Minnesota grapes. While the vines mature, they continue to develop their own wine-making expertise, and that of their customers.

Li'l Ole Winemaker Shoppe

10101 Market Street Cedar Creek Mall • Rothschild, WI 54455 • 715-355-9700 or 1-877-355-9701 • www.LilOleWinemaker.com

Location: Exit 185 at I-39/Highway 51 to the Cedar Creek Mall, center court.

Hours:
Monday–Wednesday, 10:00 am–7:00 pm
Thursday and Friday, 10:00 am–9:00 pm
Saturday, 10:00 am–7:00 pm
Sunday, 11:00 am–5:00 pm

Tasting: Complimentary

Tours: None

Signature wines:
Dandelion: from the kids in the neighborhood, a classic country wine
Apple Fumé: slightly smoky-flavored apple wine
Vineyard Royal: made from Léon Millot, a French hybrid grape

Events: Occasional; check website.

MUNSON BRIDGE WINERY

No branding committee came up with the name for this winery. No focus groups were held or questionnaires passed out in malls to determine customer preference. No one considered names like "Withee or Without Thee" or "Cows Du Roam."

For Tom Rohland, it was simple. As a child in Withee, he had tossed a fishing line into the Black River near the farm where he grew up. He always liked looking at Munson's farm, the big Victorian frame house on the road, with its historic hip-roofed red barn. When he was ready to enter the dairy industry, he bought that farm. And when he decided it was time for a new venture, it was easy to chose the name. Munson Bridge Winery is just steps away from the bridge from which Rohland fished as a child.

Twenty years in the dairy business taught Rohland a lot about farming, including how difficult it is to sustain an independent family farm. Like most farmers in the area, he's taken jobs to keep the bills paid. But he grew up in central Wisconsin and has no interest in venturing elsewhere. When a friend nearby began raising grapes, Rohland realized that his hobby of making fruit wines could grow into an agritourism enterprise. With that, he and his wife, Sheri, set about creating a winery that would be not only an attraction for those traveling between Eau Claire and Wausau, but would also provide a center for community activities.

Planning took several years. Even so, when the winery opened in 2007, the tasting room was not complete. Anything a hundred years old is going to hold remodeling surprises. In this case, the foundation of the old hipped barn was discovered to be unstable. Time and expense created a more stable foundation. When eager guests arrived for opening night, they found a half-finished tasting room. But nothing deterred them from celebrating the first winery in Withee.

Rohland tries to use local fruit, to support local producers. He makes a semisweet white wine from rhubarb, a blush "wedding wine" from raspberries, several wild elderberry blends (with cherry and blueberry), and a sweet crabapple. Four cranberry wines round out the list. Rohland expects to make grape wines as local production gets underway.

Beyond plans for expansion of the wine list, Rohland works to create a friendly setting for families as well as adult visitors. On a large lawn behind the farmhouse with its stunning gardens, children play beside a calming pond where dragonflies dance. A patio stretches from the tasting room to the pond, so picnickers can enjoy a reflective moment. Inside, local art decorates the walls of the spacious tasting room, which opens onto the winery production area, both built into an addition to the historic barn, now used for wine storage.

Events are an integral part of the Munson Bridge vision. A monthly campfire brings local musicians together with wine lovers to enjoy the pastoral setting beside the pond. A harvest fest brings community members and visitors together for scheduled and spontaneous activities. Shari has opened the farmhouse for meetings and conferences, for which she caters meals from the farm kitchen. As their enterprise expands, Tom and Shari Rohland have one main goal: to sustain and celebrate farm life. Visitors find a relaxing environment, but behind that calm surface, Munson Bridge is busy as the fish-filled pond that is their signature setting.

Munson Bridge Winery

W6462 Bridge Road • Withee, WI 54498 • 715-229-4501 • www.munsonbridgewinery.com

Location: Between Chippewa Falls and Wausau; from WI-29 take exit 118 to County Road T through Withee, turn left on Bridge Road, approximately 2 miles.

Hours:

May 3–December 21:

Friday, noon–6:00 pm

Saturday, 11:00 am–6:00 pm

Sunday, 1:00 pm–4:00 pm

Private group tours and tastings year-round by appointment

Tasting: Complimentary

Tours: By arrangement

Signature wines:

Toby's Wild Plum: semidry, made from wild-crafted fruit

Sunset Blush: cranberries and apple, sweet yet tart

Julia's Raspberry: "wedding wine" for any palate

Events: Monthly campfires with music; September harvest festival.

TENBA RIDGE WINERY

Back in Alsace, that disputed territory that has moved back and forth between German and French control for the last three centuries, John Patrick Gill's grandfather made wine in the regional style. His was no industrial winery. Instead, like other farmers and burghers in the area, Jean François Gill made enough for his own use and to share with neighbors.

It is that heritage that Gill called upon in creating Tenba Ridge Winery. After retiring in 2004, John and his artist wife, Kiyoko Fiedler, moved to an eighty-acre paradisial valley in Trempealeau County, where the central plain bumps up against the Driftless Area. It is a land of swelling hills and horse farms, of narrow country lanes winding past Amish farms, of

Alcohol Creep

Another name for a lounge lizard? No, it's the term used to describe a recent tendency toward production of super-alcoholic wines. While a typical wine rests between 10 to 12 percent alcohol, wines of 14 to 16 percent are now available—about the level of a fortified wine or port in the old days.

The higher alcohol is said, by fanciers of the high-octane stuff, to better carry flavors and aromas than traditional wines. But generations of wine drinkers have been able to distinguish Sauvignon Blanc from Chardonnay without pyrotechnical vinification. What's going on here?

Some blame global warming. The world's classic wine regions tend to be hot, and they are growing hotter. More heat means more sugar in the grapes; more sugar translates into more alcohol. In addition, a longer season means that grapes can hang on the vines longer, growing sweeter as they do so. With such sugary grapes, winemakers can make

a high-alcohol dry wine rather than leaving left-over sugar as residual sweetness.

Others blame the trend on industry tastemakers who prefer "hot" wines to more modest ones. To accommodate such tastes, hardier strains of yeast have been developed that keep transforming sugar into alcohol long after the typical yeast would have perished in an ocean of alcohol. The natural alcohol limit for wine is steadily being pushed upward by such techniques.

Alcohol creep has vociferous partisans and equally eloquent detractors. The trend seems likely to last, and a few Upper Midwestern wineries make warmish wines to meet the new demand, although most keep within conventional ranges. Another reason to make sure you taste lightly and have a designated driver for winery visits.

drifts of wildflowers and shady butternut groves. From a ridge with a grand view over miles of hills and valleys, the couple set about creating a new life.

Gill had kept up the heritage of home wine-making and saw the potential for a winery in this scenic region. But his ambitious business plan turned out to be wrong. "At the end of the first year," he says with a touch of astonishment, "we were at where we'd pegged for year five." Tenba Ridge Winery was up and running, with eighteen thousand bottles coming off the line every year since.

Other wineries have huge stainless steel fermenting vessels; Gill has a battery of six-gallon plastic buckets for primary fermentation. Then the wine is siphoned into a glass vessel or carboy for secondary fermentation. Final aging takes place in small steel barrels, which line the win-

ery tasting room as well as the tiny thirteen-by-nineteen-foot winery production area.

Gill's passion is wine-making, not growing, so he starts with pressed grape juice, plus a small amount of apple juice to add sweetness and body. Working with Kiyoko, who as "the nez" (nose) of the winery sets the standard of taste, Gill determines the yeast variety and level of fermentation for each wine. Tenba's wines range in style from dry reds to semisweet whites, and crisp fruit wines are also offered.

Although no food is served, Tenba encourages visitors to bring food to eat either on the spacious deck or indoors around a pleasantly designed table surrounded by bar chairs, beneath a ceiling crowded with Kiyoko's handmade baskets. "We're closed in winter," John Gill says, "but one day last February the phone started ringing at 10:00 AM, people wanting to

Microvinification

Those who practice microvinification are living examples of the "small is beautiful" philosophy. Although most commercial wineries use large stainless steel tanks for fermenting their wines, a few practitioners go in the opposite direction, employing the same equipment that a home winemaker might use to create basement wines. Only instead of a couple of carboys in the laundry room, these winemakers have dozens, each holding approximately six gallons of fermenting wine.

Microvinification also means intense record-keeping, so that among hundreds of fermenting and aging wines, the winemaker knows which are ready for bottling and which need more time in the barrel. But for partisans of this approach, the handcrafted appeal of small-batch wine, like the appeal of microbrewed beer, makes such limitations welcome. It allows for careful adjustment dur-

ing the fermenting process. Slight differences occur between different batches, like the differences between two versions of a handmade basket.

Artisanal wines are attracting attention lately, although some experts argue that careful wine-making can be done on any scale. The snob appeal of a bottle of handcrafted wine, however, has led to small-batch wines being created even by large commercial wineries, often to be sold at premium prices.

Small-batch production is now part of the world of beer, bourbon, even soft drinks. There is little question that it will remain part of the wine world. In Europe, the garage winery is less common than it was a generation ago, as the "large is profitable" movement strengthens. Yet the *garagistes,* as owners of tiny wineries are called in France, make up in awards what they lack in market share.

know if the winery was open. By mid-afternoon the place was full. People just wanted to come out to the winery and watch the snowfall. I warned them though, they'd better have four-wheel drive!"

Although no public events are scheduled at Tenba Ridge, as Gill puts it, "serendipity often strikes," and such events as the snowfall spectacle are common. Far enough from urban centers to be a day's outing but close enough to be a destination, Tenba Ridge fills its niche as an elegant country home that just happens to be open for wine tastings and purchase, with an informed and companionable host eager to share his joy in wine.

Tenba Ridge Winery

N27587 Joe Coulee Road • Blair, WI 54616 • 608-525-2413 • www.tenbaridgewinery.com

Location: In Wisconsin, exit I-94 at Black River Falls, take County Road C west to Joe Coulee Road, turn right; from Minnesota, Highway 53 to County Road C east, then from C turn north on Joe Coulee Road.

Hours:
May–December:
Friday, Saturday, Sunday, 10:00 am–5:00 pm, as well as holidays that fall on Mondays. Other times available by appointment.

Tasting: Small fee, waived with purchase

Tours: None

Signature wines:
Le Chapeau Rouge: pinot noir, vinified dry with a hint of apple
La Vin Aromatique: semidry Gewürztraminer, vinified with apple
Boysenberry Apple: sweet, refreshing, well-balanced fruit wine

Events: Occasional; check website.

Up North

THIS IS WHAT YOU THINK OF AS "UP NORTH": Sapphire lakes strung into glittering necklaces, miles of unbroken forest, fireweed like magenta plumes. Loons laughing on summer nights. Aurora twisting through a moonless sky above spangled snowdrifts.

And the people. Sassy middle-aged waitresses for whom the terms "insult" and "friendly teasing" are synonymous. Businessmen who close the store when the fishing's good. Gone-to-ground intellectuals who mix paranoia with utopia. Indian Fancy Dancers, proud of a timeless heritage. Hardworking, hard-playing tradespeople. Idealistic trust-funders, artists, inventors, off-the-beaten-trackers, and it's-god's-countryites.

You know you're there when you cross the divide between broad farm fields and the northern forest cut by bright swift rivers. It's the divide between settled and wild. Yes, there are pockets of farmland and urban communities up north. But even the tamest areas feel wild, and even the nicest people seem to have a streak of wildness in them.

This land has two seasons: tourist season, and the rest of the year. During the short splendid summer, visitors flock north towing canoes, powerboats, children, pets, and expectations. They camp out in the Nicolet or Chequamegon national forests, or on Rainy Lake or Itasca. Or they check into a streamside motel. Or they head back to that upscale resort where the family has spent its summers for a generation or four. They stay for a weekend, a week, a month. Or they move lock-stock-and-barrel into the family cabin and stay for the season.

Then the tourists depart, and aside from the winter sports crowd, the land is returned to its year-round residents. Many tourism-related businesses shut their doors, but enough remain open so that visitors find all they need in terms of accommodations, food, and entertainment. And that, increasingly, includes wineries.

The Canadian Shield forms a granite backbone for the land, frequently breaking through the thin topsoil in gray faceted masses. The area has long found an economic base in mineral extraction. Gold and silver appear in small amounts, and copper was mined by Native Americans for craft and trade. More extensive and economically significant were the deposits of iron ore ("red gold"), so valuable to the newly industrializing America that boomtowns rose and fell around the mines during the late nineteenth century. The Great Gogebic Boom, named for a range of low hills in northeastern Wisconsin, was a speculative frenzy almost at the level of the Sutter Creek strike that launched the California gold rush. When high-grade Bessemer ore was found in the region, a get-rich-quick investment craze swept the nation.

Profits were made at first both by miners paid premium wages and by speculators who flipped their stocks. There was ore to be mined, on a grand scale; a million tons were shipped in one year from the Norrie mine alone. But as night follows day, bust follows boom. In the summer and fall of 1887, the bottom fell out when outrageously overvalued stocks crashed as the pace of mining slowed. The irony is that there was indeed plenty of ore, which was slowly extracted over the next hundred years, but that was no consolation to those bankrupted by the boom.

A slightly longer boom in the lumber industry had the same result: so vigorously did the lumber barons execute their business that the land was denuded. Beginning in 1850 and extending to 1920, white pines were cut at a staggering rate. Forests do not regrow quickly, so the industry went from providing more than a third of the nation's lumber in 1890 to less than 10 percent in 1920. An excellent overview of the area's timber industry can be found at the Forest History Center in Grand Rapids, Minnesota.

Today's forests are second-growth, with trees nowhere near the ten-foot-diameter white pines taken to build the region's metropolitan centers. Many neighborhoods of Milwaukee and the Twin Cities trace their lumber to this region; most of the lumber used to rebuild Chicago after the 1871 fire came from the north woods. What timber is left is used mainly for pulp. But trees still standing can also produce profits. The biggest industry left up north is tourism.

It's also one of the region's oldest. Railroads built to take ore and lumber out of the region also brought in people. Advertising campaigns in the latter part of the nineteenth century extolled the virtues of wilderness vacations. By the turn of the century, resorts catering to wealthy clients from Chicago and other eastern cities were a fixture in the region; a few still operate, but most have converted to condominiums, which, together with motels and campgrounds, form the backbone of the local tourist economy.

Although surrounded by the north woods, a different ecosystem can be found on the Bayfield Peninsula, which juts out into Lake Superior in northwestern Wisconsin. There, protected by water on three sides, a small orchard paradise has grown up, with farms focusing on berries and apples. With the Apostle Islands just offshore, Bayfield has been a magnet for visitors for more than a century. On a clear summer day, sailboats fill a sparkling bay and vacationers throng shops and restaurants with stunning hillside vistas. Harvest festivals and leaf-peeping, winter sports and spring wildflowers extend the season.

Both visitors and year-round residents have embraced the region's wineries, which make wine from local fruits and berries or from imported grapes and juice; one ambitious winery has even planted a vineyard. All note the prevalence of fishing widows among their customers, especially among the midlife to older crowd; wine tasting is a great way to while away long days ashore. But locals, too, enjoy the wineries, especially during those quiet times between the close of fishing season and the arrival of the first snowmobile.

Up North Minnesota

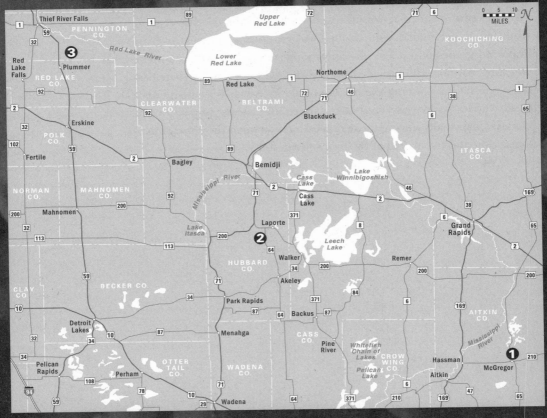

1. Minnestalgia Winery 2. Forestedge Winery 3. Two Fools Vineyard

MINNESTALGIA WINERY

It's "Minnesota" and "nostalgia"—the feeling that comes over one on tasting wild plum sauce your granny used to make when you were at the cabin. Or when you smell the pungent fragrance of highbush cranberries. Or when you drink wild grape juice whose taste makes you want to jump in the car and drive to the lake—in December.

When folks in the Upper Midwest speak of "the lake" and "the cabin," they don't just mean a place but a state of mind, a relationship between humans and nature cherished over generations, somewhere where sunsets last long into the night, just before the loons began laughing.

It is this feeling of connection between people and wild land that inspired Lori Gordon and Jay Erckenbrack to start Minnestalgia Winery in 1990 in McGregor, on a crossroads in cabin country. They dreamed of a winery using only native fruits, sustainably harvested. But they started first with other specialty food products, like syrups from lingonberries and chokecherries, jams from blueberries and blackberries, and jellies from crab apple and hawthorn. Then they moved on to wine.

Although they knew wine-making basics, they asked Robin Partch of Northern Vineyards to help them establish a formula for successful wine production. Together, they settled on a practice of making wines that start with honey wine (also called mead) blended with wild fruit wines. Rather than call them "fruit wines," a phrase that Lori feels puts off those who imagine a syrupy softness, the Erckenbracks call their line "alternative wines."

They buy fruit from wild-harvesters who pick plums, berries, grapes, and other ingredients. "For some of our harvesters, it's a good steak dinner," Lori says. "For others, it's school clothing for the kids. We buy from a lot of retirees—old loggers, they really know where to get the fruit." In addition to individuals, the winery buys from the Leech Lake, Red Lake, and White Earth reservations, under an arrangement that permits harvesters to bring fruit to a central facility. Although the fruit is raised without pesticide sprays or herbicidal assistance, it is not technically "organic," a regulatory definition that does not cover wild foods.

Although open year-round, Minnestalgia sees its busiest season during the summer, when its cheerful tasting room is busy with cabin folk and tourists. During the off-season, the winery sells by mail order and directly to those hardy souls who don't want to wait for a summer day to enjoy a taste of the north country.

Minnestalgia Winery

41640 State Highway 65 • McGregor, MN 55760 • 1-866-768-2533 • www.minnestalgiawinery.com

Location: Just north of the intersection of State Highway 210 and State Highway 65 (the only stoplight in McGregor), on the east side of the road heading north.

Hours:
January–April:
Monday–Saturday, 10:00 am–6:00 pm
May–December:
Monday–Saturday, 10:00 am–6:00 pm
Sunday, noon–5:00 pm

Tastings: Complimentary

Tours: By request

Signature wines:
Blackberry Honeywine: smooth semisweet red
Great Gray Barrel Select: oaked blackberry
Highbush Cranberry Honeywine: semisweet blush, somewhat tart

Events: Rarely; check website.

FORESTEDGE WINERY

According to the popular (and in some quarters, roundly hated) movie *The Big Chill*, after the sixties ended the hippies all got haircuts, bought suits, and went corporate. Not so Paul Shuster, who proudly claims to be a back-to-the-land hippie—"heck, I'm old enough that I really should have been called a beatnik"—who never gave up his youthful philosophy.

In the early 1970s, Paul and his wife, Sharon, went looking for a place where they could raise a family in a beautiful and healthful natural setting. They found it in the lake district of north-central Minnesota, where they envisioned a winery that would use local produce. The slab was poured in 1978, but it was twenty years before Forestedge Winery came to be.

In the meantime, Paul and Sharon made fine wooden kitchen tools to sell at arts fairs across the nation, building up a network of similarly minded artists. They also brought up their children, providing part of the family's food from their extensive gardens. When the children moved away—"and they all still have gardens," Paul says proudly—the couple decided the time had come to build on that twenty-year-old cement pad. With partner John Wildmo, they set out to make wine sustainably—using no imported juice or fruit, and relying as much as possible on the Shuster land, especially the rhubarb that formed part of the original "hippie homestead" plot. Vinified dry, the rhubarb combines with strawberries and blueberries in wines that tend toward the dry rather than sweet end of the taste spectrum.

With Sharon as winemaker, the team works with other Minnesota fruit growers to produce approximately eight thousand gallons of wine each year. In addition to wine tasting, Forestedge hosts a gallery with local artisans, many of whom are also featured at the annual outdoor arts fair

---

Wild Fruits and Wine

Once, all wine was made from wild fruits. Before grapes were cultivated, small sour wild grapes were all winemakers had. Today, few wines use wild grapes, and most fruit wines are made from domesticated plants as well.

Wild fruit grows rampantly in northern Minnesota. Some fruits are native, while others were European or, in a few cases, Asian plants that escaped from cultivation. The north offers small wild plums that grow in dense thickets; wild black raspberry with silver-mauve canes and intense seedy fruit, and its ruby cousin, the red raspberry; juicy blackberry, hidden amid thorns; low-growing tart lingonberries and rich bog blueberries. People who know the northland know the way each season brings its special fragrances and flavors.

Using wild fruits challenges the winemaker. In the first place, the harvest is unpredictable. A good raspberry year might be a dreadful year for blackberries; a year with plenty of plums might be one where elderberries dry up before picking. Wild plants are more restricted in distribution than cultivated ones, so a winemaker must work with what the region and season produce.

In addition, weather influences acid and sugar levels, sometimes dramatically. One year the raspberries might be sugary, while the next they turn tart; amounts of rain in the growth cycle can cause such changes, as can unseasonable heat. So the winemaker must constantly and methodically measure the fruit's qualities to assure the best possible result.

late each summer. The farm with its magnificent gardens and peaceful patio offers a destination for those who need "a vacation from their vacation," jokes Paul. For tourists enjoying the lake environment and "cabin people" who have been coming to Leech Lake for generations, a stop at Forestedge has become part of summer.

Forestedge Winery

35295 State Highway 64 • Laporte, MN 56461 • 218-224-3535 • www.forestedgewinery.com

Location: Take State Highway 200 west from Laporte; turn south on State Highway 64; winery is on the right.

Hours:

mid-May–December:
Tuesday–Saturday, 10:00 am–5:30 pm
Sunday, noon–5:00 pm

Tastings: Complimentary

Tours: By request

Signature wines:

Rhubarb Wine: crisp, light, not bitter
Headwaters Classic Red: soft but flavorful chokecherry and rhubarb
Black Currant Wine: full bodied, fruity red

Events: Art Fair at the Winery, third weekend in August.

TWO FOOLS VINEYARD

Starting from almost anywhere, you have to drive north to get to Two Fools. If you're in Thief River Falls, Baudette, or International Falls, you can drive south, but from Bemidji, Grand Rapids, and Duluth—to say nothing of those tropical cities like Brainerd and Minneapolis—you head for the North Star.

Rhubarb, the Unlikely Wine Ingredient

More than a thousand rhubarb plants fill curving beds, all offspring of a single rhubarb plant Sharon Shuster planted more than two decades ago. Like most gardeners, Shuster planted the rhubarb as a "pie plant" (one of its pioneer names), but now it forms the basis of Forestedge's signature wines.

Rhubarb is related to sorrel and other plants in the buckwheat (Polygonaceae) family. Like garden-invading burdock, another relative, rhubarb spreads from rhizomes, underground root sections that keep sprouting when cut, making it easy to spread and hard to eradicate. Indigenous to Asia, where it has been cultivated for centuries as food and medicine, rhubarb was not popular in Europe until the seventeenth century, in part because it needs to be sweetened to be palatable as food

Rhubarb's leaves contain oxalic acid, which is toxic in large doses. Mixed with garlic, rhubarb leaves make an effective nonpolluting insecticide spray. But the stalks are entirely safe to eat and, because the plant appears early in spring, rhubarb is welcomed as an early indicator that the garden season has come again.

An acre of rhubarb plants produces approximately ten thousand pounds of stalks. To make wine, experts advise freezing the stalks before crushing them, as this breaks cell walls and produces more juice. Naturally low in sugar, it will not ferment sufficiently for preservation unless sugar is added; even so, the finished wine will be naturally tart. For those who prefer dry wine, rhubarb makes an excellent fruit wine as well as a base for blending with other fruits.

Two Fools is so far from any other winery—two hours north of the nearest one—that it almost deserves a section to itself. But if you're in Fargo and looking to do some wine touring, you no longer have to board a plane for Bordeaux. In fact, groups from the rural Upper Midwest crowd into Two Fools, even on days when it's not advertised as open. On nice days, they sit on the patio overlooking the vineyard; on days of rough weather, there's a friendly welcome in the tasting room.

A vineyard located at 48 degrees latitude, at least a hundred miles farther north than wine grapes are supposed to grow? Unlikely as it sounds, Carol and LeRoy Stumpf have planted three and a half acres of Minnesota grapes on a flat glacial plain between Thief River Falls and Plummer. From a mile away, a visitor might think the directions were wrong, but once behind the poplar windbreak, it's clear that vines are thriving. Ten years ago, this would have been impossible, but due to the breakthrough breeding program at the University of Minnesota, wine-worthy fruit grows in a previously unlikely corner.

Stumpf, a Democratic-Farmer-Labor (DFL) state senator for almost three decades, runs the winery on weekends. He and his wife had a garden where the vineyard now stands, and he credits Carol with coming up with the idea for the vineyard. Casting about for "something exotic" to grow, Carol Stumpf suggested that the couple become the farthest-north growers of the new U of M breeds. The vineyard was planted in 1999, predominantly in Frontenac, with Marquette following later; smaller plant-

How High Can They Go?

Grapes are growing on the Minnesota-Canada border and fifty miles north of Québec. What's next? Vineyards in Alaska? (Stop laughing. Alaska already has several wineries that make wines with native or cultivated fruit. Fireweed mead is reputed to be sensational.)

As unlikely as northern Minnesota seems as a wine region, how about Inner Mongolia? Genghis Khan consumed wine raised in the gorges around Turpan, where a grape museum now displays the land's wine heritage. Wild vines thrive in Mongolia, whose government is promoting a revived wine trade. The grapes in the region are disease resistant, making organic growing possible and even profitable.

Minnesotans Tom Plocher and Bob Parke are renowned for their travels in search of cold-hardy grapes, travels that have recently focused on Mongolia. Authors of *Northern Winework*, the two join their expertise (Plocher as breeder, Parke as winemaker) to explore the possibilities of obscure vines. They have also worked extensively with Swenson varieties, their work influencing both viticulture and vinification of those varieties.

In addition to exploring grape culture in Inner Mongolia, Plocher has traveled to China, where in Heilongjiang and Jilin provinces grapes are raised successfully. As demand for western-style wine has grown, the three-thousand-year-old tradition of Chinese wine-making has been revived. Although *vinifera* vines grow, the grapes do not ripen fully, producing an acidic wine. At latitudes parallel to St. Paul, Plocher has found wineries using the Chinese grape *Vitis amurensis* in breeding. Plocher's work and his generous sharing of his discoveries suggests that cooperation among northern breeders will result in even more impressive scientific breakthroughs in future years.

ings of Sabrevois and Prairie Star provide grapes for blending.

Carol also contributed the name to the enterprise. Many wineries bear geographical names, so the pair considered Wyandot Wines for the nearby river. But Carol was reading a book about the "two fools" who first settled the Red River Valley, and how much mockery was directed toward them before the immense fertility of the region was discovered. "Two Fools" it became.

Since the winery opened in 2005, response has been enthusiastic, not only from wine drinkers, but from potential growers as well. The Stumpfs hosted a midwinter growers meeting and were delighted that several dozen came to learn about vineyard planting possibilities. From that meeting, more than six new vineyards have been planted.

Two Fools offers more than a dozen wines, including specialty fruit wines from local apples, gooseberries, and other fruits. Until the vineyard is producing, red and white wines are made from imported grapes; they range from the expected, like Merlot and Pinot Noir, to less-common varietals like Vidal Blanc and Orange Muscat. As the vineyard grows to maturity, more of the wines will be estate-grown.

Two Fools Vineyard

12501 240th Avenue SE • Plummer, MN 56748 • 218-465-4655 • www.twofoolsvineyard.com

Location: Between Thief River Falls and Plummer; take State Highway 59 to County Road 3 (Center Street), turn east, go 4 miles to 240th Avenue SE, turn south; 2.5 miles to the winery.

Hours:
June–October:
Saturday and Sunday, noon–5:00 pm

Tasting: Complimentary

Tours: By arrangement

Signature wines:
Chambourcin: French-American hybrid, dry
Vidal Blanc: dry white French-American hybrid
Blackberry: blended with grape, a sweet dessert-style wine

Events: Occasional; check website.

Up North Wisconsin

1. Bayfield Winery 2. Brigadoon Winery 3. HookStone Winery 4. Three Lakes Winery
5. White Winter Winery 6. Woodland Trail Winery

BAYFIELD WINERY

Fifteen years ago, orchardists in the Bayfield Peninsula had a problem. Tourists flocked in, but they stayed along the shore, looking out across the deep blue waters of Lake Superior to the Apostle Islands. Many came to sail, for the waters near Bayfield offer the only deepwater sailing in the region. Others came to enjoy the arts and culture of an area renowned for over a century as a resort destination. Others came to shop or sunbathe. But they didn't go up the hill.

Up there on the hilltop is a microclimate where fruit trees bloom and bear, much farther north than orchards are expected. The combination of the climatic protection of the lake's waters with the wind-stopping shield of the islands means that apples, pears, cherries, and bramble fruits grow superlatively on the six-hundred-foot-high bluffs of the Bayfield Peninsula. Winding country roads bring the traveler to one charming farm after another, each with a shop selling jams and jellies, antiques and crafts, and fresh fruit.

But most tourists stayed at the bottom of the hill. In the early 1990s, Renate and Scott Hauser thought long and hard about the problem. Their Superior View Farm, right above the town of Bayfield, was started in 1908 by Scott's great-great-grandfather. When he arrived, the land was already planted in apples; some of today's apple trees are over a hundred years old. Now, the orchard with its two thousand trees covers thirty hilltop acres.

Apples sustained the family for decades. Then, when World War II interrupted the usual shipments of bulbs and perennials from flower-filled Holland, the Hausers saw a new opportunity. The garden business they began then still thrives, with flowers shipped out in spring and fall to those interested in cold-hardy plants. But during the busy tourist season, the farm was

quiet. How to get the visitors to take that five-minute drive from town?

The Hausers found the answer right under their noses. Renate made wine. Developing her hobby into a business was the obvious next step. "It was a hobby that outgrew the house," she laughs.

Bayfield Winery was established in 1995, at a time when "wineries were just taking off," Renate remembers. "Back then, we were the new puppies. Now we're the tried-and-true." They readily give advice to new winery owners from their experience of developing a successful farm-based winery.

Renate makes ten of their twelve wines from apple bases, ranging from a tart and crisp dry style to a more familiar, softly sweet cidery style from an antique recipe she found while reading the works of Thomas Jefferson. Working with apples is different than working with grapes, she explains, because the former have less residual sugar than the latter and are not quite as acidic. Having developed skill with fruit wines, Renate is not tempted to return to making wine from grape juice or concentrates. "We have fruit here," she says simply, "so I make fruit wines."

The tourists are coming up the hill now, and not just for the wine. Renate describes what the farm offers as "agritainment." Most of their visitors are city people, whose children have not seen where their food originates. "This is where this country began, with the farmers," she says, "but many children never have a chance to experience a farm. We offer educational family entertainment."

Just as the farm's name promises, there is a superior view. On clear days, it's possible to see all the way to Hancock, Michigan, from the viewing spot on the top of the barn. That historic structure was built from a Sears Roebuck kit in the early 1920s of planks dragged up the hill by horse-drawn wagons. But many visitors miss that view, because they're out sailing on sunny days and flock to the winery when it rains. "A nice sunny day, it'll be quiet around here most of the day. But if it's a cold, windy, rainy day, people think it's perfect for the winery," Renate explains. They don't know what they're missing.

Bayfield Winery

86565 County Road J • Bayfield, WI 54814 • 715-779-5404 • www.bayfieldwinery.com

Location: Northwest of Bayfield 2.5 miles on County Road J.

Hours:
May–October:
Daily, 10:00 am–5:00 pm

Tastings: Complimentary

Tours: By arrangement

Signature wines:
Sneewittchen: "Snow White," a dry apple wine in the German style
J. D. Hauser's Grand Reserve: apple, aged in oak; limited release
Hauser's Colonial: semidry, made from three-hundred-year-old recipe

Events: First weekend in October, Bayfield Apple Festival; September, Apple Harvest Days.

The Lake Effect

What is it with wine and water? While climate and latitude, as well as soil quality, help to create the tastes of great wine, proximity to water is important. River valleys provide hillsides on which vines happily cling and stretch, while the water itself provides protection from climatic extremes. Think Bordeaux. Think Rhine and Rhône.

When winegrowers refer to a "continental climate," they do so in a tone of menace. Growing grapes far from water does not appeal for a simple reason: water freezes at 32 degrees Fahrenheit. If you have a big enough body of water, the residual heat in the water will keep the surrounding air somewhat warm. Thus land near water is warmer than that farther inland. Rivers offer some protection from cold, but the Great Lakes are much better, because their surface area is so much vaster. Unlike the shallower Great Lakes, Lake Superior rarely

freezes. As a result, the Bayfield Peninsula is protected on two sides by heat-retaining waters.

Although the Superior shores are too far north for most wine grapes, other Midwestern wine regions hug the shores of the Great Lakes. Michigan's premiere wine district stretches along Lake Michigan; Ohio's, along Lake Erie. The famous grape-juice territory around Franconia in New York, where miles of Concords stretch along upper Lake Erie, shows that even in areas of high snowfall, grapes can thrive if subzero temperatures are kept at bay by the lake.

Whether cold-hardy grapes will eventually thrive on the shores of Lake Superior, time will tell. But history shows that the protective cloak of lakeshore warmth helps make grapes happy, so the possibility lies open.

BRIGADOON WINERY

Brigadoon is Dave Welbes's favorite musical. The classic love story by Lerner and Loewe is set in a Scottish town trapped in time. To keep Brigadoon from changing beyond recognition when the modern era began, its clergyman prayed that it would disappear, to be seen one day every hundred years, after which it faded into the mists once again.

Parts of northern Wisconsin feel like that, seemingly unchanged from a more bucolic era. Welbes found his own private Brigadoon when his family moved to the Tripoli area and he met his own "Bonnie Jean," now his wife, Linda; the high-school sweethearts settled in the area and devoted themselves to family life, seeing one daughter gain her PhD in biochemistry and another devote herself to culinary arts. Welbes himself worked as a tradesman, but after thirty-eight years as an electrician, he began to look for a new profession.

Welbes had a curious hobby: he liked to read about wine. He vividly remembered a neighbor from his childhood in south Milwaukee. Every year, an elderly woman the kids called Grandma Barzamian made wine from backyard grapes and let the children taste it. The rich Chianti-like taste stayed with Welbes, and he wondered how she had made that memorable wine. For fifteen years, he read about *terroir,* grape varieties, fermentation, and aging. Did he imagine he would become a winemaker? Not at all. This was the eighties and nineties. He was in Wisconsin. There were no wineries in Wisconsin—at least, none he had ever heard of.

When he learned about the burgeoning Upper Midwestern wine industry, the dream of Brigadoon Winery was born. In 2002, Dave and Linda began to make wine. They wanted to open with wine they had made, rather than buying bulk wine while their own aged. So for more than three years, they made wine, bottled it,

tasted it, figured out how to make it better, and saved the best for release. When Brigadoon Winery opened in 2006, they were ready with seventeen varieties of wine.

Meanwhile, they planted a vineyard. The site is not propitious. There are no hills, though there is enough of a gentle slope that cold air drains away. And Brigadoon is in northern Wisconsin, at the far extreme listed for even the new cold-hardy varieties. Undeterred, the Welbes planted the mild white Brianna and the sharp Louise Swenson, as well as a mix of other Swenson and University of Minnesota breeds. Dave and Linda not only make the wine for Brigadoon; they work the vineyard, too. They also tend the tasting room, the entry to which is planted in a dozen different kinds of heather, in keeping with the Scottish theme. Their wines range from the somewhat conventional (Merlot and Pinot Noir) to the highly personal (a Chianti, blended of a secret mix to replicate the memorable wine of Grandma Barzamian).

Welbes does not disdain fruit wine in pursuit of an ideal grape wine for urban sophisticates. He treats it as he would a fine wine grape. "It helps," he readily admits, "to have a daughter with a PhD in biochemistry. I call her when I get stuck." Welbes has found that fruit varies in sugar and acid content far more than grapes do. "Some people make fruit wine the same every year," he shakes his head, "but the raspberries, say, might be more tart one year. If you don't measure, you can't produce a consistent product."

After having vinified the fruit, he ages it for a year to let it mellow—another unconventional treatment, for fruit wine is often released upon bottling. In addition to raspberry, blackberry, and the ubiquitous cranberry, Welbes also produces a mixed raspberry-blueberry wine. Welbes finishes his wine list with fruit-based dessert wines, aged in oak and fortified with cognac.

Although the winery is down a dirt road and away from the major tourist traffic, wine lovers found it immediately and came back bringing friends. "I love it in the hunting season, on a rainy day," Dave smiles. "Halfway through the morning you've got the hunters coming in, getting out of the weather. Pretty soon you've got the hunting stories, and then they're looking for a gift to bring the wife." But it isn't just locals who patronize the winery. One of Welbes's favorite customers is a woman from Napa Valley with a summer home in the area. "She says she doesn't like their wine that much. But she does like ours."

Brigadoon Winery

2170 Clifford Road • Tripoli, WI 54564 • 715-564-2280 • www.brigadoonwinery.com

Location: From U.S. 51, take U.S. 8 west to Clifford Road; turn right.

Hours:

May 1–December 31:
Monday–Saturday, 9:00 am–5:00 pm
January 2–May 1:
Monday–Saturday, 10:00 am–5:00 pm
Closed Sundays and Easter, Thanksgiving, Christmas, and New Year's Day

Tastings: Complimentary

Tours: By request

The Tastes-Like Question

Those who grow cold-hardy grapes and make wine from them face one big hurdle in public acceptance: people have never heard of the varieties. Tending to favor wines with familiar names, a customer might assume that she'll like a Merlot over a Maréchal Foch, a Chardonnay over a La Crescent.

Unfortunately for winegrowers and makers, this bias sometimes continues after the tasting. "Well, that's not bad, but I still like the Merlot better," may indeed mean that the taster likes the Merlot better. But it also can indicate a discomfort with the unfamiliar. While some tasters appreciate novelty, others find the wine-tasting process intimidating and retreat to their comfort zones. Thus many Upper Midwestern wineries offer one white and one red made with imported *vinifera* juice or grapes, for that timid part of the market. These rarely sell except at the winery. Why, after all, should a liquor store offer locally made Pinot Noir or Chardonnay instead of less-expensive, fine-quality wine from Oregon or California respectively?

To help wine tasters learn about the new varieties, the University of Minnesota, with several cooperating organizations, has published a tasting wheel that compares similar-tasting *vinifera* wines with cold-hardy wines, then links them to food. Turn the dial to "lamb," for instance, and you'll find St. Croix and Frontenac suggested to replace Merlot and Cabernet Sauvignon. Turn it to "pasta—white sauce," and you'll find Prairie Star and Frontenac Gris to replace Pinot Grigio and Chardonnay.

When tasting, be open to the new varieties. Comparing them to traditional *viniferas* is a good first step. If you know you like a hearty Barbera, for instance, ask the server if they have anything in that taste profile. Some wines made from Foch, for instance, satisfy the same tastes as the Barbera (although others are soft enough to pass for a Merlot). Be exploratory. There is likely to be a cold-hardy wine out there to surprise you.

Signature wines:
Chianti: dry and smooth with medium oak
Good Old Summertime: blueberries and raspberries fermented together
Northern Lights Raspberry: semisweet, aged in oak, fortified with cognac

Events: Memorial Day open house.

HookStone Winery

In a town with the largest sculptured fish on earth, what makes more sense than a fishing-themed winery?

HookStone is named from a legend that Native Americans in the region made fishhooks out of stone. Unlikely as that sounds—shell or bone being more common materials—there is evidence from California that some Indian cultures did prefer stone for the tool, and Ojibwe people may have hit upon the same idea. Like an arrowhead, a hookstone was made of stone carefully chipped away and formed into a hook strong enough to catch a muskie or walleye.

Northern Wisconsin's fish-rich rivers were well-known to the Ojibwe, who fished at night, attracting fish to the surface using flaming torches. The nearby Lac du Flambeau ("Lake of Flames") was named by voyageurs impressed with the haunting sight of hundreds of birch-bark canoes filling the lake, whose waters reflected the fishing fires.

When Rick Halajcsik was looking for a name for his winery in Hayward, the tie-in with local fishing culture was irresistible. After all, Hayward is home to the Freshwater Fishing Hall of Fame. Hundreds of thousands of tourists come to the area every year, drawn by the region's renowned lakes, streams, and rivers. What better theme for a regional winery?

Thus wines like Muskie Merlot and Walleye Blush were born. Halajcsik already made wine

as a hobbyist. He and his wife, Liz, were living in Oceanside, California, but they yearned to return to the Midwest. Liz's family had vacationed in Hayward for eighty years, so they knew the area's tourism industry and envisioned a winery as a strong addition.

HookStone opened in 2006, and by its second season, HookStone produced thirty-three thousand bottles, all from California or Washington grapes and juice. The wine is made in the storefront winery on Hayward's main street, then packaged with labels appropriate to its theme. Wildlife artist Scott Zoellick provided four paintings for the labels. Panfish Port shows the fish rising from a misty lake, while Northern Pinot Noir offers an underwater portrait of the famous fish. Beyond wine, HookStone provides unusual food products more readily found in a sophisticated urban neighborhood than in the north woods of Wisconsin. Flavored olive oil, olive salsa, pesto, and mustards share shelves with the wine. The Halajcsiks attempt to make the wine-tasting experience accessible even to those unfamiliar with winery etiquette.

HookStone Winery

10588 North Main Street • Hayward, WI 54843 • 715-634-9463 • www.hookstone.com

Location: Downtown Hayward.

Hours:
Memorial Day to Labor Day:
Daily, 10:30 am–6:00 pm
Other times by arrangement

Tasting: $4, includes souvenir glass

Tours: By request

Signature wines:
Muskie Merlot: medium bodied, aged in oak
Walleye Blush: cranberry and white Zinfandel
Vacationland: fragrant Viognier

Events: Occasional; see website.

Go Vintners?

If the Midwestern wine industry keeps growing, we may see the day when sports teams proudly wear wine-related names. A tradition already exists of teams bearing names related to regional industries—the Packers, the Brewers. The wine trade brings its own language and potential for team naming, for instance:

- Minnesota Vikings can become Minnesota Viniferas.
- Minnesota Twins can become Minnesota Terroirs.
- Minnesota Wild can become Minnesota Wild Fruit.
- Milwaukee Brewers can become Milwaukee Vignerons.

- Milwaukee Bucks can become Milwaukee Two-Buck Chucks.
- Green Bay Packers can become Green Bay Stompers.

And of course:

- Milwaukee Wave can become Milwaukee Wine.

The college football team names, however, present a peculiar challenge. Both states' teams are named for burrowing critters who bother farmers (gopher and badger, for those who have not been paying attention). Parallel threats to winegrowers are unappealing. Minnesota Phylloxera? Wisconsin Anthracnose? Might take a bit more work.

THREE LAKES WINERY

One Wisconsin winery got its start in California. But John McCain was not inspired by the state's famous vineyards. No, it was the abundant fruit in backyards and orchards that drew the attention the Oshkosh native. After mastering apricot and plum wine, McCain got the idea of trying cranberries. He was, after all, from Wisconsin.

Among his grape-wine-drinking California buddies, the cranberry wine was a hit. With their support, McCain moved his family back to Wisconsin in 1972 to make cranberry wine commercially. He had grown up vacationing every year in the north woods, so he selected Three Lakes as his base. More than three decades later, his sons Scott and Mark are winemaker and manager of the state's largest fruit winery.

Mark McCain encounters prejudice against fruit wines among those who consider themselves worldly. "It used to annoy me," he admits, "but now I think of it as the start of the educa-tional process." Typical Americans endure years of "grape-wine indoctrination," to the point where they fail to see the potential quality of non-grape wines. "I encourage them to do a sampling and an unbiased comparison, then to let the palate decide. If they don't like it, I don't mind, but I don't appreciate being criticized by someone who has never tried the wine."

One of the few second-generation winemakers in the region, McCain was a partner with his father and brother until his father's recent retirement. The business still involves most of the family. Mother Maureen still enjoys working in the winery, as she did when she was the sole bottle-washer and sales staff. Marla Shane, Mark's wife, serves as designer and marketing expert; she is responsible for labels, which feature evocative depictions of the fruit within.

Since the winery opened, there has been a sea change in American society regarding wine. "I can remember when there were a thousand wineries in the nation," Mark recalls, but by 2006, the number had grown to more than fifty-five hundred. This growth has been matched by increasing awareness of wine, which translates into greater sales. In 2006, U.S. wine sales passed the three-hundred-million-case mark, driven by several trends: great market visibility for wine, greater acceptance of wine as an everyday adjunct to dining, and more interest in wine among younger consumers.

These trends translate into stronger sales for all wines, including fruit wines. Three Lakes continues to make apricot and cranberry wines, but beginning with the introduction of berry wines in the 1980s, the line has steadily increased to seventeen wines. Lately, kiwi and passion fruit have been added. One surprise hit started as a novelty. When the town started a Pumpkin Fest several years ago, the winery issued a pumpkin wine. It sold out within a day, and Three Lakes makes it regularly now.

Life has not changed much in Three Lakes since the winery opened. Most retail business is still condensed into the seventy-five-day summer. Families still come, generation after generation, to enjoy the north woods with its exuberant outdoor culture. Visitors touring the winery now include people who remember taking a tour when they were children. "People enjoy coming back and seeing the changes at the winery, as well as what has stayed the same," McCain says with satisfaction.

Three Lakes Winery

6971 Gogebic Street • Three Lakes, WI 54562 • 1-800-944-5434 • www.cranberrywine.com

Location: Downtown Three Lakes, at the intersection of U.S. 45/32 and County Road A.

Hours:
Open daily year-round
Monday–Saturday, 9:00 am–5:00 pm
Sunday, 10:00 am–4:30 pm

Tasting: Complimentary

Tours: Free guided tours May–October; self-guided November–April

Signature wines:
Cranberry Wine: whole-fruit fermented heritage wine
Pumpkin Wine: Available seasonally; dry and surprising
Lady Gold: Slightly sweet apricot wine

Events: First weekend in July, open house; first weekend in October, Cranberry Fest; second weekend in October, Pumpkin Fest.

WHITE WINTER WINERY

People used to come into the Upper Midwest's only dedicated meadery and say, "Huh?" Or perhaps something like, "Oh, yeah, mead, isn't that what Beowulf drank?"

It's not surprising. Mead has had a low profile since the Renaissance or thereabouts. In America, "wine" is generally understood to be fermented grape juice, but the word actually covers any type of fruit-based fermented beverage—as distinct from beer, which is grain-based. Spirits ("hard liquor") belong to an entirely different category of drink. Whether grain-based like bourbon, vegetable-based like vodka, or fruit-based like cognac, liquor requires distilling. In the United States, since Prohibition, distilling has been rigidly controlled. At present, the Upper Midwest has no legal distillers.

But mead is enjoying a renaissance, with more than seventy meaderies in the nation, up from twenty-two a few decades ago. This expansion correlates to increasing public awareness. Although other wineries in the Upper Midwest make mead as a part of their product line, only White Winter Winery makes mead and related products its entire business.

Mead-maker Jon Hamilton comes from a beekeeping family. His father's family, then of International Falls, has kept bees for generations, a family industry that continues with Jon's uncles in Nebraska. Hamilton recalls hives behind their house in Brooklyn Center when he was a child. "It must have made an impression," he says, "because a few years ago I found my first research paper, from eighth grade, and it was about beekeeping."

After high school, Hamilton went to Northland College in Ashland, where he met his wife, Kim; both attended the University of Wisconsin in Superior, Jon in community psychology, Kim in education. Then came a short spell in Kenosha. "We told ourselves we would be there two years. Exactly to the day, we were driving our U-Haul back north." That was in the late 1980s, and the couple has never left.

Not long after moving, the Hamiltons began to make mead from the bees they kept for a hobby. "We were producing three to six hun-

dred pounds of honey a year from ten hives. We had a lot of fun, but we weren't getting a good return. We wanted a value-added product, and that turned out to be mead." They visited meaderies around the country to learn how to develop a business. Then, in 1996, they opened their doors for business. For a few years, Hamilton worked fulltime at the Ashland hospital, then drove to Iron River to work another full shift making mead. In 2000, he retired, devoting himself entirely to White Winter.

One quick result was that the business grew from thirty-eight hundred gallons a year to thirteen thousand. Hamilton would like to grow further, envisioning a state-of-the-art, energy-efficient, purpose-built building. "I can diagnose grandiosity when I hear it," the former therapist laughs, "and this comes close, but it's sustainable. I'd like to look at solar, wind, a zero-net energy building," one that leaves a light carbon footprint but still permits him to move up to twenty-five thousand gallons or so annually.

The Seventy-Five-Day Summer

It gets crowded at Three Lakes Winery in the summer. If you're a city-dweller, you don't notice, because "crowded" is a relative term. A busy day in Three Lakes does not include traffic jams, mobbed parking lots, or long lines for service. It means that the pourer serves two people at the same time at the samples counter.

That only lasts a few months: the "seventy-five-day summer" of local fame. The majority of tourists arrive between Memorial Day and the middle of August. A few come for fall festivals. A generation ago, the end of October saw the summer cabins locked up tight and the roads virtually deserted.

But over the past decade, the region has seen a slight but noticeable shift in demographic patterns.

Most of the old resorts—where people stayed a week or a month and, as they departed, reserved the same time for the following year—have been transformed into condominium developments. Many old cabins have been replaced with four-season homes. People whose families have come up north for generations now look at the region as a place to live permanently. Some of those former cabins now harbor start-up Internet businesses. Others are home to people who telecommute to a large metropolitan area. Trading the stress of an urban lifestyle with a big paycheck for a quiet life with less money is a choice some eagerly make. The era of the seventy-five-day summer may be waning.

Sustainability is important to the Hamiltons. They chose not to make grape wines because grapes don't grow in Iron River. The Bayfield Peninsula is, however, "one of the premier bramble fruit areas of the country," Hamilton explains. "Its microclimate is also excellent for apples, pears, and cherries. We want to use what's in our backyard," rather than using fossil fuel to transport grapes or juice across a continent or farther.

Recycling is also part of the operation. "The pomace, the waste from fruit, goes into the compost," Hamilton says. "We use cellulose filter sheets, so they can get shredded and reused." He is working on a process whereby the oak chips used in aging can be dried for barbeque chips.

The Hamiltons are proud that their produce comes from within a hundred and fifty miles. They have built a network of fruit-growers and beekeepers who provide their raw materials. Their meads run from very dry to sweet "honeymoon" wine and include some melomels, meads flavored with fruits like blueberry and raspberry. Perhaps their most unusual offering is brackett, a carbonated mead that resembles ale and is offered in traditional and oaked styles; brackett is historically connected with Scandinavian cultures, while the more traditional wine-like meads appear to have been Western European in origin. Response to the winery and its products has been strong, if seasonal. "We do 75 percent of our business in the seventy-five days of summer," Hamilton says, "but we have a strong local following. This is a great community." His voice catches a bit. "It brings tears to my eyes, the people up here have been just so good to us." Then he laughs. "And a good thing is, we don't take ourselves too seriously. We want to make this business fun. And it is."

White Winter Winery

68323 Lea Street • Iron River, WI 54847 • 1-800-697-2006 • www.whitewinter.com

Location: South side of Highway 2 in Iron River.

Hours:
Summer:
Monday–Saturday, 10:00 am–5:00 pm
Sunday, 11:00 am–4:00 pm
Winter:
By appointment
Closed all major holidays

Tastings: Complimentary

Tours: By appointment

Signature wines:
Black Mead: dry melomel (fruit mead) made with black currants, lightly oaked
Cyzer: Old English–style apple-mead cider
Oak Brackett: robust, nutty ale-like beverage

Events: Occasional; check website.

WOODLAND TRAIL WINERY

How many people in the Upper Midwest have the same dream? Get out of the rat-race, move to some serene rural area, start a business? Have done with traffic and stress, crowds and hassle? Be your own boss?

Thousands, certainly, maybe hundreds of thousands. Every summer they come north, heaving great sighs of satisfaction as they settle down for a week of fresh air and beautiful vistas. Then, all too soon, it's time to head south again, always with promises to return for a longer visit—or maybe to live.

Armin Baumann had that dream. With his wife, Adrienne, and their children, Baumann came up to Lakewood for decades. Their children grew up boating and fishing, gathering wildflowers, relishing the friendliness of the people on the edge of the Nicolet National Forest. And, like all visitors, they talked about making it their home.

Unlike others, however, Armin and Adrienne lived their dream. In 1989, they opened Woodland Trail Winery, the first winery in the area to focus on making wines from grapes brought in from California, New York, and later, southern Wisconsin. Armin Baumann had spent a lifetime as a Milwaukee wine salesman, and he saw an opportunity to expand into wine-making. He also saw that predictable tourists made the north woods an excellent location for a winery offering an education in the craft.

Close to twenty years later, Woodland Trail Winery offers over fifty different wines. In the

To Dream the Sustainable Dream

Some Upper Midwest wineries, ignoring local fruit, import juice or grapes from a major wine region. At the farthest extreme of the continuum from the all-California-all-the-time wineries stands Jon Hamilton, who produces an entirely local product. In a region renowned for its fruit and honey, he sees no reason to import anything. "Use what we have" is his guiding philosophy.

Sustainability is difficult to measure as well as to achieve. For instance, new FDA regulations permit a mix of honey with up to 49 percent corn syrup to be marketed as "honey." That ubiquitous corn syrup, found in everything from soda pop to cereals, typically comes from agribusiness operations, as often in China as in the Midwest. Midwestern beekeepers thus compete against diluted honey, much cheaper to produce and of arguable purity.

One way to ensure the quality of the product used for their mead, the Hamiltons have found, is to buy directly from producers. "We work with four beekeepers," Jon Hamilton says. "And I mentor people through the local beekeepers association." Sustainability, to Hamilton, is based on relationships as much as on price and availability. "Supporting others is good business," he argues. "We are on a first-name basis with our suppliers, and those relationships have been instrumental in our success." The Hamiltons feel so strongly about sustainability that their winery's mission statement includes their ethical standards. "Too many times we, as consumers, look only for the cheapest price without considering the hidden costs of buying out of our area. Costs such as the hydrocarbon emissions of shipping cheap, mass-grown, corporate-farm-raised produce across the country. Costs of importing cheap honey harvested in foreign countries at a fraction of the actual production cost and dumped into the U.S. market. Costs of substandard wages and living conditions for people who have little choice if they want any work at all."

The question of sustainability is one that winemakers, like other small business owners, struggle with every time they pay a shipping bill or look with dismay on the detritus of grape-crushing. Given the U.S. tax code that allows for enormous write-offs in the early years of a winery's business, some wealthy California investors have built their country estates around wineries; think of the proximity of Hollywood to some of the world's prime wine real estate. Native vegetation that holds erosion-prone hillsides in place is then ripped up to create vineyards heavily reliant on fertilizer and pesticides. That cheap bottle of California Chardonnay may be subsidizing the sixth home of a rock star.

tasting room, at a sleek wooden bar, Baumann guides the taster through a series of wines ranging from a semidry Seyval Blanc to a hearty Barbera. Although many offerings are familiar *viniferas*, he also makes wine from unusual grapes: Aurore, an old grape bred by the renowned nineteenth-century French breeder Albert Seibel; Traminette, a descendent of Gewürztraminer bred at Cornell University for cold-hardiness; and Catawba, another nineteenth-century variety that derives from an apparently accidental cross between a native American and a *vinifera* grape.

Baumann also offers fruit wines. In a few cases, he mixes fruit with grape wines to produce slightly sweet dessert wines, like Fusion, made with Merlot and raspberries. Baumann makes white wines from juice; because white wines do not ferment on their skins, transporting the whole grape would waste energy. But red wines, which gain their color and some of their flavor from maceration or fermentation of the tannic red skins, are brought in whole and crushed on the premises.

Like other winemakers in the region, Baumann finds most customers are summer people, although he has a steady clientele among locals as well. As the person most likely to be pouring and discussing wine as well as making it, Baumann has noticed trends over the years that Woodland Trails has been open. He sees the "fishing widows," the women who come in during the day when their men are out fishing. But increasingly, he sees young couples coming in together. Younger men, he notices, seem at home in the tasting bar. "You find the young men here, and the retired men with their wives, but middle-aged, it's mostly women," he muses.

Although he calls himself retired, the word scarcely describes the life of a man who keeps fifty different wines in stock and greets people daily during the summer season. But it was his dream when he left Milwaukee, a dream he still lives.

Woodland Trail Winery

17153 Big Hill Road • Lakewood, WI 54138 • 1-800-643-9520 • www.woodlandtrail.com

Location: Highway 32 to Big Hill Road; up the hill and to the right.

Hours:
Daily, year round, 9:00 am–6:00 pm

Tasting: Complimentary

Tours: By arrangement

Signature wines:
Merlot: softly tannic and dry
Cabernet Sauvignon: classic rich red, aged in oak
American Riesling: spätlese, or late-harvest style

Events: Occasional; see website.

Is This a Trend?

Dozens of wineries in the Upper Midwest have been opened by people who are, as it used to be delicately said, "of a certain age." Whether in business or academe, in law or psychotherapy, in engineering or the trades, many of the region's winemakers had successful careers before they launched their wineries.

The trend is national, according to the *Wall Street Journal*. Older winemakers, reporter Christine Larson points out, typically have more financial resources than younger ones. Later-life winery operators also have experience, often both in winemaking and in business. They want to use those resources to create a better life for themselves. Murli Dharmadhikari of the Midwest Viticulture and Enology Center at Southwest Missouri State University says, "People who start wineries as a retirement thing are usually looking for something more creative than what they did earlier, something they can share with their friends and family."

But running a winery is hard work. Whether or not a vineyard is involved, the wine industry calls for long hours as well as hard physical labor. Equipment can be expensive; some consultants say that a typical outlay is $250,000, although one winemaker in northern Wisconsin cuts that dramatically by finding hobby winemakers who enter the business and then, exasperated, give up. "There is a lot of fine equipment for sale secondhand," he confides.

Even with a solid financial basis, a winery keeps making demands of its owners. "Retiree" winemakers aren't sitting on the deck every evening relishing a new wine. They are in the cellar taking measurements, worrying over stuck fermentations, or hand-sterilizing hundreds of bottles. Or on the phone, trying to find enough grapes to meet their needs. Or filling out the apparently endless federal and state forms necessary to keep their license current. Or in the tasting room, hearing one more time about someone's much-better-tasting Merlot offered in Napa.

It's hard, monotonous, tiring, often discouraging. And the retired winemakers of the Upper Midwest could not imagine doing anything else.

Bibliography

Bray, Edmund C. *Billions of Years in Minnesota: The Geological Story of the State.* St. Paul: The Science Museum of Minnesota, 1977.

Burnham, J. C. "New Perspectives on the Prohibition 'Experiment' of the 1920s." *Journal of Social History* 2, no. 1 (Autumn 1968): 51–68.

"Club." *Time,* August 1, 1927.

Dammenbaum, Jed. "The Origins of Temperance Activism and Militancy Among American Women." *Journal of Social History* 15, no. 2 (Winter 1981): 235–52.

Engelman, Larry. *Intemperance: The Lost War Against Liquor.* New York: The Free Press, 1979.

Fox, Hugh F. "The Consumption of Alcoholic Beverages." *Annals of the American Academy of Political and Social Science* 109: Prohibition and Its Enforcement (September 1923): 137–44.

Grant, Edwin. "Scum from the Melting Pot." *American Journal of Sociology* 30, no. 6 (May 1925): 641–51.

Hardin, Achsah. "Volstead English." *American Speech* 7, no. 2 (December 1931): 81–88.

The Heritage of Sauk City. Sauk City, WI: Pioneer Press, 1931.

Hudelson, Richard, and Carl Ross. *By the Ore Dock: A Working People's History of Duluth.* Minneapolis: University of Minnesota Press, 2006.

Jackson, David, and Danny Schuster. *The Production of Grapes and Wines in Cold Climates.* Wellington, New Zealand: Daphne Brasell Associates and Gypsum Press, 2001.

Jackson, J. C. "The Work of the Anti-Saloon League." *Annals of the American Academy of Political and Social Science* 32: Regulation of the Liquor Traffic (November 1908): 12–26.

Kerr, K. Austin. "Organizing for Reform: The Anti-Saloon League and Innovation in Politics." *American Quarterly* 32, no. 1 (Spring 1980): 37–53.

Krosch, Penelope. *With a Tweezers in One Hand and a Book in the Other: The Grape-Breeding Work of Elmer Swenson.* Minneapolis: Minnesota Grape Growers Association, n.d.

Kyvig, David E. "Women Against Prohibition." *American Quarterly* 28, no. 4 (Autumn 1976): 465–82.

Larson, Christine. "Tending Your Own Vineyard Isn't Always Fun in the Sun." *Wall Street Journal* (Eastern edition), March 25, 2002.

"Last Men." *Time*, August 4, 1930.

Martin, Lawrence. *The Physical Geography of Wisconsin*. Madison: University of Wisconsin Press, 1965.

McGinty, Brian. *Strong Wine: The Life and Legend of Agoston Haraszthy*. Stanford, CA: Stanford University Press, 1998.

Ostergren, Robert C., and Thomas R. Vale, eds. *Wisconsin Land and Life*. Madison: University of Wisconsin Press, 1977.

Plocher, Thomas, and Robert J. Parke. *Northern Winework: Growing Grapes and Making Wine in Cold Climates*. Hugo, MN: Northern Winework, 2001.

Rorabaugh, W. J. *The Alcoholic Republic: An American Tradition*. New York: Oxford University Press, 1979.

Stanislawski, Dan. "Dionysus Westward: Early Religion and the Economic Geography of Wine." *Geographical Review* 65, no. 4 (October 1975): 427–44.

Stewart, Ella Seass. "Woman Suffrage and the Liquor Traffic." *Annals of the American Academy of Political and Social Science* 56: Women in Public Life (November 1914): 143–52.

Sullivan, Charles. *Zinfandel: A History of a Grape and Its Wine*. Berkeley: University of California Press, 2003.

Swinchatt, Jonathan, and David G. Howell. *The Winemaker's Dance: Exploring Terroir in the Napa Valley*. Berkeley: University of California Press, 2004.

Tyrrell, Ian R. *Sobering Up: From Temperance to Prohibition in Antebellum America, 1800–1860*. Westport, CT: Greenwood Press, 1979.

Wilson, James E. *Terroir: The Role of Geology, Climate, and Culture in the Making of French Wines*. London: Mitchel Beazley, 1998.

Woodbury, Marda Liggett. *Stopping the Presses: The Murder of Walter W. Liggett*. Minneapolis: University of Minnesota Press, 1998.

Pronunciation Guide

VINIFERA VARIETIES

Barbera: *Bar-BEAR-a*

Beaujolais: *Bo-zho-LAY*

Bianco Classico: *Bee-ANKH-o CLASS-ee-ko*

Bordeaux: *Bor-DOUGH*

Cabernet Sauvignon: *Cab-er-NAY Saw-vin-YON*

Chardonnay: *CHAR-dun-AY*

Chianti: *Key-AHN-tee*

Gamay: *Ga-MAY*

Gewürztraminer: *Gu-VERTZ-tra-me-nor*

Merlot: *Mer-LOW*

Muscat: *MUS-cat*

Pinot Grigio: *Pee-no GREE-zhe-o*

Pinot Noir: *Pee-no NWAR*

Riesling: *REES-ling*

Sauvignon Blanc: *Saw-vin-YON Blonk*

Zinfandel: *ZIN-fan-dell*

NORTHERN VARIETIES

Aurore: *A-ROAR-a*

Baco Noir: *BACK-o NWAR*

Beta: *BET-ta*

Briana: *Bree-AN-a*

Cayuga: *Ca-YOU-ga*

Edelweiss: *AY-del-wise*

Esprit: *Es-PRE*

Frontenac Gris: *Fron-ta-nak GREE*

Frontenac: *FRON-ta-nak*

Landot Noir: *Lan-do NWAR*

Léon Millot: *Lay-on Mil-LOT*

Maréchal Foch: *MAR-aysh-ell FOSH*

Marquette: *Mar-KET*

Noiret: *Nwar-ET*

Sabrevois: *Saa-bre-VWA*

Seyval: *SAY-vahl*

Seyval Blanc: *SAY-vahl BLONK*

St. Croix: *Saint-CROY*

St. Pepin: *Saint-PEP-in*

Traminette: *Tra-min-ETTE*

Vignoles: *Vee-NOLES*

Index

Aamodt, Chris, 60
Abel, Tim and Sarah, 127–28
Acid in grapes, 17, 42, 58, 125, 166, 167, 168, 171, 173
Aeppeltreow (winery), 49, 113–15
Agave, 20
Agritourism, 44, 69, 140, 148, 156
Alexandria Runestone, 82
Alexandria, MN, 81
Alexis Bailly (winery), 48, 66–68
Algoma, 9, 123, 132–34
Alpenglow (grape), 41
Alsace, 67, 157
Angelic Organics, 89
Anoka Sand Plain, 80
Anoka, MN, 84–86
Anthony, Susan B., 27
Anti-Saloon League, 28–31
Apple Barn (winery), 49, 112
Apple wine, 4, 39, 60, 81, 85, 115, 126, 138–39, 140, 150–51, 171–72
Appleton, 123, 125–27
Aramon, 16
Arena, WI, 94
Arnois, Roland, 87
Aurore (varietal), 66, 100, 153, 181
Autumn Harvest (winery), 49, 150–51
AVA (American Viticultural Area), 106, 131

Bacchus/Dionysus, 14, 18
Baco Noir (varietal), 66, 141, 143
Baco, François, 152–53
Bailly family, 66
Baraboo, WI, 11, 94
Barneveld, WI, 94, 96
Battle of Somme, 66
Baumann, Armin and Adrienne, 179–81
Bayfield (winery), 48, 171–72
Bayfield Peninsula, 162, 171–72
Bees, 61–62, 177–79
Bemidji, MN, 72

Bentley, R. D., 145
Beta (varietal), 39, 40
Big Ole, 79, 81
Biodynamic wine, 89
Blair, WI, 157–59
Bloomer, Mrs. Samuel, 56
Bluebell (varietal), 28, 48
Borucki, Bob and Peg, 99
Boscobel, WI, 95
Botany of vine, 17–18, 38
Botham (winery), 48, 96–98
Botham, Peter, 96–98
Bowers, James, 139
Brackett, 176–78
Brehn, Richard, 75
Brianna (varietal), 41, 173
Brigadoon (winery), 49, 173–75
Brink, John, 112
Brix, 87, 127
Brown, Joseph Renshaw, 55
Burr Oak (winery), 49, 152–54

Cade, Loren, 102–3
Caledonia, MN, 65
Canadian Shield, 161
Cannon Falls, MN, 68–70
Cannon River (winery), 49, 68–70
Capone, Al, 34, 144
Captain's Walk (winery), 49, 124–25
Carlos Creek (winery), 81
Catawba (varietal), 102, 181
Cave of the Mounds, 94
Cedar Creek (winery), 48, 115–17
Central Minnesota (wine region), 79–92
Central Wisconsin (wine region), 148–59
Chamberlin, Laura and Troy, 57
Chambourcin (varietal), 100, 105
Chancellor (varietal), 153
Chasselas (varietal), 98
Chateau St. Croix (winery), 49, 57–58
Cheese with wine, 99

Chippewa Falls, WI, 150–51
Chisago City, MN, 61
Christen, Johan, 75
Cider, 113–14
Cloquet, MN, 59
Closser, Mike and Gail, 154–55
Concord (varietal), 99, 119
Concord, WI, 118–20
Cooking with wine, 76
Cooperative Movement, 59
Coquard, Philippe, 96, 106–8, 116
Cornell University, 16, 61, 181
Coulee Region, 94
Cranberries, 199, 140, 156, 173, 176
Crofut Family (winery), 49, 82–84
Crofut, Don, 82–84
Cyser/Cyzer, 115, 179

Dalles, 55
Danner, Steve, 116–17
Death's Door, 141
DeBaker, Steve and Andrea, 130–31
DeChaunac (varietal), 96, 99, 153
Delaware (varietal), 100
Demeter certification, 90
Dodgeville, WI, 94
Dolomite, 5, 11–12, 64
Dom Pérignon, 75
Door County (wine region), 136–46
Door County, 94, 122, 125, 130
Door Pensinula (winery), 48, 139–41
Dorsey, M. J., 38
Driftless Area (wine region), 94–108
Dry/sweet continuum, 101
Duluth (glacial lake), 55

East Central Wisconsin (wine region), 122–34
Ebert, Dustin, 73–75
Edelweiss (varietal), 40, 68, 102, 127
Egypt, 14
Eighteenth Amendment, 29–33
Elk River, MN, 84–86
Elkhorn, WI, 112
Elvira (varietal), 100

Erckenbrack, Jay, 165
Esprit (varietal), 41

Falconer (winery), 49, 70–72
Falconer, John, 70–72
Feder, Ben, 4
Federal limit on wine-making, 72
Fiedler, Kiyoko, 157–59
Fieldstone (winery), 49, 86–87
Finger Lakes Region, 143
Finger Lakes, 16
Finnish heritage, 59, 72
Foch, Ferdinand, 66–67
Fontaine, Lynn, 110
Fontana, WI, 112
Forestedge (winery), 48, 166–67
Foxy flavor, 15, 42, 153
French Paradox, The, 74
Frontenac (varietal), 43, 61, 68, 82, 88, 102,
    104, 127, 128, 140, 155, 168
Frontenac Gris (varietal), 45, 49, 60, 82, 88,
    104, 127
Fruit wines, 81, 125–27, 130–31, 138–39,
    150–51, 156, 158, 165, 167–69, 173–74,
    176–77, 179–81

Garvin Heights (winery), 49, 72–73
Geology of Midwest, 8–12, 55, 64, 79, 94, 110,
    122, 161
Gewürztraminer (varietal), 70, 98, 102, 104,
    105, 143, 181
Gill, John Patrick, 157–59
Gilruth (Volstead), Nellie, 30
Ginsburg, Allen, 123
Glacial Lake Wisconsin, 148, 152
Glaciation, 10–12, 64, 110
Goff, John, 56
Goman, Kyle and Bobbi, 117
Goose Lake (winery), 49, 84–86
Gordon, Lori, 164–65
Gordon, WI, 55
Granite Falls, MN, 30, 35, 91
Grantsburg (glacial lake), 55
Great Gogebic Boom, 161-62

Great River North (wine region), 55–62
Great River South (wine region), 64–77
Green Bay, WI, 100, 122, 124
Greenleaf, WI, 127–28

Haislet, Sam, 66
Halajcsik, Rick and Liz, 175
Hall, Peter, 56
Hamilton, Jon and Kim, 178–79
Haraszthy, Agoston, 20–24, 26, 38, 48, 106,
    107, 146, 182, 48, 106, 146
Haraszthy, Arpad, 23–24
Haraszthy, Eleanora, 21, 22, 23
Harmony, MN, 64
Hastings, MN, 66–68
Hauser, Scott and Renate, 171–72
Havumaki, Sulo, 72
Heipas, Marv, 125
Hemstad, Peter, 39, 40, 44–45, 60, 102
Highland, WI, 101
Home wine-making, 154
HookStone (winery), 49, 175
Hot (superalcoholic) wine, 157
Hybrid grapes, 16

Ice wine, 57
International Falls, MN, 34
Iron Range, 32
Italian wine, 129

Jacobson, Steve and Judy, 112
Janesville (varietal), 39
Johnny Appleseed, 114
Johnson, Hugh, 20
Johnson, Steve, 128–30
Jordan, MN, 82–84
Judgment of Paris, 132–33

Kay Gray (varietal), 41, 102
Kehl, Peter, 22, 106
Keillor, Garrison, 80
Kennedy, Steve and Judy, 152–53
Kerrigan Brothers (winery), 49, 125–27
Kickapoo River, 94

Koehler, Jim and Paul, 123
Kuhlmann, Eugene, 16, 153
Kvale, Rev. O. J., 35

La Crescent (varietal), 45, 49, 60, 68, 82, 88,
    104, 115, 127
La Crosse (varietal), 41, 72, 102, 104, 127,
    129
Lake Agassiz (glacial lake), 79
Lake Geneva, WI, 112
Lake Lillian, MN, 90–92
Lake Michigan, 12
Lake Huron, 12
Lake Pepin, 64, 102
Lake St. Croix, 55
Lake Wobegon, 8
Lambeau, Curly and George Calhoun, 123
Landot Noir (varietal), 43
Landwehr, Troy, 125–27
Lanesboro, MN, 64, 75–76
Laporte, MN, 166–67
Last Man's Club, 55–56
Lautenbach family, 138–39
Lawrie, Tim, 143–44
LedgeStone (winery), 49, 127–28
Léon Millot (varietal), 66, 96, 140, 153
Lewis, Sinclair, 80
Ligget, Walter, 91
Lil' Ole Winemaker (winery), 49, 154–55
Limestone, 9, 94, 143, 152
Lockwood, Charles, 56
Lorelei (varietal), 41
Louise Swenson (varietal), 4, 39, 41, 72, 128,
    173
Lowe, Anne, 70
Luby, Jim, 44, 47
Lunt, Alfred, 110

MacGregor, David, 39, 41
Madison, WI, 110
Maenads, 14
Maloney, Maureen and John, 68–70
Mansfield, Anna Catherine, 46
Mardi, Paula and Georg, 88–90

Maréchal Foch (varietal), 4, 60, 61, 70, 88, 96, 99, 100, 102, 103, 104, 107, 116, 128, 140, 152, 153, 174

Marquette (varietal), 45–46, 60, 61, 72, 102, 155, 168

Marquette, Father Jacques, 16

Martin, Dennis, 58

Mason Creek (winery), 117–18

Mather, Increase, 26

Mazomanie, WI, 94

McCain family, 176–77

McCarthy, Joseph, 123

McGinty, Brian, 20

McGonigle, Charles and Milissa, 113–15

McGregor, MN, 165

McIlquham, Jon, Jim, Marykay, 150–51

Mead, 82, 165, 177–79

Mesabi Range, 59

MGGA (Minnesota Grape Growers Association), 44, 52, 71, 72, 127

Microvinification, 158

Milano, Angelo, Maria, 128–30

Milwaukee, WI, 110

Minchurnetz (varietal), 89

Mineral Point, WI, 94

Minnesota Department of Agriculture, 86

Minnesota Farm Winery Law, 85

Minnesota River, 79

Minnesota State Fair, 60, 128

Minnestalgia (winery), 165

Mississippi River, 64

Moen, Irv, 90–92

Mondavi, 31–32

Monroe, WI, 94

Morgan Creek (winery), 48, 88–90

Morgan, MN, 86–87

Morrow, Elisha, 124

Mount Horeb, WI, 94

Munson Bridge (winery), 49, 156–57

Munson, T. V., 39

Names for wine, 118

Nativism, 27

Negret, Vincent, 58

New Glarus, WI, 98–99

New Lisbon, WI, 152–54

New Ulm, MN, 88–90

Newton Valley, 102

Niagara (varietal), 105, 130

Niagara Ledge/Escarpment, 11–12, 122, 131, 136

Nicolet, Jean, 124

Niedecker, Loreine, 110

Northern grape varieties:

Aurore, 66, 100, 153, 181

Baco Noir, 66, 141, 143

Beta, 39, 40

Bluebell, 28, 48

Brianna, 41, 172

Catawba, 102, 181

Chambourcin, 100, 105

Chancellor, 153

Chasselas, 98

Concord, 99, 119

DeChaunac, 96, 99, 153

Delaware, 100

Edelweiss, 40, 68, 102, 127

Elvira, 100

Esprit, 41

Frontenac, 43, 61, 68, 82, 88, 102, 104, 127, 128, 140, 155, 168

Frontenac Gris, 45, 49, 60, 82, 88, 104, 127

Gewürztraminer, 70, 98, 102, 104, 105, 143, 181

Janesville, 39

Kay Gray, 41, 102

La Crescent, 45, 49, 60, 68, 82, 88, 104, 115, 127

La Crosse, 41, 72, 102, 104, 127, 129

Landot Noir, 43

Léon Millot, 66, 96, 140, 153

Lorelei, 41

Louise Swenson, 4, 39, 41, 72, 128, 172

Maréchal Foch, 4, 60, 61, 70, 88, 96, 99, 100, 102, 103, 104, 107, 116, 128, 140, 152, 153, 174

Marquette, 45–46, 60, 61, 72, 102, 155, 168

Minchurnetz, 89

Niagara, 105, 130
Petite Jewel, 41
Pinot Nero, 145
Pinot Noir, 45–46, 98, 102, 141, 169, 175
Prairie Star, 41, 68, 82, 169
Riesling, 61, 70, 96, 104, 106, 141
Rosette, 153
Sabrevois, 41, 68, 82, 102, 127, 168
Seyval Blanc, 96, 128, 143
Shannon, 41
St. Pepin, 41, 68, 72, 88, 127, 129, 140
Steuben, 105
Summersweet, 41
Swenson Red, 41, 48
Swenson White, 41
Traminette, 104, 105, 141, 143, 181
Trollhaugen, 41
Vidal Blanc, 141, 143, 168
Vignoles/Ravat, 51, 104, 128, 143, 153
Worden, 105
Northern Minnesota, 161–62
Northern Vineyards (winery), 48, 58–59
Northern Wisconsin, 161–62

Ohman, Cindy, 84–86
Olde Country (winery), 49, 90–92
Orchard Country (winery), 48, 138–39
Organic wine, 89
Osceola, WI, 39, 40

Packers, Green Bay, 122
Paper, Jim, 48, 115–16
Parallel 44 (winery), 49, 128–30
Parke, Bob, 4, 168
Parker, Robert, 96
Partch, Robin, 58–59, 165
Paul, John, 71
Payette, Tom, 143
Pecatonica River, 94
Penokean orogeny, 9
Penokee range, 9
Perry, 115
Peterson, Kevin, 61–62
Petite Jewel (varietal), 41

Phylloxera, 15, 152–53, 176
Pierquet, Pat, 41–48
Pinot Nero (varietal), 145
Pinot Noir (varietal), 45–46, 98, 102, 141, 169, 175
Plocher, Tom, 4, 168
Plummer, MN, 167–69
Pollan, Bob and Rob, 139–41
Popularity of wine, 57
Pottery, 71
Prairie Star (varietal), 41, 68, 82, 169
Predation, 87
Prohibition, 2–36, 91, 119, 156
Pruning, 14
Pulque, 20
Pumpkin wine, 177

Quast, Charlie, 86–87
Quast, Paul, 60
Québec, 12, 168

Rating wine by numbers, 96
Ravat, J. F., 152–53
Red Oak (winery), 49, 141–43
Red Wing, 65, 70–72
Refrigeration, 113
Regulation, 69
Reiburn, Tim, 102
Rhubarb wine, 156, 166–67
Riesling (varietal), 61, 70, 96, 104, 106, 141
Riestau, Karrie, 76
River Warren (glacial), 79
Rochester, MN, 73–75
Rogers, Bucky, 75
Rohland, Tom, 156
Root River, 75
Rosette (varietal), 153
Rothschild, WI, 154–55
Rush, Benjamin, 26

Sabrevois (varietal), 41, 68, 82, 102, 127, 168
Salem Glen (winery), 49
Sauk Centre, MN, 80, 82
Sauk City, WI, 20

Sauk Prairie, WI, 94

Sbragia, Ed, 8

Scenic Valley (winery), 75–76

Schell, August, 88

Schmiling, Aric and Brad, 132–34

Seibel, 16

Seibel, Albert, 152–53, 181

Seppanen, Linda and Marvin, 72–73

Seyval Blanc (varietal), 96, 128, 143

Shane, Marla, 176

Shannon (varietal), 41

Shushnoff, Cecil, 42

Sibley, Henry, 55

Simon Creek (winery), 49, 143–45

Sips of History Trail, 82

Sogn Valley, 68

Southeastern Wisconsin (wine region), 110–20

Spring Green, WI, 94

Spring Grove, MN, 64

Spurgeon (winery), 48, 100–102

Spurgeon, Glenn, 35, 100–101

St. Croix (varietal), 41, 82, 129

St. Croix Falls, 55, 57–58

St. Croix Vineyards (winery), 48, 60–61

St. Pepin (varietal), 41, 68, 72, 88, 127, 129, 140

St. Urho, 72

Stanton, Elizabeth Cady, 27

Starks, Bob, 102–3

Steiner, Rudolf, 89

Steuben (varietal), 105

Stillwater, 55, 58–61

Stone Mill (former winery), 48, 115

Stone's Throw (winery), 145–46

Stumpf, LeRoy and Carol, 168–69

Sturgeon Bay, WI, 141–43

Sugar River, 94

Summersweet (varietal), 41

Superior View Farm, 169–71

Sustainability, 88, 156–66, 169–71, 180

Shuster, Paul and Sharon, 166–67

Swedenborg, Emmanuel, 114

Swenson Red (varietal), 41, 48

Swenson White (varietal), 41

Swenson, Elmer, 16, 39–41, 48, 57, 61, 68, 152

Swenson, Louise, 39

Taliesin, 94

Tannin, 138, 181

Tenba Ridge (winery), 49, 157–59

Terroir, 4, 8, 9, 12, 83, 86, 140, 173

Three Lakes (winery), 48, 176–77

Three Rivers Wine Trail, 61

Tobacco, 102–3

Traminette (varietal), 104, 105, 141, 143, 181

Trollhaugen (varietal), 41

Trout Springs (winery), 48, 130–31

Turco, Russel, 145

Two Fools (winery), 49, 167–69

University of Calfornia, Davis, 146, 151

University of Minnesota, 16, 38–47, 48, 70, 72, 85, 86, 102, 155, 168

Up North (wine region), 161–82

Upper Midwestern Wine Regions:

    Central Minnesota (wine region), 79–92

    Central Wisconsin (wine region), 148–59

    Door County (wine region), 136–46

    Driftless Area (wine region), 94–108

    East Central Wisconsin (wine region), 122–34

    Great River North (wine region), 55–62

    Great River South (wine region), 64–77

    Southeastern Wisconsin (wine region), 110–20

    Up North (wine region), 161–82

Vernon County Vineyards (winery), 49, 102–4

Vetrano, Michael, Bill, and LaVerne, 118–20

Vetro (winery), 49, 118–20

Victory Memorial Drive, Minneapolis, MN, 66

Vidal Blanc (varietal), 141, 143, 168

Vignoles/Ravat 51 (varietal), 104, 128, 143, 153

Viking Altar Rock, 82

Vikings, 82

Vinum, 14

Virginia, MN, 32, 72

Viroqua, WI, 103

Viste, Cassie Lautenbach, 138–39

Vitis (grape species), 14

Vitis muscadine (muscadine grape), 15

Vitis aestivalis (summer grape), 15

Vitis labrusca (fox grape), 15, 38, 40, 42, 153

Vitis riparia (riverbank grape), 15, 39, 42, 43, 45, 66, 67, 82

Vitis rotundifolia (round-leaved grape), 15

Vitis rupestris (sand grape), 15, 16

Vitis vinifera (wine-making grapes), 4, 14, 15, 16, 21, 44, 45, 46, 60, 61, 66, 67, 70, 72, 79, 91, 96, 102, 103, 106, 124, 136, 140, 141, 143, 145, 146, 152, 153, 154, 168, 174, 181

Volstead, Andrew, 30–36

Von Stiehl (winery), 48, 124, 132–34

Von Stiehl, Charles, 132

Wagener, Nicholas and Gigi, 141–43

Walnut Grove, MN, 64

Washington County Historical Society, 56

Weggy (winery), 49, 104–5

Weglarz, Marion, 104–5

Wein (German), 14

Welbes, Dave and Linda, 173–74

Western Uplands, 94

Wheeler, Wayne B., 31

White Winter (winery), 177–79

Widman, Dick, 140

Wilcox, A. J., 38

Wilder, Laura Ingalls, 64

Wildmo, John, 166–67

Wilson, Eva, 84

Wilson, Woodrow, 32

Wine and health, 74

Wine tourism, 57

Winehaven (winery), 48, 61–62

Winona, 64, 72–73

Wisconsin Apple Growers Association, 126

Wisconsin Dells, 11, 148, 152

Wisconsin River, 11, 16, 106, 148

Wisconsin State Fair, 128

Wisconsin Winery Association, 52

Withee, WI, 156–57

Wollersheim (winery), 22, 48, 106–8

Wollersheim, Bob, 96, 100, 104, 106–8, 116

Wollersheim, Julie, 106–8

Women in wine, 150

Woodland Trails (winery), 48, 179–81

Worden (varietal), 105

Zinfandel, 20, 21, 23, 145, 155

Zoellick, Scott, 175

Zumbro River, 74

Tasting Notes

WINERY

DATE VISITED

VISITED WITH

WINES TASTED

FAVORITE WINE(S)

MEMORABLE FEATURES

WINERY

DATE VISITED

VISITED WITH

WINES TASTED

FAVORITE WINE(S)

MEMORABLE FEATURES